THE ROMAN MARBLE SCULPTURES FROM THE SANCTUARY OF PAN AT CAESAREA PHILIPPI / PANIAS (ISRAEL)

AMERICAN SCHOOLS OF ORIENTAL RESEARCH
ARCHAEOLOGICAL REPORTS

Kevin M. McGeough, Editor

Number 17

The Roman Marble Sculptures from the Sanctuary of Pan
at Caesarea Philippi/Panias (Israel)

THE ROMAN MARBLE SCULPTURES FROM THE SANCTUARY OF PAN AT CAESAREA PHILIPPI/PANIAS (ISRAEL)

By

Elise A. Friedland

AMERICAN SCHOOLS OF ORIENTAL RESEARCH • BOSTON, MA

The Roman Marble Sculptures from the Sanctuary of Pan
at Caesarea Philippi/Panias (Israel)

by

Elise A. Friedland

Cover illustration: Drawing of head of Athena wearing an Attic helmet (cat. 2); by Lorene Sterner.

The American Schools of Oriental Research © 2012

ISBN 978-0-89757-087-9

Library of Congress Cataloging-in-Publication Data

Friedland, Elise A.
   The Roman marble sculptures from the Sanctuary of Pan at Caesarea Philippi/
Panias (Israel) / by Elise A. Friedland.
      p. cm. -- (American Schools of Oriental Research archeological reports ; no. 17)
   Includes bibliographical references (p.) and index.
   ISBN 978-0-89757-087-9 (alk. paper)
 1. Baniyas (Damascus, Syria)--Antiquities, Roman--Catalogs. 2. Marble sculpture,
Roman--Catalogs. 3. Excavations (Archaeology)--Syria--Baniyas (Damascus)--
Catalogs. I. Title.
   DS99.B23F75 2012
   733'.50939434--dc23
                                 2012039663

Contents

List of Illustrations

Unless otherwise noted, all photographs are by the author.

List of Tables

Acknowledgments

This book is a revised and updated version of my doctoral dissertation (Friedland 1997). First and foremost, I thank Zvi Ma'oz, director of the Excavations of the Sanctuary of Pan at Caesarea Philippi (Banias), and Zvi Gal, former director of Publications of the Israel Antiquities Authority, for generously granting me permission to study and publish the marble sculptures discovered at the site. Both Sharon Herbert and Andrea Berlin are responsible for my affiliation with the excavations, and they, along with the other members of my dissertation committee, Elaine Gazda and John Pedley (co-chairs) as well as David Potter have provided me with unfailing professional, intellectual, and personal support from the moment that I began this project up to the present. John Humphrey has also served as an invaluable mentor. Many Israeli colleagues were extraordinarily generous in welcoming me and sharing unpublished material and ideas with me. Warmest thanks go to Rivka Gersht, Moshe Fischer, Gideon Foerster, Ze'ev Weiss, Gaby Mazor, Arthur Segal, Peter Gendelman, and Rina and Arnon Angert. At the Israel Antiquities Authority, Ruta Peled, Joe Zias, Rivka Birger, Danny Syon, Hava Katz, Naomi Sidi, Donald Ariel, and Moshe Hartal offered all manner of assistance and support for my work. Benjamin Isaac, Moshe Fischer, and John Wilson were extremely kind to provide me with pre-publication drafts of their manuscripts on material related to the Paneion statues. Ariel Heimann and Naomi Porat of the Weizmann Institute of Science conducted the original isotopic analyses on ten select pieces and generously discussed their results with me; Susan Walker and Norman Herz graciously compared the results of isotopic analyses with their databases of classical marbles. In addition, Elizabeth Bartman, R. R. R. Smith, Mark Fullerton, Gerhard Koeppel, Sandra Knudsen, Susan Kane, Lea Stirling, Rebecca Schindler, Helen Dizikes Sanders, Diane Conlin, Ellen Perry, Steven Tuck, and Melanie Grunow Sobocinski all read portions of this manuscript and offered invaluable comments. Kenneth Holum, Jodi Magness, Marilyn Stewart, Elizabeth Fisher, Pierre and Patricia Bikai, and Barbara Porter have also offered valuable support and sage advice. K. Paul Bednarowski provided assistance with the Greek phrases noted in the text. During my time at The George Washington University, Eric Cline has provided constant support and invaluable mentorship.

For the production of this volume, special thanks are due to Kevin McGeough, editor of ASOR's Archaeological Report Series, for his energy, enthusiasm, and guidance. In addition, I thank Susanne Wilhelm of ISD for her keen eye and expert copyediting. Lorene Sterner, with her ever-present attention to detail and long experience with archaeological graphics, converted original black and white negatives to digital scans and deftly created the maps and plans. Any errors that remain are, of course, my own.

Funding for my doctoral research came from the American Research Institute in Turkey and the University of Michigan's Horace H. Rackham School of Graduate Studies, Interdepartmental Program in Classical Art and Archaeology (IPCAA), and Rackham Pre-Doctoral Fellowship program. Post-doctoral support was provided by a Margo Tytus Fellowship from the Department of Classics at the University of Cincinnati; Rollins College, Winter Park, FL; The George Washington University, Washington, DC; and a Council of

American Overseas Research Centers Senior Fellowship at the American Center for Oriental Research in Amman, Jordan.

Finally, I would like to thank my parents, Drs. Joan and Sigmund Friedland, my sister, Dr. Shea Friedland, my grandparents, Gwendolyn Gertz†, Estelle† and Benjamin Friedland†, and Jack J. Angert†, and my aunt, Mitzie Friedland-Stell, for their constant love and support. Andrew M. Smith II, my life and academic partner, deserves special mention for his constant intellectual and personal support, as does our daughter, Eleanor, who has decided (at age 6) to join her parents and write her own books.

This volume is dedicated to my devoted parents.

Abbreviations

NOTE: In addition to the following abbreviations, ancient authors and their works are cited according to the abbreviations used in the *Oxford Classical Dictionary*, 3rd rev. ed.

CCCA   M. J. Vermaseren. 1977–1989. *Corpus Cultus Cybelae Attidisque* (CCCA) 1–7. Leiden: Brill.

DAIR   Deutsches Archäologisches Institut, Römische Abteilung, n.d., *Index der Antiken Kunst und Architektur.* New York: Saur.

ESI   *Excavations and Surveys in Israel.* English Edition of *Hadashot Arkheologiyot,* Archaeological Newsletter of the Israel Antiquities Authority.

LIMC   Ackermann, H. C., and Gisler, G.-R. Redaction. *Lexicon iconographicum mythologiae classicae.* Vols. 1–8 (1981–); Supplement (2009). Zurich: Artemis.

MadrMitt *Mitteilungen des Deutschen Archäologischen Instituts, Madrider Abteilung.*

NEAEHL   E. Stern, H. Geva, and J. Aviram (eds.), *The New Encyclopedia of Archaeological Excavations in the Holy Land.* New York 1993; Jerusalem 2008 (Supplement, Vol. 5).

NSRV   1993. *The Cambridge Annotated Study Bible, New Revised Standard Version.* Notes and references by Howard Clark Kee. New York: Cambridge University.

PAT   Hillers, D. R., and Cussini, E. 1996. *Palmyrene Aramaic Texts.* Baltimore, MD: Johns Hopkins University.

Chapter 1

The Roman Marble Sculptures from the Sanctuary of Pan at Caesarea Philippi/Panias

Problems, Approaches, Context

In 1992, after four seasons of excavation at the Roman Sanctuary of Pan at Caesarea Philippi/Panias (modern Banias, Israel), a deposit of broken, white marble sculptures was discovered in one of the buildings atop the elevated terrace of the sanctuary. During this season and that following, over 200 fragments of statuary were recovered.[1] From these, twenty-eight marble sculptures and one limestone piece representing Graeco-Roman deities and mythological figures may be reconstructed.[2] They range in date from the second half of the first through the late fourth or early fifth centuries AD. Scale varies from colossal to miniature. Subjects include a colossal head of Roma or Athena (cat. 1), life-size heads of Athena (cats. 2–3), Zeus or Asklepios (cat. 4), Apollo or a Muse (cat. 6), and Dionysos (cat. 7), a life-size torso of a nymph (cat. 11), a life-size leg of a Capitoline/Medici Aphrodite (cat. 13), a two-thirds life-size Artemis Rospigliosi (cat. 15), and ten small-scale statuettes, including a torso of a dancing satyr (cat. 20) and a weary Herakles (cat. 21). Only one portrait, a rare genre in this region, may be associated with the site: an over-life-size bust of Antinous (reportedly discovered at Caesarea Philippi/Panias in the mid-1800s; see Appendix 4, fig. 95).

The Sanctuary of Pan at Caesarea Philippi, also called the Paneion, originated in the Hellenistic period, sometime before 200 BC. A rural shrine to the pastoral god Pan, it was centered on an enormous natural grotto in the southwestern-most slopes of Mount Hermon (the southern extension of the Anti-Lebanon Mountain Range) (fig. 1). From beneath the grotto issue abundant springs, and the site was famous as one of the sources of the Jordan river. In 19 BC, Herod the Great constructed a temple to Augustus in front of the grotto, and in 2 BC, Herod's son, Philip, founded a city several hundred meters to its south. Thus began two centuries of architectural embellishment (19 BC–AD 220). During this period, the Sanctuary of Pan evolved into a metropolitan religious center of Roman Syria (later Syria Phoenicia), whose cult figures included not only Pan, but also the nymphs, Zeus, Nemesis, and Augustus/Roma. Thus, the site offers an invaluable opportunity to examine the character and function not only of a Roman-period sanctuary, but of a Graeco-Roman religious center situated within the Semitic milieu of the Roman Levant. From the start, the excavations yielded architectural, numismatic, and epigraphic evidence, all of which indicate that the sanctuary was fairly Hellenized. However, it is the significant number of high-quality, large-scale marble sculptures, unusual in the Levant, that provide the clearest and most abundant evidence for the

Fig. 1   *Map of the region of Caesarea Philippi/Panias during the Roman period (by Lorene Sterner).*

sanctuary's mainstream, Hellenistic, and later Roman character.[3] This volume constitutes the first study of these sculptures and has two goals: first to identify and catalogue the individual sculptures from the Paneion, then to assess the significance of the group within the contexts of the Roman-period Sanctuary of Pan, the broader region of the Levant, the wider Roman empire, and modern Roman sculptural studies.

THE SCULPTURES AS *IDEALPLASTIK*

At the core of this study is a group of twenty-seven sculptures that belongs to a genre known in the scholarship by the German term *Idealplastik* ("ideal sculpture"). This term was coined by W. Trillmich in the 1970s to describe Roman marble sculptures that represent divine or semi-divine figures in a classical style but are not exact "copies" of classical works assigned to renowned Greek masters (Trillmich 1973; 1979). Trillmich argues that these Roman sculptures should not be thought of as accurate or inaccurate "copies" of single Greek masterpieces, but rather as variations of a central ideal model of a particular mythological subject — hence the term *Idealplastik*.

The majority of the Paneion sculptures may be classified as *Idealplastik*. However, I have chosen not to refer to them as such, but more generally as "Roman marble sculptures" and "mythological sculptures," as this study, although initially sculptural, also focuses on the architectural, historical, and religious context of the sculpture and is meant to be accessible to scholars of varied specialties. I use these terms, therefore, to refer to marble sculptures carved during the Roman period in a classical style that represent Graeco-Roman deities and mythological figures at any scale.[4] As such, these sculptures display standard, repeated depictions of mythological figures that were carved, purchased, and displayed throughout the Roman Empire and "whose meaning was instantly clear to everyone, the visual equivalent of clichés" (Marvin 1993: 169). Thus, their presence at Caesarea Philippi demonstrates that at least some patrons — and viewers — in the eastern provinces were conversant in the visual vocabulary of the Graeco-Roman world.

THE LEVANT: A VIABLE VENUE FOR ROMAN MARBLE SCULPTURE?

For the purposes of this study, I situate the site of Caesarea Philippi, which became part of the Roman province of Syria Phoenicia after AD 93, within a sub-region of the Roman Near East known as the Levant. The Levant encompasses the Roman provinces of Syria Coele, Syria Phoenicia, Syria Palestina, and western Arabia (roughly modern Lebanon, Syria, Israel, and Jordan), a largely coastal region. To a certain extent, from the Persian period onward, this area has been viewed as a single unit geographically, historically, and politically.[5] The majority of marble statuary discovered in the Near East is found along this coastal strip and in Transjordan, while fewer marble artifacts have been found in Mesopotamia or Arabia.

To date, scholars have overlooked the Levant as a place where Roman marble statuary is likely to be found. Traditionally, the Levant has been viewed as a region in which the effects of Hellenization begun by Alexander the Great succeeded only in creating pockets of Hellenistic civilization amidst the indigenous Near Eastern cultures and Semitic religions (Millar 1993). Scholars seem particularly taken with this phenomenon in Judaea/Syria Palestina, where they note that artistic manifestations of Hellenistic religion were explicitly prohibited by the second commandment, which forbade the creation and worship of graven images.[6] An article entitled "Greek and Roman Sculpture in the Holy Land" exemplifies the tendency of scholars to view the region as uniformly Semitic ("Holy Land") and thus to interpret instances of mainstream Graeco-Roman art as exceptional (Vermeule and Anderson 1981). More recently, J. Elsner called Judaism "the most uniconic (indeed anti-iconic) of religions," claiming not just that Jews themselves were disinterested in or opposed to art, but that they inhabited an environment virtually free of classical visual forms, with Roman Palestina — home to Rabbinic Jews, Christians, and pagans alike — being almost wholly bereft of icons (Elsner 1998: 215). B. S. Ridgway went so far as to claim that "areas with a strong religious tradition of their own, as for instance the Holy Land, did not greatly favor the import of classical works" (Ridgway 1984: 89).

In addition, mainstream scholarship on Roman sculpture has neglected the Levant, because the region is known to have no native source of marble, nor a local tradition of carving it. Furthermore, significant finds of Roman sculpture in the Levant are relatively recent, and many, such as those from Beth Shean/Scythopolis, await publication. Those finds that are studied tend to be published individually in articles that focus on the formal and iconographic details of single pieces rather than in synthetic monographs that consider their broader sculptural, architectural, historical, and cultural contexts. However, the Paneion sculptures (and similar finds from other Levantine sites) offer overwhelming evidence against prevailing assumptions that the Levant had no use for the marble statuary so profusely displayed in public contexts throughout the other provinces of the Roman empire.

HISTORY OF THE SCHOLARSHIP ON ROMAN MARBLE SCULPTURE FROM THE LEVANT

During the past seventy years, there have been two different types of studies on Roman marble sculpture discovered in the Levant: first, the publication of statuary discovered at individual, excavated sites, and second, more general surveys of the sculpture found in the sub-regions of Syria, Arabia, Palestine, and the Decapolis. The following review will focus on the discovery, publication, and interpretation of statuary from specific archaeological sites in order to locate the present study of the Paneion sculptures within its broader historiographic context. Since it is important to consider the material from each site in relation to the importation, use, and meaning of marble artifacts in the region as a whole, the conclusions of general surveys will also be noted.

Before the 1980s, few major groups of marble statuary had been discovered in the Levant. Finds tended to be random, limited in number, and often only loosely associated with a fully-excavated architectural context. Most statuary discovered in the region was studied by excavation directors, published as part of archaeological site reports, and rarely presented in relation to the wider land-scape. For example, six marble sculptures found in the nymphaeum at Byblos were published in J. Lauffray's 1940 excavation report on the monument; four statues from the stadium and the temple precinct at Samaria-Sebaste were described by J. W. Crowfoot, J. Iliffe, and J. M. C. Toynbee in the third volume of the 1957 site reports; three statues from the theater at Amman were catalogued by El Fakharani in a 1975 article on the excavations; and two statues from the Temple of Allat at Palmyra are recorded by Gawlikowski in his 1977 article on the excavations of the temple. In addition to these reports by excavators, a handful of isolated finds from various sites throughout the region were published by J. Iliffe in short articles (Iliffe 1932; 1933a; 1933b; 1934; 1951). For the most part, these publications provide little more than iconographic and stylistic analyses of the pieces. They consist largely of catalogue entries that describe and identify the pieces, discuss comparanda, suggest dates, and engage in *Kopienkritik* (the association of these Roman-period sculptures with earlier Greek masterworks). Some scholars describe the marble and attempt to identify its origins. Few include discussions of the workshop associations or training of the sculptors, and fewer still consider their finds of marble statuary within the broader context of the importation of marble artifacts to the Levant. Interpretation of the pieces in relation to the architectural context with which they are associated is often brief (Lauffray 1940: 26–27; Crowfoot et al. 1957: 71; El Fakharani 1975: 398, 400; Gawlikowski 1977: 262), and little attempt is made to view them as part of a larger, regional phenomenon.

For many of these issues, scholars were restricted by the current state of research, particularly in marble studies. Isotopic analysis had not been developed and accepted as a viable method for probing the quarry origins of marble artifacts. J. B. Ward-Perkins was just beginning to formulate, lecture on, and publish his model for the structure and operation of the imperial marble trade (Ward-Perkins 1951; 1980; Dodge and Ward-Perkins 1992). Moreover, the importation and use of marble statuary in the Levant was just being recognized as a phenomenon. In his 1951 publication of the Icarus and Daedalus group from Amman, Iliffe notes that "a full knowledge of Roman Imperial art in [the] remote region of … the Decapolis would probably remove grounds for surprise at the existence of such … purely classical work[s] in a Semitic context" (1951: 706).[7] Iliffe was clearly aware that he was one of the pioneers in establishing the corpus of marble statuary from the Levant.

Two pre-1980 publications of statuary discovered in this region stand out from those mentioned above. In his lengthy catalogue entries on the twenty-odd sculptures discovered in the 1959–1964 excavations at Caesarea Maritima, A. Frova addresses such issues as the initial architectural context of each sculpture and its marble type, the importation of marble artifacts to the region, and the possibility of local carving workshops at Caesarea Maritima (Frova 1966: 193–215, 305–10). Even more synthetic is the 1970 reassessment of the sculptural group from the late Roman villa at Antioch by the sculpture specialist D. M. Brinkerhoff. The group of 277 fragments of marble sculpture discovered in the excavations at Antioch-on-the-Orontes comprises one of the largest bodies of marble statuary found in the Levant before the 1980s. While the initial 1938 and 1941 excavation reports by R. Stillwell published basic catalogue entries on the sculptures (much like those noted above), Brinkerhoff's 1970 re-study of the group from the late antique villa constitutes a watershed in the contextualized interpretation of marble statuary from this region. Building upon M. Stuart's model for the circulation of imperial portraits (1939) and Ward-Perkins' early articles on the marble trade (1951; 1958), Brinkerhoff considers the Antioch sculptures in the context of Roman-period sculptural production and distribution (Brinkerhoff 1970: 43–46). He addresses the origins of the marble, the workshop affiliations of the sculptors, the centers of sculptural production in the East, and methods of distribution of statuary. Brinkerhoff also considers the meaning of the classical style of the Antioch pieces within their predominantly Oriental context (Brinkerhoff 1970: 46–49). Finally, he considers the Antioch cache within the intellectual and religious milieu of the early Christian age, the era in which the sculptures were last displayed (Brinkerhoff 1970: 53–62). Brinkerhoff's broader perspective on the Antioch pieces was significantly affected by the

publication in 1961 (by H. F. Mussche) and in 1965 (by E. Will) of two surveys of marble statuary from Syria (Brinkerhoff 1970: 47). Both of these articles discussed the distribution of marble statuary in this region and the relationship of material, style, and iconography to cultural setting.

In the past thirty years, there has been a florescence in the archaeology of Roman-period Israel, Jordan, and Syria. Increased excavation has swelled the corpus of marble statuary discovered in the Roman Levant (Vermeule and Anderson 1981; Israeli 1992; Humphrey 1995: 7). Since the early 1970s, systematic excavations have been carried out throughout the port city of Caesarea Maritima, yielding well over 200 fragments of marble statuary (*NEAEHL* 1: 271–72; *NEAEHL* 5: 1656–57, 1665). Beginning in 1980 and particularly since 1986, excavations of the city center of Beth Shean/Scythopolis have yielded a similarly large quantity of marble sculptures (*NEAEHL* 1: 223; *NEAEHL* 5: 1616, 1623, 1636). The other major discovery of marble statuary in this region since 1980 is the group from the Sanctuary of Pan at Caesarea Philippi studied here.

Thus, in the early 1980s, marble statuary from the Levant began to enter the mainstream of scholarship on Roman sculpture. In 1981, as multiple marble sculptures were emerging from excavations, C. Vermeule and K. Anderson co-authored the article that surveyed Greek and Roman sculpture discovered in Israel.[8] Although Vermeule and Anderson concluded that the corpus of marble statuary from Roman Palestine was small, especially in comparison to that from Asia Minor, they listed the major Roman-period ideal sculptures, portraits, and reliefs known from the region and briefly discussed issues of display context, patronage, origins, and the importation of marble statuary to Palestine. A handful of other articles also appeared in the 1980s and early 1990s that survey classical statuary from the region (Parlasca 1989; Weber 1990; Wenning 1991; Israeli 1992). However, as noted above, in 1984, in her discussion of the distribution of Roman copies of Greek originals, B. S. Ridgway (citing Vermeule and Anderson) still dismissed the Levantine coast as a viable market for Roman sculpture (Ridgway 1984: 89). Clearly, full recognition of the extent and significance of the Levantine corpus awaited further discoveries and publications.

The interpretation and growing recognition of the ever-expanding corpus of marble sculpture from the Levant is currently being furthered by archaeologists who engage sculpture specialists to study and publish the sculptural finds from their excavations. To date, R. Stucky's 1993 volume on the 169 Roman sculptures from the Temple of Eschmun at Sidon is the only monograph, other than Brinkerhoff's, on a large group of marble statuary from a single architectural context in the Levant. The publication of Caesarea Maritima marbles, assigned to sculpture specialist R. Gersht, has resulted, since the mid-1980s, in multiple English-language articles that focus on individual sculptural types, provide catalogue entries for groups of related pieces, and address issues of the origins of the sculptures (Gersht 1984; 1987; 1995a; 1995b; 1996d); she has also published articles on various themes represented in sculptures discovered at Caesarea Maritima or in Israel generally (Gersht 1996b; 1996c; 2008; Gendelman and Gersht 2010). For Jordan and Syria, the archaeologist and sculpture specialist T. Weber has published statuary discovered at the individual sites of Pella (1993) and Gadara (2002), a catalogue of all of the sculptures discovered in Roman-period Jordan (Weber 2002), and a catalogue of sculptures from the cities and villages of central and southern Syria in the National Museum of Damascus (2006). Currently, along with his colleagues Detlev Kreikenbom, Karl-Uwe Mahler, and Mustafa Koçak, Weber is compiling the corpus *Sculptures from Roman Syria II: The Marble Sculpture*, which will include all known material from Roman-period Lebanon, Syria, Jordan, and Israel. Once the corpus is assembled and published, the next phase of this project will involve writing more analytical interpretations of the material.

Recent advances in marble studies have also greatly affected the interpretation of marble statuary discovered in the Levant. On the scientific front, isotopic and other chemical analyses have been conducted on material discovered in Roman-period Israel, Syria, and Jordan. Z. Pearl's 1989 master's thesis, entitled *Archaeological Marble in Israel: Chemical and Mineralogical Analysis*,

was groundbreaking. Subsequently, Pearl and his mentor M. Magaritz have published joint studies with archaeologists and sculpture specialists on the origins of marble sculpture, sarcophagi, and architectural elements from various sites in Israel, particularly Caesarea Maritima and Beth Shean (Pearl and Magaritz 1991a; 1991b; Gersht and Pearl 1992; Fischer and Pearl 1998). Fischer has continued this work by publishing synthetic analyses of the chronology and distribution of marble imported from specific Greek and Anatolian quarries to Roman Israel (Fischer 2002; 2009a; 2009b). For Syria, D. Wielgosz has recently undertaken a comprehensive research program to analyze the origins of marble sarcophagi and statuary (Wielgosz 2000; 2001; 2008; Wielgosz et al. 2002), and in Jordan work has been done on architectural marble from Gadara/Umm Qais (Al-Bashaireh 2003; 2011) and the Small Temple at Petra (Reid 2005: 113–14, 202–4), as well as on sculptural marble from Gerasa (Friedland 2003) and Philadelphia/Amman (Friedland and Tykot 2010; 2012).

For the position of the Levant within the imperial marble trade, M. Fischer has pioneered the application of Ward-Perkins' models to the importation, distribution, and use of marble in Israel (Fischer 1988; 1991; 1994; Fischer and Stein 1994; Fischer and Grossmark 1996). His book on *Marble Studies: Roman Palestine and the Marble Trade* surveys marble architectural decoration, sculpture, and sarcophagi found in Israel and analyzes the contexts, both architectural and cultural, in which these imported marble artifacts were used (1998). The work of A. Ovadiah and Y. Turnheim on the Severan theater frieze from Beth Shean provides a contextualized study of the architectural marble from a single monument and addresses issues such as technique, style, and the ethnicity of the artisans.[9]

Thus, the contextualized study and publication of large groups of marble statuary associated with specific architectural contexts in the Levant is a fairly recent endeavor. As noted above, because many of the finds of marble statuary in Israel and Jordan are so recent, and because they are often published in short articles or as parts of excavation reports that focus mainly on their formal and iconographic characteristics, most Roman sculpture specialists have overlooked the Levant as a potential venue for marble statuary. The present study of the sculptures from the Sanctuary of Pan at Caesarea Philippi will, following Brinkerhoff and Stucky, endeavor to contribute another contextualized analysis to the scholarship on marble sculpture from the Levant. As well, it is hoped that it will further efforts to include the corpus of marble statuary from this region in the mainstream of scholarship on Roman sculpture.

HISTORICAL CONTEXT OF THE SCULPTURES

The Greek names for Banias — Paneas, Panias or Paneias — derive from the feminine form of the adjective πάνειον, which refers to the site's vast natural grotto that was dedicated to the god Pan sometime in the third century BC (Ma'oz 1993a: 136–37). The site received its Roman name, Caesarea Philippi, in 2 BC when Herod the Great's son, Herod Philip, built a city here and named it "Caesarea" to honor the emperor Augustus and "Philippi" to distinguish it from his father's Caesarea Maritima on the coast (Joseph. *BJ* 2.167–69). In AD 61, Agrippa II, whose capital was at Caesarea Philippi, renamed the city Neronias in honor of Nero (Joseph. *AJ* 20.211) and commemorated this refoundation in a series of city coins (Meshorer 1984–85: 39, pl. 7B, C, D). This name seems to have been maintained, at least on coins minted at the city, through the years of the Jewish Revolt; however, the name by which the site became known in the second and third centuries AD is Caesarea Panias. The official name of the city that appears on the reverse of coins minted at the site from the period of Marcus Aurelius to Elagabalus is Καισ(αρεία) σεβ(αστὴ) ἱερ(ὰ) καὶ ἄσυ(λος) ὑπὸ Πανείου (Meshorer 1984–85: 38, 49, no. II, 5–7; 50, no. III, 9; nos. IV, 11–12; 51, nos. V, 13–14; nos. VI, 15–17; 51–52, nos. VII, 19–21). In Jewish sources of this period, the city is referred to as Keisarion or Kisrin, and the grotto as Pamias or Panias (Ma'oz 1993a: 136). In the fourth century AD, the name Caesarea was dropped and the town was referred to solely as Panias.

The identification of modern Banias as Caesarea Philippi is secure, since the grotto and springs that provide the Hellenistic name for the site, still survive, and the modern Arabic name — Banias — is clearly derived from the Hellenistic and Roman period name, Panias.

The site of Panias is first mentioned by Polybius, who notes that the Seleucid king Antiochus III won a victory over the Ptolemaic general Scopas in 200 BC at τό Πάνιον, the cave of Pan (16.18). From this reference, it can be assumed that the grotto was firmly associated with Pan by 200 BC (Wilson 2004: 4–6; Ma'oz 2007: 6–8). The cave must have been dedicated to the deity sometime in the third century BC, perhaps by the Ptolemies, who were known to have constructed a Paneion in Alexandria and whose dynastic cult of Dionysos was associated with the worship of Pan (Ma'oz 1993a: 137; 2008: 1587; Wilson 2004: 2–4). As a consequence of the victory at Panias in 200 BC, the site fell under Seleucid rule (Grainger 1990; Wilson 2004: 4–6). During the late second and first centuries BC, Panias and its territory became part of the Ituraean kingdom, which included much of Lebanon (Wilson 2004: 6–9). Following Pompey's conquest of the Levant in 64 BC, a reduced Ituraean kingdom, which included Panias, was ruled first by Lysanias (64–34 BC) and later by Zenodorus (23–20 BC) (Millar 1993: 37; Schürer 1973, 1: 243). Upon the death of Zenodorus in 20 BC, Augustus granted his territories, namely Panias and the neighboring Ulatha, to Herod the Great who had been appointed client king of Judaea in 40 BC (Joseph. *AJ* 15.344–64; Wilson 2004: 9–11).

The transfer of Panias to the kingdom of Herod began a new era of Roman association and eventually domination, which encouraged the architectural embellishment of the site. Josephus tells us that, after Herod accompanied Augustus on his visit to Syria in 20 BC, the client king dedicated a temple to the emperor near the grotto at Panias (Joseph. *AJ* 15.363; *BJ* 1.404–6; Wilson 2004: 10). The construction of an Augusteum at Caesarea Philippi may be seen in several lights (Wilson 2004: 11–16). It is certainly in keeping with Herod's Hellenization of his territories. It also follows Herod's pattern of adulation of his imperial patron via the foundation of cities named for Augustus, which had as their focal points temples to Roma and the emperor (for example, Caesarea Maritima and Sebaste). On a local level, the establishment of

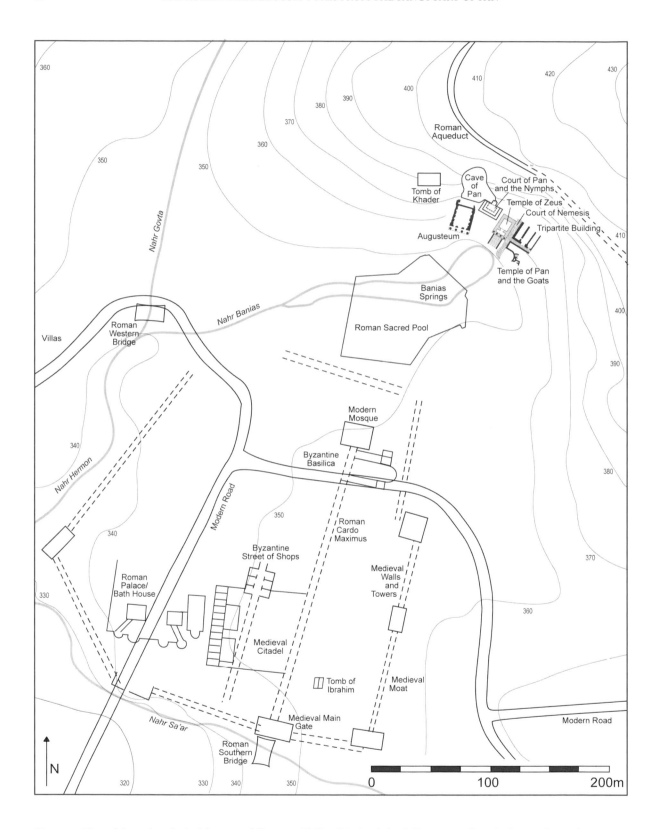

Fig. 2   Map of the archaeological features of Caesarea Philippi/Panias (after Wilson 2004: fig. 1; by Lorene Sterner).

Fig. 3　　The springs at Banias, the Cave of Pan, and the terrace at the Sanctuary of Pan (photo by Gugganij, 2007).

the Sanctuary of Pan, the review of the archaeology focuses solely on the sanctuary *temenos*. To date, only one significant fragment of a marble sculpture has been discovered in any of the other excavations at or around the city of Caesarea Philippi.[13]

The focal point of the sanctuary, the enormous, natural grotto, occurs in a 30-m-high vertical rock scarp in the southwestern slopes of Mount Hermon (fig. 3). Immediately to the east of this grotto, a natural rock terrace (c. 76 m long by 20 m deep) juts out from the foot of this rock scarp. Approximately 10 m below this terrace and 40 m south, the springs of Banias emerge from two underground ravines that run beneath the terrace, perpendicular to the façade of the scarp.

In the early Hellenistic period, the site does not seem to have been architecturally embellished. To date, the only Hellenistic remains discovered are two retaining walls, probably dated to the second

century BC, which cut across the southern end of the terrace (Ma'oz 2008: 1588). These may indicate that a road passed through the sanctuary across this terrace. Such minimal architectural remains, as well as the ceramic finds from Stratum VI, indicate that at this time the site was merely a road-side sanctuary with activities focused around the natural grotto (Berlin 1999: 29–31; Ma'oz 2008: 1588).

The first construction at the site is Augustan in date: a rectangular hall placed directly in front of the natural grotto. Following this, from the middle or later first century AD, a series of buildings was laid out atop the elevated terrace from west to east in "horizontal stratigraphy," with the earliest construction on the far western side of the sanctuary and the latest building occupying the easternmost edge of the terrace. Unlike the Augustan building, which sits in front of the grotto, these structures were built up to and abutted the rock scarp itself.

OVERVIEW OF CHAPTERS

This publication consists of two major parts: a catalogue that documents the statues and the interpretive text that analyzes this assemblage within its local, regional, and empire-wide contexts. The analysis of the statuary is supported and aided by the nearly-complete excavation of the sanctuary and the discovery and interpretation of large bodies of architectural, ceramic, epigraphic, and numismatic evidence.[21]

The catalogue of the sculptures from the Paneion (placed at the end of this volume) records the twenty-nine reconstructable pieces found in the 1988–1994 excavations of the sanctuary. In addition to recording the vital statistics for each piece, these catalogue entries focus on the identification and discussion of the subject of each piece, the stylistic comparanda that may relate it to a particular sculptural workshop or chronological period, and its date of manufacture. These identifications, workshop associations, and dates of production are then used throughout the book to discuss broader issues related to the sculptural group as a whole, such as the origins of the group, the chronology of sculptural dedication at the sanctuary, and the nature of worship at the sanctuary. Two appendices provide information regarding other sculptural fragments discovered at the site. The first presents a tally of small, non-restorable sculptural fragments recovered during the 1988–1994 excavations. The second describes an over-life-size bust of Antinous (fig. 95) reportedly found at the site in the mid-1800s, "rediscovered" on the art market by H. Meyer in 1983, and sold again by Sotheby's in 2010 to a private collector.

As noted above, there is no native source of marble in the Levant, nor a local tradition of carving marble. Thus, the discovery of a large body of marble statuary, such as that found at the Paneion, poses questions regarding its origins and acquisition. In Chapter 2, "The Origins of the Sculptures: Marble Provenience, Technical and Stylistic Characteristics, Production, and Acquisition," I consider the three factors relevant to the origins of the Paneion sculptures: the geological origins of their marble, the carving tradition in which their sculptors were trained, and the place where they were carved. Isotopic analyses of 15 of the sculptural fragments and petrographic studies are employed to determine where the marble of the sculptures was quarried. These scientific results are compared with workshop attributions for the sculptures, derived from analyses of style and carving techniques, as well as from similarities of Paneion pieces with specific comparable statues. Both the scientific and the art historical analyses indicate that the pieces are associated with the workshops of western Asia Minor and "Asiatic style," in material, style, and technique. This leads to questions of whether the Paneion pieces were imported fully-carved or worked locally and by whom, how sculptural patrons might have acquired these imported pieces, and which were the possible ports of entry into the Levant.

Since imported marble sculptures carved in an Asiatic style were not readily available in most Levantine cities and were probably more expensive and conspicuous than sculptures worked in local stone and carved in a local tradition, the dedication of imported marble statuary in the Levant is a notable phenomenon. Chapter 3, "Patronage, Chronology, and Display: Patterns of Sculptural Dedication at the Sanctuary," considers who was dedicating this statuary, when they were dedicating it, and how these dedications related to the architectural development of the sanctuary. From literary, epigraphic, architectural, sculptural, and numismatic evidence, it becomes clear that statues were dedicated at the sanctuary from the first century AD through the late fourth or fifth centuries AD, with the majority of dedications erected in the first through third centuries. Initial patrons seem to have been Herodian client-kings, though in the second and third centuries AD the patrons were local Romanized religious and civic officials.

The sculptural evidence from the Paneion, more so than the epigraphic and numismatic material, provides plentiful and important information regarding the pantheon of deities worshiped and honored at the sanctuary. Knowledge of the breadth of the sanctuary's pantheon and the nature of the individual deities worshiped there shows that the Sanctuary of Pan expanded beyond its original rural, Pan-centered worship and attracted dedications to numerous Olympian deities, as well as more personal demi-gods. Chapter 4, "The Subjects of the Sculptures: The Graeco-Roman Pantheon of the Sanctuary of Pan," analyzes the iconography of the sculptural fragments discovered at the sanctuary. In addition to at least two (probably four) of the five known cult deities of the sanctuary, a host of other "visiting deities," not cited in either the numismatic or epigraphic evidence, were worshipped or honored via sculptural dedications.

This publication provides important documentation and synthetic analysis of the surviving sculptural dedications from a major provincial Graeco-Roman sanctuary. As discussed in the concluding chapter, "The Function and Meaning of the Sculptures: The Sanctuary of Pan as a Graeco-Roman Cult Center in the Levant," the Anatolian marble, Asiatic style, Hellenistic types, Romanized local patrons, and Graeco-Roman subject mat-

ter of the sculptures from the Paneion suggest that our Levantine sanctuary was both highly Hellenized and Romanized. As such, it stands in direct contrast to other religious centers in this region, where Semitic deities such as Eschmun and Allat were (in the Roman period) conflated with classical gods such as Asklepios and Athena. The Paneion sculptures also offer important evidence for the role of the Levant in the imperial marble trade and the dialogue on cultural interaction or "Romanization" in this far-flung eastern region. Thus, far from there being no market for marble sculptures in the Levant, patrons at sites such as Caesarea Philippi seem to have acquired and dedicated great numbers of high-quality large-scale marble statuary to communicate their assimilation to and participation in mainstream Graeco-Roman culture.

NOTES

1   This number includes seven limestone fragments, six of which are so poorly preserved that it is difficult to determine whether they belonged to sculpture or architectural decoration. Only one limestone fragment discovered at the sanctuary, the base of a statuette of Kybele or Dea Syria (cat. 23), was clearly part of a sculpture.

2   The sculptures are currently in the Beth Shemesh storage facility of the Israel Antiquities Authority.

3   Though Josephus states that Herod used "white marble" for the temple that he built at Caesarea Philippi/Panias (*BJ* 1.21.3), there is no archaeological evidence for the use of architectural marble at the site, and there is little evidence for the large-scale import of marble artifacts of any sort to this region before the second century AD (Fischer and Stein 1994). Thus, though some scholars have taken Josephus' words at face-value and assumed that Caeasarea Philippi and other Herodian sites regularly employed marble in the first century BC, this scenario must be rethought.

4   Portraiture will be clearly noted as such (e.g., cat. 24). The single limestone sculpture from the Sanctuary of Pan (cat. 23) will be discussed separately, since it too is excluded from this genre of *Idealplastik* because of its material and style.

5   In the Persian period, this region constituted a satrapy named Ebirnâri, or "the land beyond the river." This name clearly reflected the perspective

of the Assyrian kings at Babylon and Susa (Avi-Yonah 1966). The Levant may be further defined as F. Millar's "Near East" minus Mesopotamia and the majority of Arabia (Millar 1993: 2–23).

6   "You shall not make for yourself an idol, whether in the form of anything that is in heaven above, or that is on the earth beneath, or that is in the water under the earth. You shall not bow down to them or worship them…" (Exodus 20: 4, 5; Deuteronomy 5:8, 9, NSRV). For Jewish figurative art despite this, see Hachlili 1988: 285–316; Fischer 1991: 140–41; Fine 2005.

7   For recent publications of this sculptural group, see Reich 1996; Hannestad 1998 and 2001.

8   Note that several of their footnotes cite recently-discovered, unpublished pieces in the storerooms at the Rockefeller Museum in Jerusalem.

9   Though see the critical review by Foerster 1997.

10   This historical fact makes it likely that there was some sort of an arena at Caesarea Philippi, although to date no archaeological evidence for this type of building has been found.

11   For example, Bishop Barachus of Panias attended the Council of Constantinople in AD 381; Bishop Olympios of Panias attended the Council of Chalcedon in AD 451.

12   The initial construction date of this road is unknown; however, a milestone, dated to the reign of Gordian III (AD 238–244) and found 4 km/2.7 miles west of

Caesarea Philippi on the road to Tyre, indicates that the road existed by the first decades of the third century AD (Isaac in press: 21–22, no. 29). For the Tyre–Damascus road, see Avi-Yonah 1966: 186, 187; Roll 1983: 145; 2002: 216.

13   V. Tzaferis, personal communication, 1998. The piece is not yet published.

14   For two clear summaries of the four most-discussed candidates and relevant recent bibliography, see Bernett 2007b: 339, n. 6, and Kropp 2009: 109–10; for the suggestion that the Augusteum was built in the city center of Panias, beneath the Byzantine church, see Wilson 2004: 14–16; for arguments that the newly-excavated Roman temple at Omrit is Herod's Augusteum, see Overman et al. 2003; 2007.

15   Ma'oz (1994–99: 97–99; 2007: 15–17; 2008: 1588) now also attributes a semicircular colonnade, depicted on a series of coins minted at Panias from AD 218/9–221/2 (Meshorer 1984–85: nos. 31–32, 38–39, 45), to Herod and tentatively locates this in front of and below the sanctuary terrace. However, because no archaeological remains of such a colonnade were located during excavations outside the cave or on the sanctuary terrace, and because appearances of structures (and statues) on coins do not necessarily translate to the existence of similar buildings at a site (Prayon 1982; Dumser 2006; Sobocinski in press), I do not discuss the proposed semicircular colonnade here.

16   The date in the inscription indicates 150 years from the foundation of the city of Caesarea Philippi by Herod Philip, which took place in 2/1 BC. Thus, the inscription may be dated to AD 148/9.

17   For coins showing a freestanding Zeus, see Meshorer 1984–85: nos. 5, 5a (Marcus Aurelius); no. 8 (Commodus); nos. 10, 10a, 10b, 11a (Septimius Severus); no. 15 (Geta); no. 19 (Caracalla).

18   For coins showing Zeus standing in a tetrastyle temple, see Meshorer 1984–85: no. 29 (Macrinus);

no. 30 (Diadumenianus); no. 37 (Elagabalus); Ma'oz 1994–99: 92–93.

19   Note that Ma'oz refers to this structure as a "temple" and names it the "Tomb-Temple of the Sacred Goats" (2008: 1589).

20   For example, the largest fragment of the left leg and support of the Capitoline/Medici Aphrodite (cat. 13) was found in the sculpture deposit (locus 705), while the joining front half of its right foot and attached base were found in one of the northern-most niches in the west gallery in the Tripartite Building (locus 726), and the back half of its right leg was found outside the temple in the street to the south (locus 195); the torso of the dancing satyr (cat. 20) was found in the main deposit (locus 705), while one of its joining arm fragments was found in the northern-most niche in the west gallery within the Tripartite Building (locus 718); the torso of the Herakles (cat. 21) was found in the street outside and to the southwest of the temple (locus 183), while its joining leg fragment was found in the northern area of the central hall of the Tripartite Building (locus 716).

21   Z. U. Ma'oz's *Paneion I: Excavation at the Sanctuary of Pan at Caesarea Philippi-Banyas, Final Report* is in press. Several specialists have been most kind in forwarding their final reports to me prior to their publication in this volume. I would like to thank Benjamin Isaac of Tel Aviv University for "Inscriptions from Banias" and Andrea M. Berlin for "The Hellenistic and Roman Sanctuary: The Evidence of the Pottery." During my doctoral work, John F. Wilson of Pepperdine University, co-director of the excavations of the city center of Caesarea Philippi, also kindly forwarded a draft of his monograph on Caesarea Philippi, now published (2004). The coins were published in 1984–85 by Ya'akov Meshorer.

Chapter 2

The Origins of the Sculptures

Marble Provenience, Technical and Stylistical Characteristics, Production, and Acquisition

Since there is no native source of marble in the Levant, all marble statuary found in this region had to be imported from the other marble-rich provinces of the empire—either as fully-carved monuments, partially-carved works, or uncarved blocks.[1] Thus, the discovery of Roman-period marble sculptures at the Sanctuary of Pan at Caesarea Philippi, as at other sites in the region, raises questions regarding their origins. In this chapter, three factors relevant to the origins of the Paneion sculptures are considered: the geological origins of their marble, the carving tradition in which their sculptors were trained, and the place where they were carved.

Scientific, technical, and stylistic evidence suggests that most of the Paneion sculptures were imported from Asia Minor (especially from the regions of Asia and Caria), probably fully-carved. Thus, in this chapter I also consider modes of acquisition of marble sculpture from Asia Minor and probable ports of entry into the Levant. The Asiatic origins of the Paneion sculptures reveal that Caesarea Philippi was one of the few sites that received significant quantities of marble statuary within a region that seems to have been selectively involved in the imperial marble trade. This importation also demonstrates notable trade connections between the eastern-most Levant and the Hellenized provinces of Asia Minor.

MARBLE PROVENIENCE: ISOTOPIC ANALYSES OF THE PANEION SCULPTURES

The marble of the majority of the Paneion sculptures has large, white, translucent crystals with no foliation or color-banding. Isotopic analysis was performed on samples taken from fifteen sculptures and the results were compared to the Classical Marble Database (data and quarry possibilities are listed in Tables 1 and 2 at the end of this chapter).[2] As is common with the results of isotopic analysis, every sample taken from the Paneion sculptures may be associated with at least two or more different quarries.[3] To further narrow the range of quarry sources, the chemical composition of ten of the Paneion pieces was tested and determined to be either dolomitic or calcitic. From these additional mineralogical analyses and the history of use of particular quarries, in all but three cases the Greek and Italian quarries may be eliminated as possible sources for the Paneion sculptures. For example, the analyses of the sample taken from cat. 4 show that the marble used to make the head of Zeus or Asklepios may have come from one of five different quarries in Asia Minor, Thasos/Cape Phaneri, or Carrara. Carrara may be ruled out as a possible quarry source, since its marble tends to be very fine-grained, and the marble of

21

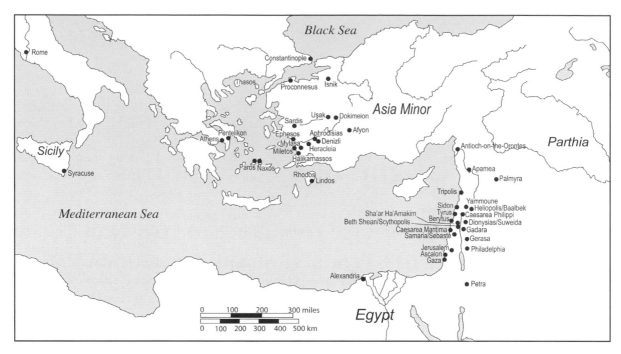

Fig. 5   Map of possible quarry origins of the sculptures from Caesarea Philippi/Panias (by Lorene Sterner).

cat. 4 is medium-grained. Likewise, Thasos/Cape Phaneri may be eliminated as a possible quarry source, since its marble is dolomitic, whereas that of cat. 4 is calcitic. In the case of cat. 25, the sample taken from the forequarters of a bovine shows that the marble used to carve this piece comes from one of two quarries in Asia Minor or from either Naxos/Apiranthos or Naxos/Apollonas. These Greek quarries may be ruled out, since historical evidence shows that both were mined only during the Archaic period and not in the Roman period when this sculpture was carved.

Thus, isotopic analyses, additional mineralogical tests, and historical evidence regarding the use of particular quarries suggest that the sampled statues from the Paneion are made of marble primarily (if not exclusively) from Anatolian quarries (further petrographic tests are needed to determine whether cats. 2, 11, and 13 come from Anatolian or Greek quarries). Because each of the sculptures from the Paneion is associated with at least two (usually more) different Anatolian quarries, and because the marbles from many of these quarries have identical physical characteristics and are difficult to distinguish from one another even by scientific methods, it is not possible to be

more specific regarding the provenience of the Paneion sculptures. Possible Anatolian quarry sources, therefore, are Afyon, Aphrodisias, Denizli, Dokimeion, Ephesos, Heracleia, İznik, Miletos, Mylasa, Proconnesos/Marmara, and Uşak; if cats. 2, 11, and 13 are not made of Anatolian marble, they are associated with the Greek quarries of Paros/Lychnites, Thasos/Acropolis, and Pentelikon, respectively (fig. 5).

It is probable that the remaining unsampled sculptures also originated in Anatolian quarries, since the marble used for the majority of the Paneion sculptures is remarkably homogenous in grain size, grain density, and the ability to take a high polish. In support of this, the results of the isotopic analyses performed on ten pieces in 1995 and on a further five pieces in 2005 provide strikingly similar quarry origins and point overwhelmingly to quarry sources in Asia Minor.

The suggestion that the marble of the Paneion sculptures comes primarily from quarries in Asia Minor and possibly Greece corresponds with the conclusions of studies of imported white marble discovered in Israel, Syria, and Jordan.[4] Using a sequential, multi-method analysis that combines chemical and mineralogical analyses to study Roman-period statuary, architectural elements, and sarcophagi,[5] Fischer and Pearl found that Roman-period marble artifacts discovered in Israel were quarried and exported almost entirely from Asia Minor and Greece, with only four pieces tentatively, but not definitively, associated with the Italian quarry of Carrara.[6] Furthermore, their results show that different combinations of quarries seem to have supplied the marble for statuary, architectural elements, and sarcophagi. Architectural marble was imported primarily from the Anatolian quarry of Proconnesos and the Greek quarry of Paros, while sarcophagi were imported from Proconnesos and Pentelikon (Fischer and Pearl 1998: 248–50, 252–55, 256–57; Fischer 2002: 320). Sculptural marble came from a much wider range of quarries in both Asia Minor and Greece, and especially from Proconnesos, Afyon, and Aphrodisias in Asia Minor and Thasos/Cape Vathy, Paros, and Pentelikon in Greece (Fischer and Pearl 1998: 248–50, 255–56; Fischer 2002: 320). Apparently, marble from these Greek quarries was used exclusively for statuary in Palestine (Fischer and Pearl 1998: 255). Similarly, for material from Roman Syria, Wielgosz employed chemical and mineralogical analyses and found that four sarcophagi from Palmyra were made of Pentelic marble (Wielgosz 2001), while nineteen statues from the same site used marble from Dokimeion, Proconnesos, Pentelikon, Thasos/Cape Vathy, and Paros (Wielgosz 2000; Wielgosz et al. 2002). Finally, for Jordan, Al-Bashaireh finds that the architectural marble from Umm Qais/Gadara comes primarily from Asia Minor, but somewhat from Greece (2003; 2011); Reid's analysis of the architectural and epigraphic marble from the Small Temple at Petra suggests that it comes from various quarries in Asia Minor (Marmara, Sardis, Uşak, Afyon), Greece (Paros, Pentelikon, and Thassos), and perhaps also from Luna in Italy (2005: 113–14, 202–4); and preliminary analyses of marble from Roman sculptures discovered at Gerasa, Philadelphia/Amman, and Gadara/Umm Qais show quarry origins in Asia Minor (Afyon, Aphrodisias, Denizli, Dokimeion, Ephesus, Heracleia, İznik, Mylasa, Proconnesos, Sardis, Uşak) and in Greece (Paros, Pentelikon, and Thasos/Cape Vathy) (Friedland 2003: 415–17; Friedland and Tykot 2010; 2012).

The overwhelming association of the Caesarea Philippi statues with Anatolian quarries and possible connections to Greek quarries should also be compared with the sources of the marble sculptures from Caesarea Maritima and Beth Shean/Scythopolis, the two sites in Roman Israel where the largest number of marble sculptures have been discovered. Interestingly, the statuary found in these two cities is not homogenous in origin. Of thirty-one sampled sculptures from Caesarea Maritima, five were made of marble from Thasos/Cape Vathy, eight were made of marble from Pentelikon, one was made of marble from Paros, eleven were made of marble from Aphrodisias/Afyon, two were made of marble from Hymettus (possibly Carrara), and five were made of marble from Marmara (Pearl 1989: table 7.2). Eight of the sculptures found at Beth Shean/Scythopolis have been analyzed so far: two come from Pentelikon, one from Paros, three from Afyon/Aphrodisias, one from Marmara, and one from Hymettus or Marmara (Pearl 1989: 50–55). In addition, the marble of the two colossal heads found at Tel Naharon near Beth Shean/Scythopolis comes from Thasos/Cape Vathy (Pearl and Magaritz 1991a: 46–47). Thus, Caesarea Maritima and Beth Shean/Scythopolis received marble statuary from multiple Greek and Anatolian quarries, whereas Caesarea Philippi seems, based on the scientific analyses done to date, to have imported statuary primarily from Asia Minor and to a much lesser degree from Greece. This distinction may be due to the fact that the comparison of Caesarea Maritima and Beth Shean/Scythopolis with the Paneion at Caesarea Philippi is somewhat uneven, since the former were large cities in which statuary was displayed in a variety of architectural contexts, while the latter is a sanctuary with a single function. However, two things should be emphasized. First, only one sculpture has been found in the extensive excavations of the city of Caesarea Philippi itself.[7] More importantly, though the Paneion sculptures were dedicated in one functional setting, they were not all erected at a single point in time as a cohesive sculptural group, but are the result of beneficence by a variety of patrons over many years. It is more likely, then, that the consistency of source material of the Paneion sculptures is due to larger patterns of trade and exchange, rather than patterns of dedication at the site itself. While still further scientific analyses of the Paneion sculptures might show that some of the marble sculpture was imported from Greek quarries, if the distinction between the sources of marble for sculpture from Caesarea Maritima, Beth Shean and Caesarea Philippi is further substantiated, it may reflect the fact that sculpture reached the cities of Roman Israel and Syria through different trade routes and ports of entry.

SCULPTURAL TRADITIONS OF THE PANEION SCULPTURES: TECHNICAL AND STYLISTIC ANALYSES

As discussed above, chemical and petrographic analyses of Roman-period sculptures, architectural elements, and sarcophagi discovered in the Roman Near East have demonstrated that the marble of artifacts imported to the region was quarried in both Asia Minor and Greece, but rarely (if at all) in Italy. Indeed, some scholars have noted that many of the imported marble sculptures found in the Levant have stylistic and technical features specific to Anatolian workshops (Iliffe 1951: 709–11; Vermeule and Anderson 1981: 11–12; Gersht 1984: 113–14; Stirling 1994: 57–76, 82–5; 2005: 92, 117–29; Hannestad 1998; 1999: 192; 2001). To assess the carving traditions with which the Paneion sculptures may be associated, their technical and stylistic features must be compared to those of sculptures carved in the workshops of Roman-period Greece and Asia Minor, both of which are known to have supplied marble statuary to the Levant.

The Paneion sculptures are characterized by the following technical features: highly-polished drapery and flesh; emphatic and plentiful drill-work in the hair and drapery; eyes with undrilled pupils, pointed inner corners, and little indication of tear ducts (other than the occasional drill hole at their inner corners); and square or rectangular neck struts (large cubic areas of roughly-worked marble left at the backs of necks).[8] Technically, the Paneion sculptures are not comparable to the statuary carved in the workshops of Roman Greece. They are easily distinguished from Attic and Peloponnesian products,[9] which share many

stylistic and technical features and are characterized by smoothed, but rarely polished, skin surfaces;[10] rasp marks left unsmoothed on drapery, shoes, arms, legs, and occasionally even on faces and necks;[11] rounded inner corners of eyes with chiseled indications of tear ducts;[12] chiseled rather than drilled hair with drill-work used only for accent;[13] and an absence of neck struts.[14] Nor are the Paneion pieces comparable to Roman-period northern Greek statues,[15] which are distinguishable from Attic and Peloponnesian works and are characterized by smoothed and often lightly polished faces, necks, and limbs;[16] occasional rasp marks left on drapery; more variation in the shape of the inner corners of eyes and the indication of tear ducts;[17] more prevalent drillwork in the hair;[18] Venus rings carved on their necks;[19] and an absence of neck struts.

The Paneion pieces are, instead, most similar technically and stylistically to the sculptures carved in the workshops of Roman Asia Minor. Though scholars speak of a unified "Asiatic" style that existed from the late first through the third century AD[20] and the definition of regional styles continues to be debated, archaeological, sculptural, and epigraphic evidence suggests that regional sculptural production centers existed in Caria (Aphrodisias), Asia (Ephesos), Pamphylia (Side and Perge), and Phyrgia (Dokimeion) from the first through the third centuries AD and beyond.[21]

Thus, in addition to connections via the general technical features noted above, several specific comparisons of the Paneion sculptures with pieces from Ephesos and Aphrodisias will illustrate that the Paneion statues may be associated with the workshops of Asia Minor in general, and with the carving centers of Caria (Aphrodisias) and Asia (Ephesos) in particular. For example, the nearly complete, two-thirds life-size Artemis Rospigliosi, accompanied on her right by a hound and hare (cat. 15), has highly polished flesh and drapery. Such high polish, especially on drapery, is common on sculptures carved in Asia Minor, but contrasts with the rasp marks frequently found on the drapery, flesh, and faces of statuary carved in Greek workshops.[22] In addition, four of the five fully-preserved heads from the sanctuary have neck struts, a technical feature most commonly associated with the workshops of Asia Minor.[23] One example from the Paneion is the life-size head of a goddess wearing a *stephane* (cat. 5), which may be identified as Hera, Hygieia, or Aphrodite based on her headpiece and hairstyle. Such neck struts are extremely rare on statuary found in Greece. Another technical characteristic of the Paneion sculptures that associates them with the workshops of Asia Minor is the emphatic and plentiful use of the drill in hair, beards, and drapery. On a head of Zeus or Asklepios from the sanctuary (cat. 4), deep drill channels outline the locks of hair and the curls of the beard. On both sides of the face, deep drill channels separate a hood of hair from the temples and cheeks. This approach to the hair, however, is not common to all Anatolian workshops, but seems most widely-used in production centers along the western coast. The "black and white" effect created by the deep drill channels seen here differs markedly from the technique used on Pamphylian works, which were carved with drill channels of varying depths that create a layered effect.[24] In contrast, the hair of sculptures carved in Greece is worked mainly with a chisel and merely accented by drillwork.[25] Another technical feature common to all of the Paneion heads and comparable to Anatolian sculptures is the rendering of the eyes. As with the classicizing head of Athena wearing an Attic helmet (cat. 2), all the Paneion sculptures have eyes with pointed inner corners and little indication of tear ducts, except for tiny drill holes at their inner corners.[26]

In addition to these technical similarities, several of the Paneion pieces are stylistically similar to individual sculptures from Aphrodisias and Ephesos. For example, the Paneion head of Apollo or a Muse (cat. 6) echoes a head from Aphrodisias often identified as Aphrodite but now thought to depict a Caryatid.[27] Comparable features include the shape of the face, the rendering and shape of the eyes, the polish of the face, and the contrast between the polished face and the heavily drilled hair (Friedland 1999: 14–15, figs. 7–10). In right profile, these same pieces appear particularly close in the drilling of the hair. Both have several deep, continuous, undulating channels piercing an otherwise solid mass of hair. This technique seems to be common to Aphrodisian sculptors, since several

other heads from the site have similarly worked hair. Another Paneion sculpture, a statuette of a satyr or faun (cat. 20), may also be associated with the workshops at Aphrodisias. The back of the creature has an S-shaped tail and uncommon rendering of the backbone, both of which find parallels in two statues from Aphrodisias: the Pan of a *spinario* group and the satyr from the small group of a satyr with the young Dionysos.[28] The spines of all of these creatures are depicted with single chisel lines that run down their backs, fork just above their buttocks, and then extend horizontally to separate the buttocks from the lower backs (Friedland 1999: 16–17; figs. 11–13). Both figures have S-shaped tails nestled into the triangular area created by these forks. Finally, the Paneion torso of a nymph (cat. 11) recalls the sculptural type, posture, and formal and technical characteristics of an Aphrodite or nymph from the Fountain of Trajan at Ephesos (Ephesos Museum no. 768; Miltner 1959: 339, pl. 183.4; Longfellow 2011: 92–93, fig. 32). Especially similar are the arrangement of the drapery around the lower hips, the position of the shell above the pubic region, the rounded edges of the drapery folds, the clean, even drill channels that indicate separations between folds, and the highly polished drapery and flesh (Friedland 1999: 17, figs. 14–15).

Many technical and stylistic characteristics of the seven pieces discussed here are shared by the other sculptures from the site. Thus, technical and stylistic similarities, as well as several direct stylistic comparisons, make the Paneion sculptures most similar to statuary created in the workshops of western Anatolia.

PRODUCTION OF THE PANEION SCULPTURES: EVIDENCE FOR CARVING MARBLE STATUARY IN THE LEVANT

Though the evidence suggests that the Paneion sculptures were carved of marble primarily from Anatolian quarries and created by sculptors trained in Anatolian workshops, it is difficult to determine more specifically where these pieces were actually carved. Evidence from shipwrecks shows that statuary was transported both fully-carved and in roughed-out or quarry-state.[29] Because finished sculptures, uncarved blocks of marble, and itinerant sculptors traveled widely throughout the Roman world, the location of carving of a single piece does not follow from either the origins of its marble or the training of its sculptor, nor can it be determined from the finished sculpture itself. At most sites that are thought to have been sculptural production centers during the Roman period we lack physical evidence for sculptors' workshops such as the one found at Aphrodisias. The same holds true for the Levant: except for one possible sculptor's workshop at Antioch-on-the-Orontes (Stillwell 1941: 117–19; Najbjerg 2001: 180, 250–51, cat. nos. 92–93), we are not able to identify any specific structure in which marble statuary was carved.

Could the Paneion sculptures have been carved in the Levant? It is important to address this issue here, as there is much debate in the literature about whether marble statues were imported to the region fully-carved or whether they were worked locally, either from roughed-out, quarry-state pieces or from entirely unworked blocks of marble.[30] On one side of the debate, there are scholars who argue that because there is no native source of marble in the region, it is unlikely that a local tradition of carving marble existed. Thus, these scholars argue that the majority of marble sculptures found in the Levant must have been imported fully-carved (Colledge 1976: 118; Fischer 2009b: 401). On the other side of the debate, there are those who argue that all marble sculptures found in the Levant and worked in a Graeco-Roman style could have been carved in this region, either by local Levantine sculptors trained in the Graeco-Roman tradition or by itinerant sculptors from the major sculptural production centers of the imperial east who had set up workshops in various cities in the Levant (Will 1965: 512; Ward-Perkins 1969; Albertson 1988: 7 n. 35; Albertson 2004: 299; Gersht 1995b).

Archaeologically, clear instances of marble carving in the region come from discoveries of quarry-state and unfinished statuary, sarcophagi, and architectural elements, but these are few in number and distinctly non-classical in style. For example, in Roman-period Israel, Caesarea Maritima preserves several important examples. First, the quarry-state, unsculpted marble protome discovered at the site demonstrates that someone was expected to complete the imported piece locally (R. Gersht believes that the piece was abandoned because the sculptor determined that the proportions were not appropriate for carving the intended portrait bust; Gersht 1987: cat. no. 58; Gersht 1995b: 36; Gendelman and Gersht 2010: 37). Second, also discovered at Caesarea Maritima are "two or more copies of the same image, of which at least one is of higher quality than the rest" (Gersht 1995b: 36). For example, two versions of Tyche of the Amazon type are known; based on the style and technique, the example found in the 1970s may be associated with a sculptor trained in one of the major carving centers of Asia Minor at the end of the first or beginning of the second centuries, while a second version found in the mid-1980s seems to have been "copied from the first by a craftsman who was skilled in carving marble, but far from the Graeco-Hellenistic tradition" (Gersht 1995b: 36). Also from this region, at Beth Shean/Scythopolis, a totally unworked block and several half-carved blocks, discovered among the architectural elements of the Severan theater frieze, suggest that the theater frieze was carved at the site (Ovadiah and Turnheim 1994: 105, 122). According to A. Ovadiah and Y. Turnheim, the style and iconography of the finished blocks, which compare more readily with Oriental prototypes than with Graeco-Roman ones, indicate that the frieze was executed by local artists (Ovadiah and Turnheim 1994: 108–11 and 121–22).[31]

In Roman Syria, the scant evidence comes from Palmyra, where two unfinished pieces were found: a torso of Apollo from the "Baths of Diocletian" (Wielgosz 2000: 96–98, figs. 1a–c; Wielgosz et al. 2002: 390, 396) and a head of Dionysos from the Colonnaded Street (Wielgosz 2000: 98, figs. 2a–c; Wielgosz et al. 2002: 395); both seem to have been shipped from Proconnesos in a semi-finished state for completion at the destination. In this instance, however, D. Wielgosz has proposed that, because the two pieces seem to have been displayed despite their clearly unfinished state, "at least in the second century AD there were no workshops in Palmyra able to complete the work" (Wielgosz et al. 2002: 398). Further evidence comes from Antioch-on-the-Orontes, where there is a purported sculptors' workshop.[32] According to the excavator's diary of March 1937, excavations on the Main Street discovered below the basalt pavement … an atelier, of which the principal room was paved with a 'pebble mosaic' … To the north, another room contained two cemented basins, and an oven, possibly for lime (Stillwell 1941: 118).

In these rooms, numerous fragments of statues were found, all in marble (except for one piece that is listed as white limestone: no. 274 a): 12 heads of men and women (cat. nos. 254–64); 1 male (no. 265) and 3 female torsos (nos. 267–68); a statuette of Aphrodite (no. 266); a thumb (no. 269); 3 feet (no. 270); 1 arm (no. 273 a); and 20 hands (nos. 271, 272, 273 b–j) (Stillwell 1941: 117–19; Najbjerg 2001: 180, 250–51, cat. nos. 92–93). In addition,

> a considerable number of other pieces, mostly fragments of feet, hands, limbs, all at small scale, were found … Along with these was a section of a very delicate Hellenistic floral relief that had been sawn up … The indications are that here was a sculptor's shop, specializing perhaps in statuettes (Stillwell 1941: 118).

According to the excavator, the supposed workshop was destroyed in the second half of the first century AD. It is tempting to follow the excavator's and Stillwell's identification of a sculptor's workshop, though there is no mention of some of the other kinds of evidence one might expect, such as sculptor's tools, marble chips, or multiple versions of the same sculptural type at varying stages of completion. The evidence for a possible lime kiln and the fragmentary nature of most of the pieces may indeed indicate that many of the products of this purported sculptors' workshop were cut up and burned during the destruction of this context.

Finally, though the production and transport of sarcophagi clearly differed from that of statuary, it should be noted here that plenty of unfinished marble sarcophagi have been found in the Levant at sites such as Tyre, Berytus, and Caesarea Maritima (Gersht 1991 and 1996a). Scholars have argued that the preponderance of unfinished sarcophagi at places like Tyre only highlights the fact that there must not have been a sculpture workshop capable of completing this kind of funerary furniture there,

though J. B. Ward-Perkins suggests that there may have been finishing workshops at Berytus and Tripolis, where more finely-finished sarcophagi have been found (Ward-Perkins 1969). However, there is some evidence to suggest that Tyre functioned as a marble yard or receiving center of both Attic and Proconnesian sarcophagi for the wider Levantine coast, and Gersht has shown that several sarcophagi found at Caesarea Maritima have moldings similar to those characteristic of sarcophagi found at Tyre, concluding that they were finished in the same Levantine workshop, whether at Tyre or elsewhere (Gersht and Pearl 1992: 238–39; Gersht 1996a).

Overall, then, except for the handful of examples described above, there is no overwhelming evidence for the sustained carving of marble in this region, and there is certainly no indisputable evidence for workshops that produced sculpture in the classical tradition. Therefore, it seems more likely that the Paneion sculptures were imported to this region fully-carved.

PORTS OF ENTRY INTO THE LEVANT AND MODES OF ACQUISITION

Through what Levantine port did the Paneion sculptures enter the region? The large numbers of marble sculptures, sarcophagi, and architectural elements found at the cities of Caesarea Maritima, Tyre, Sidon, and Berytus make all of these possible ports of entry into the Levant for the goods of the imperial marble trade. Scholars have focused on the ports of Caesarea Maritima and Tyre as major entry points along the Levantine coast and the most likely locations for marble yards that received and stored statues and stones for carving and building. Although it is likely that Tyre was a receiving center for sarcophagi and perhaps for architectural blocks, there is no evidence for whether or not the port received statuary and if so in what state (fully-carved, partially-carved, or as uncarved blocks). However, while Sidon and Berytus should not be ruled out as possible ports of entry, if the marble yards at Tyre did receive statuary, this is the most likely port of entry for the Paneion sculptures, since Caesarea Philippi is located just 47 km (29 miles) east of Tyre along the Tyre–Damascus road (Roll 1983: 145; 2002: 216).

More specific mechanisms for the commission and transport of the Paneion sculptures from Asia Minor (and perhaps Greece) to Panias are harder to ascertain, because both specific evidence for these statues and more general information for the circulation of marble statuary via the marble trade is so paltry, especially in comparison to that for sarcophagi. Still, it is important to consider how these marble sculptures may have made their way from the quarries of Anatolia to their final display contexts in the Sanctuary of Pan. The fact that each of the Paneion sculptures seems to have been a single dedication and that there do not seem to have been any major programmatic sculptural groups at the sanctuary makes it likely that each piece was purchased on an *ad hoc* basis. I present here two possible options by which patrons of the sanctuary could acquire statuary. First, it is possible that they engaged in so-called "'mail-order' shopping for statues" (Dodge 1991: 38), as witnessed in the famous passage from Arrian. Upon completing an inspection of some building projects ordered by Hadrian at Trapezus on the Black Sea, Arrian writes to Hadrian:

> As for the statue of yourself, it is fine as regards the pose — it is pointing towards the sea — but it is a poor likeness and not good work. Please send a statue worthy of yourself in this same pose… [The temple, Arrian goes on to say, dedicated to Hermes and a local hero, Philesios, is acceptable; but the statue of Hermes is poor work.] If you think fit, please send a fresh Hermes about 5 feet high … and one of Philesios, 4 feet (Arrian, *Periplus* 1–2, trans. by Dodge 1991: 37–38).

Individual patrons of the Sanctuary of Pan could have "ordered" particular sculptures via agencies in the Levant who contacted marble quarries and sculptors' workshops in Asia Minor to acquire the desired piece. This is an especially likely scenario for the larger and heavier pieces, since we know from shipwrecks that statues tended to travel as single items amidst cargoes of other stone objects (e.g., architectural and funerary), and it seems unlikely that heavy statues would be moved around without a clear buyer already identified on the receiving end (Russell 2011: 149–50). A version of this system was used by Cicero to stock his villa in Italy with statuary acquired in Greece and is recorded in his famous letters to Atticus (Cicero, *Letters to Atticus*, 1.7, 2.2, 3, 4.2, 5.2, 6.3–4, 7.3, 8.2, 9.3, 10.5; Marvin 1993: 161–68, 180–83), though Cicero personally arranged for the shipping of the pieces separately from their purchase by his representative, Atticus (Cicero, *Letters to Atticus*, 4–5; Russell 2011: 149).

In the context of the enormous prefabrication, standardization, and stockpiling documented for sarcophagi and architectural elements, however, it seems prudent to consider another scenario. A second option is that perhaps marble yards such as those at Tyre would stock pre-carved statues of gods, goddesses, and mythological figures, so that patrons from nearby cities such as Caesarea Philippi, Sidon, and Berytus could "shop" there for desired sculptures. This "indirect trade" in finished statues, that is, the shipping and marketing of marble statues without a secured buyer at the endpoint, is especially likely for smaller-scale statues (of which there are plenty of examples from Caesarea Philippi). Such statuettes are more portable, less costly, not destined for architecturally-specific spaces that have particular requirements for dimensions, and therefore more easily sold from marble yards (Russell 2011: 150). There is evidence for this sort of indirect trade in fully-carved statuary in Philostratos' description of the life of Apollonius of Tyana, in which Philostratos discusses a merchant in Piraeus who is selling a cargo of statues of deities from Asia Minor (Philostratos, *Life of Apollonius of Tyana* V.20; Russell 2011: 150). A similar scenario for the sale of pre-carved statuary from marble yards or workshops has been envisioned for the sculptors' workshop discovered at Aphrodisias where, Rockwell suggests, sculptors displayed fully-finished statuary outside their shop to attract customers who might come to browse (Rockwell 1991: 140–41).

Thus, based on geographic proximity and the finds of multiple sarcophagi at Tyre, the Paneion sculptures probably entered the Levant through this port city, after which they were transported to the site via the Tyre–Damascus road. The statues may have been ordered directly from the quarries or associated marble carving centers of Asia and

Caria (and elsewhere) through agencies located somewhere in the Levant; in addition or alternately, some may have been shipped even without pre-established buyers to the proposed marble yard at Tyre, where patrons like those from Caesarea Philippi went to shop for imported dedications.

CONCLUSION: THE ANATOLIAN ORIGINS OF THE SCULPTURES

The scientific, technical, and stylistic evidence all suggest that the Paneion sculptures are most likely to have been made largely of marble from quarries in Asia Minor and carved by sculptors associated with renowned sculptural workshops there. Isotopic analyses suggest that many of the Paneion sculptures are made of Anatolian marble. Their stylistic and technical characteristics, as well as comparisons to individual pieces from Ephesos and Aphrodisias, associate many of the statues with the sculptural workshops of Asia and Caria. Although it is difficult to know for certain where the pieces were carved (in Asia Minor or in the Levant), the meager evidence for marble carving workshops in the Levant that produced sculptures in the Graeco-Roman tradition makes it probable that the Paneion sculptures were imported to the region fully-carved. Based on geographic proxim-

ity and evidence for the location of marble yards at Tyre, the Paneion sculptures probably entered the Levant through this major port city. They may have been "mail-ordered" by patrons via local agencies who contacted quarries and sculptural workshops in Asia Minor, or the sculptures could have been stockpiled, like sarcophagi and architectural elements, at a marble yard where patrons went to "shop" for desired sculptural dedications.

Of course, it should be noted here that the importation of statuary was an extremely expensive undertaking. Not only would our Levantine patrons incur the cost of the quarrying and carving of the statues, they would also have to pay the costs of transport, which were hefty enough for seaborne cargo, but which could be staggering for the movement of statuary on land (Russell 2008: 112–20). Such a significant economic undertaking offers further insights regarding the patrons and their goals in erecting these imported marble dedications, made so expensive not only by their material (unavailable locally) but also by their transport both via sea and land to the Sanctuary of Pan. Thus, the foreign material, Graeco-Roman artistic tradition, and serious expense resulting from the movement of these statues demonstrate that those who paid to import and dedicate these pieces were invested heavily in a broader, Mediterranean realm.

NOTES

1   For a preliminary version of this study, see Friedland 1999. For the absence of marble in the Levant, see Fischer 1988: 162; 1991: 142, n. 149; 1998: 29; 2002: 317; and Pearl 1989: 2. Instead of marble, many sculptural, architectural, and funerary monuments in the Levant were made of locally-available limestone, sandstone, and basalt.

2   For isotopic analysis, see Craig and Craig 1972; Manfra et al. 1975; Herz and Wenner 1978; 1981; Coleman and Walker 1979; Germann et al. 1980; Walker 1984; Herz 1987; 1990; Herz and Waelkens 1988; Moens et al. 1990; Gorgoni et al. 2002; Pentia et al. 2002; Lazzarini et al. 2002; and Attanasio et al. 2006. For the use of multiple methods to determine marble provenance, see Pearl 1989: 14–28 and Attanasio et al. 2002. In 1995, shortly after the discovery of the statues, ten pieces

were sampled and subjected to isotopic analyses; for the scientific report, see Heimann and Porat 1995: 18–29. Thanks are due to Dr. Norman Herz of the University of Georgia, who in 1996 and again in 2007 compared Heimann and Porat's data to his Classical Marble Database to provide the updated possible quarry origins of the Paneion sculptures listed in Table 1. In 2005, I sampled five further statues from the Paneion, and Dr. Herz graciously analyzed those samples and provided the possible quarry origins listed in Table 2; this publication consitutes the first official report of the results of the five pieces sampled in 2005. Because samples were taken by different people and analyzed in different laboratories, I have chosen to report the results for the statues sampled in 1995 and 2005 separately.

3 For the limitations of isotopic analysis, see Manfra et al. 1975; Germann et al. 1980; and Attanasio et al. 2006: 28–30, 213–66.

4 In addition to the specific studies discussed below, see Pensabene 1997.

5 Fischer and Pearl 1998: 247–59, based on Pearl 1989; Fischer et al. 1992; Fischer 2002; 2009a; and 2009b. For a discussion of Fischer and Pearl's methodology and the need for a sequential, multi–method analysis of white marbles, see Pearl 1989: 14–28.

6 This finding accords well with Russell's observation that "generally speaking, very little stone from the western Mediterranean appears to have travelled to the eastern Mediterranean at all" (2011: 144).

7 V. Tzaferis, personal communication, 1998. This piece is not yet published.

8 For an important discussion of sculptural technique in the Roman world (as well as in other ancient civilizations), see Rockwell 1993.

9 For Attic and Peloponnesian workshops, see Ridgway 1981: 437–43; De Grazia 1973; Sturgeon 1989: 114–21; Sturgeon 2003. This description of the stylistic and technical features of Attic and Peloponnesian statuary is based on first-hand inspection of the pieces displayed in the National Archaeological Museum and the Agora Museum in Athens, the Olympia Museum, and the Corinth Museum and storerooms (thanks are due to Charles K. Williams and Nancy Bookidis of the American Excavations at Corinth for allowing me access to the Corinth materials).

10 Ridgway notes that the majority of the sculptures from Corinth do not have the high surface polish characteristic of pieces from Asia Minor (1981: 444). This observation is echoed by Sturgeon (1975: 294, 300) and De Grazia (1973: 55). Similarly, Perry notes the lack of high surface polish on the statuary from the nymphaeum of Herodes Atticus at Olympia (1995: 167).

11 Other scholars have noted this rasped finish on the drapery and flesh of sculptures found at Athens (Graindor 1915: 272), Olympia (Perry 1995:167), Corinth (Ridgway 1981: 440; Sturgeon 1975: 281, 300; 1989: 115; 1995: 503; De Grazia 1973: 55), Isthmia (Sturgeon 1987: 6), and Argos (Marcadé 1957: 452). Graindor suggests that rasping of faces may have been intended to depict the grain or texture of skin. He notes that on the Attic portraits of the Cosmetes, rasping of the face appears on heads datable from the Antonine period until the time of Galens, during and after which the faces of the Cosmetes are entirely polished (Graindor 1915: 273). However, rasping of the face may be found on portraits from

Corinth dated as early as the Julio-Claudian period (for example: Augustus S-1116; Gaius Caesar S-1080; Lucius Caesar S-6). Sturgeon argues that the rasping of faces and drapery at Corinth is either a workshop-specific trait or a preference of a particular period (1995: 503). Rasping of flesh is found on the legs of the Versailles Diana in the National Archaeological Museum of Athens (NAM no. 3567); the torso of the Diadoumenos from Delos in the National Archaeological Museum of Athens; the right hand and neck of the portrait of a draped woman (Faustina the Younger?) from Olympia (Λ159); the abdomen around the attached shell on the nymph from the Baths of Eumenes on the Lechaion Road at Corinth (S-1429). Rasping of faces is found on both mythological and portrait statuary, including ten portraits of Cosmetes from Athens (NAM nos. 386, 388, 389, 390, 395, 402, 406, 408, 409, 411; see Graindor 1915); many of the portraits from Olympia, such as the young Lucius Verus (Λ166), Faustina the Elder (Λ155), the draped woman (Faustina the Younger?, Λ159), and the draped girl (perhaps the daughter of Marcus Aurelius, Λ160); many of the Julio-Claudian portraits from Corinth, including Augustus as priest (S-1116), Gaius Caesar (S-1080), Lucius Caesar (S-6), and the young Nero (S-1088); and several mythological pieces from Corinth, such as the head of Dionysos (S-194) and the head of Tyche. Often, these tool marks follow the contours of limbs, faces, or necks. This is particularly clear on the Amazon from the theater at Corinth (S-3723), where rasp marks run vertically on vertical drapery folds and follow the contour of the boots around the legs. In some cases, rasping seems to have been used to create patterns on drapery. For example, the skirt of the cuirassed figure from Olympia thought to represent Marcus Aurelius (Λ150), has, on the pleats of its skirt, tool marks on opposite sides carved in opposing diagonals, so that they slant inward, both pointing at the central pleat, which was smoothed.

12 Examples of eyes showing such tear-ducts include the unknown Cosmete from Athens (NAM no. 409); the cuirassed emperor thought to be Titus (Λ126), Antinous (Λ104 and 208), Antoninus Pius (Λ165), and the portrait of a draped girl, perhaps the daughter of Marcus Aurelius (Λ160), all from Olympia; the head of Dionysos (S-194), the head of Tyche, and the head of Apollo Kitharode (S-814) from Corinth.

13 Restrained use of the drill is noted in pieces from Athens (Graindor 1915: 272), Corinth (Sturgeon 1989: 115; De Grazia 1973: 54), Isthmia (Sturgeon 1987: 6), and Argos (Marcadé and Raftopoulou 1963: 186–87).

14 Several sculptures found in Greece have neck struts; however, these pieces are usually markedly different from other Greek works and may therefore have been imported or carved by sculptors who were not part of Attic, Peloponnesian, or northern Greek workshops. For example, the reclining male atop the lid of an Attic sarcophagus displayed in the National Archaeological Museum in Athens (NAM no. 1497) has an elongated neck strut; however, the figures on this sarcophagus lid are known to have been recarved and the neck strut may be a result of the conversion of a female figure into a male (see museum label). The Apollo Kitharode found in the west end of the Forum at Corinth (S-774) has a neck strut, comparable in size, shape, and delineation from the neck with that on the Paneion head of a goddess wearing a *stephane* (cat. 5). The Apollo, however, does not compare in marble or technique to the other pieces found at Corinth. Its marble has much larger crystals than the usual fine-grained Pentelic marble common at Corinth and has occasional bluish-gray streaks rather than being pure white. In addition, the drapery is highly smoothed and the flesh is polished. Based on these technical features and the fragmented rendering of digitations over the ribs, Ridgway suggests that the Apollo was imported from Aphrodisias or that Aphrodisian sculptors and their marble were imported to Corinth (1981: 444). A head of Dionysos (T-1044) in the Corinth storerooms also has a neck strut. Unfortunately, its surface is too badly eroded to determine its original finish. Finally, the portrait herm of an unknown Cosmete (NAM no. 389) has a small area of marble left at the back of its neck that may be viewed as a neck strut, although it is narrower and shallower than typical examples. This particular strut is even more of an oddity, since none of the other portrait herms of Cosmetes displayed in the National Archaeological Museum have such a neck strut.

15 The following conclusions are based on first-hand examination of sculptures displayed in the Thessaloniki Museum and the Dion Museum.

16 For example, three colossal heads from the Agora area of Thessaloniki, now displayed in the Thessaloniki Museum, have highly polished faces and necks: the head of Athena (Thessaloniki Museum no. 877; Despinis et al. 1997: 99–101), the head of a deity (no. 878; Despinis et al. 1997: 120–22), and the head of a bearded deity (no. 886; Despinis et al. 1997: 119–20). The torso of the young water-bearer (Thessaloniki Museum no. 895; Despinis et al. 1997: 128–29), which originally decorated a public fountain house northwest of the Agora in Thessaloniki, has a polished torso, as does the statue of Harpokrates from the Serapeion (Thessaloniki Museum no. 844; Despinis et al. 1997: 115–16). The Hygieia and Panakeia from the group of Asklepios' family, the Dionysos Lykeios, and the cult statue of Isis-Tyche, all from Dion, have polished flesh (although their drapery is rasped).

17 The following examples have pointed inner corners of the eyes, but lack arcs chiseled on the inner eyeball to indicate tear ducts: the female head from the Serapeion (Thessaloniki Museum no. 1010; Despinis et al. 1997: 46–47); the female head from Thessaloniki (Thessaloniki Museum no. 1011; Despinis et al. 1997: 48–49); and the water-bearer from northwest of the Agora in Thessaloniki (Thessaloniki Museum no. 895; Despinis et al. 1997: 128–29). Many of the later portrait heads have eyes with rounded inner corners that curve sharply downward.

18 For example, the head of a bearded deity (Thessaloniki Museum no. 1017; Despinis et al. 1997: 109–10) has a lot of drillwork in its hair; not only are locks separated by drill channels, but individual strands of hair within these locks are separated by drill lines. Pronounced drillwork may also be seen in the hair of two colossal heads from the Agora in Thessaloniki (the head of a deity, no. 878, Despinis et al. 1997: 120–22; and the head of a bearded deity, no. 886, Despinis et al. 1997: 119–20) and in the hair of the head of a female, perhaps Isis, from the Serapeion in Thessaloniki (Thessaloniki Museum no. 2490; Despinis et al. 1997: 114–15).

19 Examples from Thessaloniki include the colossal head of Athena from the Agora (Thessaloniki Museum, no. 877; Despinis et al. 1997: 99–101) and the colossal head of a deity from the Agora (Thessaloniki Museum no. 878; Despinis et al. 1997: 120–22). Examples from Dion in the Dion Museum include Aigle from the group of Asklepios' family, the head of Demeter (no. 200), the Dionysos table stand (no. 79), and the three busts done in "local style" (nos. 393, 394, and no number).

20 On the unified "Asiatic style," see Ridgway 1984: 89; more recently, see Pensabene 2011: 38–40.

21 For sculpture from Antonine, Severan, and late antique Asia Minor, see Filges 1999. Evidence for sculptural production at Aphrodisias comes from the discovery of two adjoining rooms filled with sculptors' tools, numerous unfinished statues, and a block of marble used as a practice surface (Rockwell 1991; Smith 1998; 2011; Van Voorhis 1998; 2008); in addition, the sculptural school at Aphrodisias has

long been known from pieces made by sculptors abroad (Squarciapino 1943; 1991). Evidence for local sculptural production at Ephesos comes from large groups of statuary designed for individual monuments, such as the Fountain of Trajan (Longfellow 2011: 77–95) and the monuments of C. L. Bassus; multiple examples of the same sculptural type, such as the five Tritons from the C. L. Bassus monuments; the *puntelli* that cover the backside of the late Antonine Dionysos from the Fountain of Trajan (Aurenhammer 1990: 19, 62); and a lintel block from the city that shows a series of scenes from a sculptor's workshop (Istanbul Archaeological Museum no. 775T; Mendel 1912–14: 78–80, no. 13; Smith 2011: 66–68; see also Schneider 1999: 37–45; Pensabene 2011: 38–40). Pamphylia also must have had one or more regional workshops as attested by the large number of sculptures found at both Perge and Side; multiple examples of the same type from these sites; two unfinished heads discovered at Side (Inan 1975: 7–8); sculptor's tools and unfinished blocks recovered from the region (displayed in the Antalya Museum); and epigraphic evidence from Side, which identifies sculptors working at the site during the Hellenistic period (Inan 1975: 7–8); for Perge, see Bravi 2011; for Perge and Side, see Schneider 1999: 38; for sculpture from Sagalassos, see Mägele 2011. For sculptural workshops at Dokimeion, see Filges 1999.

22 For high polish on pieces from Asia Minor, see Ridgway 1981: 444. For rasping left on flesh and drapery of Attic and Peloponnesian pieces, see n. 11, above.

23 Inan and Rosenbaum 1966: 10; Inan and Alföldi-Rosenbaum 1979: 3; Ridgway 1984: 87–88; Hollinshead 2002: 138–41. Neck struts appear more commonly on pieces from Pamphylia and Pisidian Antioch, but also on pieces found in Nicomedia, Pergamon, Miletos, Ephesos, and Aphrodisias. Although neck struts do appear on pieces found elsewhere in the empire, their occurrence is isolated and rare. The best-known group comes from the North African sites of Carthage, Cyrene, Lepcis Magna, Utica, and Thuburbo Maius (Braemer 1990: 189–95). However, because this North African group is so small in comparison to the numerous examples from Asia Minor, their neck struts seem best interpreted as evidence that these sculptures were either imported from Asia Minor or created by itinerant Anatolian sculptors. Several scholars have suggested that neck struts were designed to protect the structurally weak neck from breakage, especially during transport (Ridgway 1984: 88; Braemer 1990: 190); however, Hollinshead points out that struts may indicate more than technical concerns (2002).

24 This conclusion is based on first-hand examination of sculptures displayed in the Antalya Museum.

25 See n. 13, above.

26 Although several technical features of this head compare to other sculptures from the Paneion group, its classicizing style and archaizing snail-shell curls distinguish it from the other sculptures preserved at the site.

27 Excavation inv. no. 66-269; Smith 2007: 212–13, 224 no. A18, fig. 16.

28 For the *spinario* group (inv. no. 67-559), see Erim 1967: 69; Mellink 1968: 143, pl. 55,6; Smith 1998: 258. For the small group of a satyr and young Dionysos (inv. no. 67-577), see Erim 1974: 767–75; Smith 1996: 60–61, fig. 62; 1998: 255–56. I thank R. R. R. Smith for directing my attention to this technical feature.

29 For example, the following sculptures were all being transported as finished pieces: the colossal marble head of Augustus in Luna marble found in the Rhône Delta wreck in France (ca. 20 BC; Parker 1992: 366); the sculptures dredged up from the floor of the Piraeus (dated to the second century AD; Parker 1992: 312; Bass 1966: 78); the sculptural group of Cupid and Psyche in Proconnesian marble found in the Punta Scifo A shipwreck off the coast of Italy (early third century AD; Parker 1992: 361); and the six marble statues found in the Lixouri wreck off the coast of Greece (Roman period; Parker 1992: 245). However, the two sculptures found in the Sile shipwreck off the coast of Anatolia in the Black Sea (dated to AD 100–125) were shipped in extremely rough quarry-state: one is a protome meant to be carved into the bust of a Flavian woman, and the other is a colossal imperial cuirassed statue, 4.5 m tall. On the Sile shipwreck, see Parker 1992: 404–5; for photos of the quarry-state sculptures, see Asgari 1978:pl. 142, fig. 17 (Trajanic woman), fig. 18 (colossal cuirassed statue). See also Russell 2011: 148.

30 For a full review the history of this debate, as well as the scientific, literary, epigraphic, and archaeological evidence for the creation of white marble statuary in Roman Syria, Palestina, and Arabia, see Friedland in press.

31 For critical reviews see Foerster 1997; Holum 2006.

32 I thank Thomas Weber for drawing my attention to this important find.

Table 1   Data from Isotopic Analysis of Marble Sculptures from the Sanctuary of Pan at Caesarea Philippi.
Samples Collected in 1995.

Cat. No.	Subject	Desc. of Crystals	Minerals	d^{18}O	d^{13}C	Possible Quarry
15	Artemis Rospigliosi	sm–med, glittering	calcite	-4.05	3.13	Afyon 32.1%, Thasos/Cape Vathy* 23.0%, Marmara 19.7%
4	Head of Zeus /Asklepios	med, glittering, flaky	calcite	-3.22	2.59	Thasos/Acropolis* 71.4%, Uşak 68.4%, Marmara 65.1%, Mylasa 59.6%, Afyon 46.0%
14	Right shoulder, upper arm, and breast	large, chunky, glittering	calcite	-2.31	2.59	Marmara 93.5%, Uşak 62.5%, Denizli 59.3%, Miletus 33.9%, Afyon 27.9%,
12	Torso of youthful, nude god (Dionysos?)	tiny, glittering	calcite	-1.69	3.74	Denizli 64.9%, Marmara 25.3%, Paros/Chorodaki 20.6%, Thasos/Cape Vathy* 16.6%, Afyon 8.3%
8	Fragment of head (Dionysos?)	large, chunky, glittering	calcite	-3.87	1.78	Aphrodisias 95.8%, Afyon 78.9%, Miletus 69.7%, Ephesus 37.5%, Uşak 37.2%
25	Forequarters of bovine	small, closely packed, translucent	calcite, feldspar	-6.44	1.71	Denizli 38.8%, Afyon 37.2%,
not catalog.	Tree limb (?) (W60/2236)	medium, translucent	calcite	-1.63	3.42	Marmara 54.4%, Denizli 41.6%, Paros/Chorodaki 32.1% (if fine-grained)
29	Base w/human and animal feet	medium, glittering	calcite, quartz	-3.36	1.15	Ephesos 65.3%, Afyon 64.2%, Aphrodisias 49.3, Miletus 19.7%
20	Torso of dancing satyr	medium, closely packed	calcite	-4.96	1.73	Afyon 81.8%, Aphrodisias 55.0%, Uşak 45.3%
1	Head of Roma or Athena	large, highly translucent	calcite	-3.71	0.93	Ephesus 86.9%, Afyon 74.1%, Aphrodisias 36.6%,
			dolomite	-3.29	1.45	Afyon 64.2%, Mylasa 45.1%, Ephesus 45.0%

Columns 4–6 repeat data presented in Heimann and Porat 1995. The quarry possibilities and percentages listed in column 7 are derived from comparing the Paneion delta figures with the Classical Marble Database in July 2007 (thanks to Norman Herz; Herz 1987; 1990; Herz and Wenner 1981; Herz and Waelkens 1988). These numbers give the percent possibility that the marble originated in the listed quarry. However, a higher percentage for one quarry rather than another does not necessarily mean that the marble comes from first quarry and not the second (Norman Herz, personal comm., June 8, 1998).
*If dolomitic.

Table 2   Data from Isotopic Analysis of Marble Sculptures from the Sanctuary of Pan at Caesarea Philippi.
Samples Collected and Analyzed in 2005.

Cat. No.	Subject	Desc. of Crystals	$d^{18}O$	$d^{13}C$	Possible Quarry
2	Head of Athena wearing an attic helmet	small crystals	3.89	-3.35	Paros/Lychnites 42.6%, Thasos/Cape Vathy* 28.1%, Afyon 13.2%
5	Head of a goddess wearing a *stephane*	large, coarse, glittering crystals	1.90	-4.88	Afyon 76.2%, Naxos/Melanes (if early classical) 75.3%, Uşak 60.4%
6	Head of Apollo Kitharode or a Muse	large, coarse, glittering crystals	2.72	-2.51	Marmara 92.7%, Denizli 69.5%, Uşak 50.8%
11	Torso of a nymph	large, coarse, glittering crystals	2.33	-2.65	Uşak 77.5%, Thasos/Acropolis* 70.4%, Marmara 70.3%
13	Left leg and support of a Capitoline/ Medici Aphrodite	small, closely packed, glittering crystals	2.61	-7.62	Penteli 93.9%, Naxos/Apirathos (if early classical) 74%, Iznik 66.9%

The quarry possibilities and percentages listed in column 6 are derived from comparing the Paneion delta figures with the Classical Marble Database in July 2007 (thanks to Norman Herz; Herz 1987; 1990; Herz and Wenner 1981; Herz and Waelkens 1988). These numbers give the percent possibility that the marble originated in the listed quarry. However, a higher percentage for one quarry rather than another does not necessarily mean that the marble comes from first quarry and not the second (Norman Herz, personal comm., June 8, 1998).
*If dolomitic.

Chapter 3

Patronage, Chronology, and Display

Patterns of Sculptural Dedication at the Sanctuary

In the Levant, the dedication of imported marble statues carved in the classical style was a deliberate act, since, as suggested in the previous chapter, these sculptures were not readily available in most Levantine cities and were certainly more costly and notable than statuary made of local stone and carved in indigenous traditions. Therefore, the discovery of a large number of imported marble sculptures such as those found at the Sanctuary of Pan at Caesarea Philippi raises related questions regarding the cultural, ethnic, and political background of their patrons; the historical periods during which they were dedicated; and their relationship to the architectural embellishment of the sanctuary.

In this chapter, I analyze the evidence for the patronage, chronology, and display of sculpture at the Paneion in order to understand better patterns of sculptural dedications at the sanctuary. Information about the patrons comes primarily from six inscriptions found at the site. A secure chronology of sculptural dedication may also be derived from these inscriptions, because they record the dates when the statuary was erected. This chronology may be extended by the stylistic dates of the sculptural fragments found at the sanctuary. A partial reconstruction of the display of sculptures at the sanctuary is derived from both the architec-

tural remains at the site and specifics regarding individual sculptural dedications recorded in the inscriptions.

THE EPIGRAPHIC EVIDENCE RELATED TO SCULPTURAL DEDICATION

Table 3 lists the epigraphic evidence for the patronage of sculptural dedication at the sanctuary in chronological order. It includes the date of each dedication, the name of its dedicator(s), the epithet of its dedicator(s), the subject represented, the deity to whom the sculpture was dedicated, the scale of the sculpture, and the type of monument with which the inscription and sculpture were associated. Of these six epigraphic references to sculptural dedications, only that on the pedestal of the bust of Antinous (Appendix 4, fig. 95) may be associated with an extant sculpture. Five of these inscriptions include exact dates of dedication, while that to the "hero Antinous," which lacks an internal date, may be securely dated based on the chronology of Antinous portraits (Lambert 1984: 209; Meyer 1991: 99, no. I 77, pl. 88).

The two earliest inscriptions are associated with freestanding sculptures not necessarily meant to be displayed in niches. The earliest is carved on a fragmentary pillar (0.54 m high, 0.34 m in di-

Table 6   Chronological Listing of Datable Sculptural Dedications from the Sanctuary.

Date	Date Derived From	Sculptural Subject	Scale
AD 63/4	Inscription	Asklepios	?
AD 88	Coin (Meshorer 1984–85:39, no. F)	Pan w/Syrinx	?
AD 88	Coin (Meshorer 1984–85:39, 43, no. G)	Tyche w/Rudder	?
Trajanic	Sculpture fragment	Face of a Goddess (cat. 9)	Life-size
Trajanic	Sculpture fragment	Nymph (cat. 11)	Life-size
Trajanic	Sculpture fragment	Torso of Nude God (cat. 12)	Life-size
AD 130–138	Sculpture with inscription	Bust of Antinous (Appendix 4)	Over-life-size
AD 148/9	Inscription	Hermes	Under life-Size
AD 148/9	Inscription	Goddess (Echo?)	Life-size
AD 169/170	Coin (Meshorer 1984–85:42, nos. 5, 5a)	Zeus Standing with Patera	?
AD 169/170	Coin (Meshorer 1984–85:43, nos. 6, 6a, 6b, 7)	Pan Playing Flute	?
AD 178/9	Inscription	Nemesis	Colossal
2nd c. AD	Sculpture fragment	Roma or Athena (cat. 1)	Colossal
2nd c. AD	Sculpture fragment	Zeus or Asklepios (cat. 4)	Life-size
2nd c. AD	Sculpture fragment	Apollo or Muse (cat. 6)	Life-size
2nd–3rd c. AD	Sculpture fragment	Artemis Rospigliosi (cat. 15)	Two-thirds life-size
AD. 201/2	Coin (Meshorer 1984-5:52, no. 26)	Tyche Seated	?
AD 220/1	Coin (Meshorer 1984-5:56, nos. 50, 59)	Pan Playing Flute	?
AD 221/2	Inscription	Echo	Miniature
Late 4th c. AD	Sculpture fragment	Eros (cat. 22)	Miniature
Late 4th c. AD	Sculpture fragment	Forequarters of Bovine (cat. 25)	Miniature
Late 4th c. AD	Sculpture fragment	Hindquarters of Bovine (cat. 26)	Miniature
Late 4th c. AD	Sculpture fragment	Fragment of Tree Trunk (cat. 28)	Miniature

Table 7   Dates and Measurements of Niches Preserved at the Sanctuary.

Niche	Date	Height	Width	Depth	Scale of Sculpture	Subject of Sculpture
Augusteum – 4 Semi-Circular	19 BC	3.10 m	1.35 m	.75 m	Colossal	?
Augusteum – 4 Rectangular	19 BC	not determin.	1.55 m	.65 m	Colossal	?
Augusteum – 2 Larger Near Cave	19 BC	not determin.	2.30 m	1.35 m	Colossal	?
Operosum Antrum	1st c. AD	n/a	3.1 m	2.8 m	Colossal	Pan Playing Flute to Three-Bodied Goat?
In *Operosum Antrum*	1st c. AD	1.35 m	.82 m	.41 m	Under life-size	?
Above *Operosum Antrum* (Victor, son of Lysimachus)	148/9 AD	1.60 m	.83 m	.67 m	Life-size	Goddess (Echo?)
Opus Reticulatum	1st c. AD	1.07 m	.56 m	.35 m	Miniature	?
East of Court of Pan and Nymphs (Victor, Son of Lysimachus)	148/9 AD	1.30 m	.68 m	n/a	Under life-size	Hermes
Nemesis Court (Valerios Hispanos)	178/9 AD	2.90 m	1.25 m	1.20 m	Colossal	Nemesis
Miniature Nemesis Court (Agrippas and family)	221/2 AD	n/a	n/a	n/a	Miniature	Echo
Tripartite Building (easternmost niche)	3rd c. AD	1.20 m	.95 m	.35 m	Under life-size	?
Apsidal Court (part of building)	3rd c. AD	not determin.	1.75 m	1.25 m	Colossal	Flute-Playing Satyr?

wall), with the two closest to the cave even larger than the other eight. The colossal head of Roma or Athena wearing a Corinthian helmet (cat. 1), discovered in the excavations of the sanctuary, may be associated with this building's sculptural program, based on its scale and its subject matter. Its height, reconstructed to approximately 2.75 m, makes it appropriate for either one of the eight colossal niches or one of the two extra-colossal niches near the grotto. If indeed the piece depicted the goddess Roma (rather than Athena), its subject matter makes it likely that this statue was displayed in one of the two larger niches at the back of the cella, which were probably enlarged to hold the cult statues of the temple (especially since the grotto seems to have been the focal point of this temple and, as such, may have pre-empted the

usual positioning of cult statues at the end of the long axis of the building). Although there is no other evidence of statuary from this building, it is likely that the niches held a colossal pendant pair of Augustus and Roma. The other eight niches may have held representations of Julio-Claudian family members and/or Olympian deities. The sculptural display on the interior of this temple, housed as it was in alternating rectangular and semicircular niches, may have been meant to echo in some way that in the Forum of Augustus, which Herod may have seen on one of his later visits to Rome — at least during its construction.[5]

The Court of Pan and the Nymphs may have had at least one, if not two sculptures or sculptural groups displayed in the *operosum antrum*, which formed the focal point of the open-air shrine. A small niche carved at the back of the artificial grotto is large enough to have housed a statue just under life-size, while the artificial cave itself, which is 3 m wide and 3 m deep, could have displayed a figure at least 2 m tall.[6] Mershorer has suggested that the sculptural group housed in this artificial cave may be depicted on several coins of the early third century AD that show Pan standing in a niche playing the flute above a cave with a fence or screen at its front (Meshorer 1984–85: nos. 35, 41); however, Maʿoz associates these and other coins with the Temple of Pan and the Goats, though he agrees that it is "likely" that a just under life-size statue of a youthful, flute-playing Pan or Satyr was installed in the smaller niche carved at the back of the *operosum antrum* (Maʿoz 1994–99: 92, 96–97). Certainly, statues representing other Pan-related subjects could also have been displayed in the *operosum antrum*.

Three other niches surrounding the *operosum antrum* also displayed statuary, although at least two were installed later than the original construction of the Court and thus their statuary was layered onto the already pre-existing sculptural program. The "*opus reticulatum* niche," probably associated with the first-century AD construction of the Court, must have held an under-life-size statue. It is equipped with a trapezoidal pedestal carved out of the natural rock of the scarp that stands 0.22 m high. Since no associated inscription remains, it is impossible to determine what subject this sculpture represented, although it is likely to have been associated with the god Pan. Inscriptions associated with the other two niches, added to the court in AD 148/9, suggest possible subjects for these two sculptures. The niche above the artificial cave held a life-size statue of a "Goddess," thought to be Echo, because the inscription is dedicated to "Pan, lover of Echo" (Isaac in press: no. 2; Aliquot 2008a: 99).[7] The niche 6 m to the east of the *operosum antrum* displayed an under-life-size statue of Hermes.

The Temple of Zeus is the only building at the sanctuary for which no sculptural display contexts are preserved. This temple, unlike the others, did not utilize the rock scarp as its back wall, but had one constructed of ashlars that blocked off this ready-made venue for sculptural display. It is likely

that at least one cult statue was displayed inside the cella against this back wall, and sculptural niches may also have been built into its now-missing sidewalls.

The Court of Nemesis preserves two niches for sculptural display. One niche, contemporary with the Court's construction and centered at its back, displayed a colossal statue of Nemesis. The associated inscription notes that the statue was displayed behind a fence, and mortises for attaching a metal grill can be found in the scarp to the left and below the niche (Isaac in press: 3–4, no. 4; Aliquot 2008a: 103, no. A/16). Such niches bounded by fences are commonly noted in inscriptions (Robert and Robert 1950: 47–49)[8] and, according to Maʿoz, become something of a symbol of the Sanctuary of Pan on the city's coins (1994–99: 93, 99, 100). The second niche, added in AD 178/9 to the east of the first one, housed a miniature statuette of the nymph Echo, 10 m above the pavement of the court (Isaac in press: 4, no. 5; Aliquot 2008a: 104–5, no. A/17). No other sculptural niches may be associated with this court, since its open-air nature meant that it had no walls. Other sculptures, however, may have been erected on pedestals throughout the court.

The Tripartite Building preserves only one sculptural display niche. An undecorated niche, large enough to hold an under-life-size statue, was carved in the rock scarp 4.7 m above the terrace floor and was probably meant to appear above the roof of the building. Because no inscription accompanies this niche, the subject of its sculpture is not known. No other sculptural display contexts are known from this structure. The compartments within the cella are at ground level and are too small to have held statuary; rather, it seems that they functioned as receptacles for ritual objects, since they were found filled with pottery and animal bones (Berlin 1999: 36–40).

The Temple of Pan and the Goats was probably constructed to showcase a statue or a sculptural group displayed in the niche built into the center of its semicircular wall. Although the height of the wall and its niche are not reconstructable, its width and depth show that it held a life-size or larger statue or a multi-figural group. Maʿoz suggests that a series of coins dated to the early third century AD, depicting a fenced-off semicircle with a niche above, in which stands a flute-playing satyr (Meshorer 1984–85: nos. 41, 49, 50), may be associated with this temple (1994–99: 95–97). If these coins do depict the Temple of Pan and the Goats, they suggest that a version of the Lysippan flute-playing satyr served as the focal point of this court.

PATTERNS OF SCULPTURAL DEDICATION AT THE SANCTUARY

The epigraphic, sculptural, and numismatic evidence suggests that sculptures were dedicated at the sanctuary from the second half of the first through the late fourth/early fifth centuries AD. Throughout this period, the dedication of imported, mainstream Graeco-Roman sculptures seems symptomatic of the dedicants' desires to be assimilated not only to a Hellenistic but also to a Roman milieu, evidenced first by Herod's foundation of the Augusteum and later by the Roman names of the patrons recorded in the dedicatory inscriptions. Although there is no epigraphic or sculptural evidence for dedications by the Herodian kings during the early architectural elaboration of the sanctuary in the late first century BC and the first century AD, architectural evidence (the ten niches in Herod's Augusteum) and numismatic evidence (the possible evidence for dedications of cult statues by Agrippa II) suggest that the majority of the sanctuary's sculptural dedications in this period were probably made by royal patrons. Dedications by private individuals, however, were not precluded during this period, as is shown by the statue of Asklepios erected by the physician Quadratus in AD 63/4.

After the Herodian period, in the second and early third centuries AD, when the sanctuary came under Roman control, epigraphic and sculptural evidence from the site shows that sculptural dedication continued to be an important means of patronizing the sanctuary. Local religious and civic officials seem to have adopted the Herodian habit of dedicating three-dimensional statuary at the Paneion. While the epigraphic and architectural evidence from this period points primarily to large-scale dedications associated with the architectural embellishment of the sanctuary, the large number of second-century AD sculptural fragments found

at the site, which are not associable with any of its architectural contexts, must have been incorporated into the decor and dedications at the sanctuary as well. Perhaps these were displayed in the cellas or on the porches of buildings on pedestals.

From the late third and early fourth century AD on, epigraphic, sculptural, architectural, and ceramic evidence shows that patterns of patronage at the sanctuary had changed drastically. There is virtually no epigraphic evidence from this period, and building activity at the site wanes. A significant number of ceramic dedications is noted, but the majority of these are inexpensive, plain, locally-made lamps (Berlin 1999: 36–40). In contrast to the large number of second-century AD sculptures, there are only two (perhaps three) miniature sculptural dedications from the late fourth century AD. Although these show that the pagan sanctuary was still functioning well into the Christian era and that it was important enough to merit a certain number of imported marble sculptures, their markedly reduced number and size shows that marble statuary was probably not the primary vehicle for patronage of the sanctuary in the late antique period.

THE CHRONOLOGY OF SCULPTURAL DEDICATION AT THE SANCTUARY IN LIGHT OF THE IMPERIAL MARBLE TRADE IN THE LEVANT

The chronology of sculptural dedication at the Sanctuary of Pan at Caesarea Philippi corresponds to the dates established for the incorporation of the Levant into the imperial marble trade. The absence of sculptural fragments dated to the Herodian period is understandable in light of the fact that the importation of marble statuary to the Levant during the Hellenistic and early Roman periods is rare.[9] If Herod and his successors did erect marble sculptures at the sanctuary, they would have had to import them from Italy or another center as special commissions, since the mechanisms of the imperial marble trade were not yet developed. In contrast to the lack of first-century AD. sculptural finds at the Paneion, the large number of second-century AD sculptural fragments discovered at the sanctuary probably reflects the infusion of marble to this region when the marble trade reached the

Levant following the Hadrianic reorganization of the quarries (Dodge 1988: 215, 217; Fischer 1994: 22–23; Fischer 1998: 40–45; Fischer 2009b: 406–8). The several fourth-century AD dedications discovered at the Paneion have parallels in the late antique marble statuary found at other Levantine sites, such as Antioch, Sidon, Byblos, and Caesarea Maritima, all of which affirm that the imperial marble trade continued to supply the Levant with mythological statuary well into the late fourth and early fifth centuries AD.[10] The absence of evidence for sculptural dedication at the site beyond the late fourth or early fifth centuries AD is in keeping with the changes in the marble trade to Roman Israel in the fifth and sixth centuries AD noted by Fischer (1994: 25; 1998: 267–73; 2002: 322–23). Although marble reached more cities in the Levant during this period, the volume of marble imported was considerably reduced, and, more importantly, the use of marble shifted away from large-scale civic and pagan architectural and sculptural monuments to smaller, liturgical artifacts such as chancel-screens and baptismal fonts (Fischer 1994: 25; Fischer 1998: 267–68).

CONCLUSION

Important patterns have emerged from the epigraphic, sculptural, and numismatic evidence for sculptural dedication at the Sanctuary of Pan at Caesarea Philippi/Panias. Although there is no epigraphic or sculptural record for Herodian dedications of marble statuary at the sanctuary, architectural and numismatic evidence suggests that during the first century AD a large number of sculptures were erected by these royal patrons as part of their architectural elaboration of the site. In the second and early third centuries AD, the dedication of marble statuary became an important means of patronizing the sanctuary; now the patrons were not Herodian client kings, but local (in some cases Semitic), Romanized, religious and civic officials. After the late third century AD, the sanctuary saw fewer and smaller sculptural offerings. In contrast to the large-scale, often architecturally-related dedications of the second century AD, these were probably the result of individual votive offerings. These late antique sculptural dedications show that the pagan sanctuary continued to function during the time when Christianity had taken hold in the city below. Their small scale and sparse numbers, however, indicate that imported marble statuary was no longer the primary vehicle for patronage of the sanctuary (the absence of epigraphic material from this period makes it difficult to know anything about the patrons of these votives).

The evidence presented in this chapter supports three important conclusions about the Sanctuary of Pan: first, the height of sculptural dedication occurs in the second and third centuries AD and is contemporaneous with the florescence of the region under Antonine and Severan rule; second, the sculptural dedication is intricately tied to the architectural elaboration of the sanctuary, which is based on distinctly Roman modes of sculptural display in aediculated interiors and exteriors (Burrell 2006: 450–62), albeit with a local twist due to the use of the cliff face as the back wall of several of the temples and open air courts; third, the sanctuary provided a venue where public officials, some of whom came from indigenous Semitic backgrounds, could demonstrate their adoption of Graeco-Roman deities and patterns of worship, including the dedication of cult and votive statues. Thus, other than the Semitic origins of at least one of the patrons and the unique setting on the terrace nestled against the cliff face, the patterns of sculptural dedication and display at the Paneion appear highly Graeco-Roman.

NOTES

1 Alternately, the name could have been bestowed on Agrippas' ancestors by Herodian dynasts in the first centuries BC or AD. It is also possible that people with names related to that of Agrippa could have received citizenship from M. Agrippa.

2 In each catalogue entry, under the section titled "Comparanda, Workshop, and Date," the particular technical and stylistic traits that associate the Paneion sculpture with more securely dated comparanda are presented and, if possible, a suggested date is noted.

3 "Christianity reached Banias at an early date; according to tradition, the town's first bishop was a contemporary of St. Paul. The Christian community was well-established in the early fourth century, when Bishop Philocalus attended the Council of Nicaea in 325 AD. Several other bishops are known in the fourth and fifth centuries" (Ma'oz 1993a: 138); for Christianity at Panias/Banias, see also Wilson 2004: 70, 78–107.

4 Based on archaeological evidence, only two buildings were standing in the sanctuary *temenos* at this period: the Augusteum in front of the natural grotto and the Court of Pan and the Nymphs built atop the elevated terrace and furnished with an artificial *operosum antrum*.

5 Herod is known to have made at least four visits to Rome, and on two of them, in 17 BC and 13/12 BC, he could have encountered the Forum of Augustus during its construction, which probably took place sometime between 19 and 2 BC. For the dates of Herod's visits to Rome, see Richardson 1996: 239, esp. n. 79, 278–79. For the dates of the construction of the Forum of Augustus and its famed sculptural display, see Geiger 2008: 53–115. For "The Impact of the Gallery of Heroes" of the Forum of Augustus outside of Rome and Italy, see Geiger 2008: 195–97. I thank one of the anonymous reviewers for suggesting this interesting connection.

6 While some of the coins on which Pan is depicted also include one or more goats standing or crouching at his feet, and while Meshorer has suggested that a three-bodied goat was once displayed in the larger artificial grotto (Meshorer 1984–85: no. 50), it seems unlikely that statues of goats were erected at the sanctuary, due to the lack of finds of sculptural fragments that may be associated with depictions of goats and the enigmatic iconography of the sculptural group suggested by Mershorer (Ma'oz 1994–99: 95–96).

7 I agree with Isaac's argument for the subject matter of the statue, rather than with Aliquot's more open and uncertain reading.

8 I owe this reference to Isaac in press: 4.

9 Vermeule and Anderson 1981: 8, figs. 13–14; Wenning 1983; 1986: 151; Pearl 1989: 30–31; Fischer 1998: 35–40; 2009a: 400–405; 2009b: 403–6; Fischer and Stein 1994. While all of these publications consider the colossal head of Alexander the Great from Beth Shean/Scythopolis to be Hellenistic, note Stewart's suggested re-dating of the head to the Severan period (Stewart 1993: 338, n. 46). Rather than attributing the rarity of marble statuary in Herodian Judaea to the absence of an organized marble trade, Vermeule proposes that early Roman statuary may have been destroyed by Jewish zealots during the Jewish Revolts of AD 116–17 and AD 132–34 (1981: 30).

10 Examples of other late antique statuary from sites in the Levant include a female portrait from Caesarea Maritima dated to the fourth century AD (Gersht 1995b: 110–13, figs. 5–8); the head of a woman from Beth Shean (unpublished, discovered by Gabi Mazor); the head of Athena from Khirbat al-Mafjar (Merker 1987: 15–20); the group from the late antique villa at Antioch (Brinkerhoff 1970); the Mithras Tauroktonos, Aion-Kronos, and herm of Hekate Triformis from Sidon, all securely dated by inscriptions to AD 389 (Jidejian 1971: 78, 88–93, figs. 214–16; Stirling 2005: 92–95; for the date, see Will 1950: 261–69); the Achilles and Penthesilea from Byblos (Lauffray 1940: 30, 31, fig. 5); a recently-discovered head from Apollonia (Fischer 2009a: 409); and multiple decorative table tops from Hama, Gan Shemuel, Beth Shean, Mi'ilia, El-Husn, Baalbek, Beirut, and Ascalon, all dated to the Theodosian period (Dresken-Weiland 1991: 306–13, pls. 32–38).

Chapter 4

The Subjects of the Sculptures

The Graeco-Roman Pantheon of the Sanctuary of Pan

Epigraphic, literary, and numismatic sources provide evidence for the worship of at least five cult deities at the Sanctuary of Pan. All are traditional Graeco-Roman deities or members of the early imperial cult. The sculptural fragments from the site not only substantiate the worship of these cult figures, but also provide a fuller picture of the pantheon honored at the Sanctuary of Pan. Of the nineteen identifiable sculptural fragments discovered at the Sanctuary of Pan, sixteen preserve distinct subjects: fifteen divine and semi-divine figures and one imperially-related portrait. To expand our understanding of the scope of worship at the Paneion, this chapter discusses the subjects represented in the sculptural fragments found at the sanctuary in light of their association with a major cult center. Which deities are represented in the sculptures erected at the sanctuary? Why are sculptures of deities other than the cult figures erected here? What is the relationship of these deities to Pan, the earliest and primary cult figure of the sanctuary? Finally, what position does the sanctuary at Caesarea Philippi hold within the broader context of pagan worship in the Levant?

To facilitate this analysis, I divide the sculptural subjects dedicated at the sanctuary into four categories: representations of the major cult deities of the sanctuary; representations of "visiting deities;" representations of emperors and imperial family members; and representations of private individuals who may have been patrons or benefactors of the sanctuary.[1] Table 8 lists the subjects, scale, and dates of the identifiable sculptural fragments discovered at the Paneion according to these categories. Within the category of "visiting deities," I have listed major Olympian gods first and demi-gods second.

Prior to a discussion of the individual deities represented in the sculptural fragments and their roles at the sanctuary, several points should be noted about the Paneion sculptures as a group. First, in terms of subject matter and iconography, all of the mythological sculptures represent standard Graeco-Roman gods, goddesses, and mythological figures in traditional Hellenistic fashion, suggesting perhaps that the sanctuary was dedicated largely to the worship of these Graeco-Roman deities as opposed to indigenous Semitic ones.[2] Second, the majority of the sculptural fragments represents deities other than those currently established as the cult figures of the site; many of these have some relation to Pan and therefore may be understood as representing part of what I will call the "circle of Pan," which seems to have been honored at this religious center. Finally, the absence of three-dimensional portraits of private individu-

Table 8   Subjects of the Sculptural Fragments Discovered at the Sanctuary.

Category of Sculpture	Sculptural Subject	Scale	Date	Catalogue Number
Cult Deities of the Sanctuary				
	Satyr	?	?	18
	Pan or Daphnis	Half Life	?	19
	Satyr	Miniature	?	20
	Nymph	Life	Trajanic	11
	Zeus or Asklepios	Life	2nd c. AD	4
	Roma or Athena	Colossal	?	1
	Roma or Athena	Life	?	3
Visiting Deities: Olympian Gods				
	Athena	Life	?	2
	Artemis Rospigliosi	Under Life	2nd–3rd c. AD	15
	Artemis of Ephesos	?	?	16
	Aphrodite	Life	?	13
	Apollo or Muse	Life	2nd c. AD	6
	Dionysos	Life	?	8
	Dionysos (?)	Life	Trajanic	12
	Eros	Miniature	late 4th c. AD	22
Visiting Deities: Semi-Divine				
	Herakles	Miniature	?	21
	Kybele	Miniature	?	23
	Orpheus or Herakles	Miniature	late 4th c. AD	25
Imperial-Related Portrait	Antinous	Over Life	AD 130–138	Appendix 4

als at the sanctuary is notable, especially in comparison to groups of sculptural dedications from other sanctuaries throughout the Mediterranean.

THE SCULPTURAL EVIDENCE FOR THE MAIN CULT DEITIES OF THE SANCTUARY

According to literary and epigraphic evidence, there were at least five main cult figures worshipped at the sanctuary: Pan, the nymphs (particularly Echo), Zeus, Nemesis, and Augustus.[3] In addition, it is certain that Roma was worshipped alongside Augustus in the Herodian Augusteum because, although we have no literary or epigraphic evidence that attests to the worship of Roma at the Paneion, Suetonius tells us that Augustus did not permit the dedication of temples to himself unless they included the worship of Roma (Suet. *Aug.* 52).[4] In keeping with this, Josephus records the dedication of a joint temple to Augustus and Roma (complete with cult images of both "deities") by Herod at Caesarea Maritima (Joseph. *AJ* 15.339; *BJ* 1.21.7). From this, scholars have extrapolated that the other temple to Augustus dedicated by Herod at

Samaria must likewise have been a joint temple to Augustus and Roma (Mellor 1975: 95). Thus, although Josephus makes no mention of the worship of Roma in conjunction with the Augusteum at Panias (Joseph. *AJ* 15.363; *BJ* 1.404–6), the city goddess of Rome must also have been one of the sanctuary's main cult deities alongside Augustus. Five of the buildings discovered at the site can be associated with one of these cult deities (the Court of Pan and the Nymphs, the Temple of Zeus, the Court of Nemesis, the Temple to Pan and the Goats, and the Augusteum). Since it is not known whether the Tripartite Building functioned as a temple or a treasury, no cult deity may be associated with this building (Berlin 1999: 36–40).

The sculptural fragments discovered at the sanctuary represent or allude to at least two, if not four, of these cult figures: Pan, a nymph, possibly Zeus, and probably Roma. Pan is the only cult figure represented by multiple sculptural fragments and is alluded to in three, possibly four, different pieces: the tree trunk with a hanging syrinx (cat. 18), which probably accompanied a satyr; the hand holding a syrinx (cat. 19), which may have belonged to a statue of either Pan or Daphnis; the torso of a dancing satyr (cat. 20); and possibly the fragment of a base with human and animal feet (cat. 29), which may represent a satyr and panther. These sculptures of satyrs, Pan, and Pan-related subjects vary in scale from miniature to half-life-size. Since none are monumental in scale, none may be readily identified as cult statues.

Pan is one of two cult deities of the sanctuary who is recorded in the epigraphic, numismatic, and sculptural evidence. Two inscriptions associated with the Court of Pan and the Nymphs record the dedication of statues to "Pan and the nymphs" and to "Pan" (Isaac in press: nos. 1a and 2; Aliquot 2008a: 100–102, no. A/14; 99–100, no. A/13, respectively). In addition, the benefactor of the Court of Nemesis identifies himself as a Priest of the god Pan in the dedicatory inscription for this court (Isaac in press: no. 4; Aliquot 2008a: 102–3, no. A/16). Furthermore, multiple issues of the city's coinage depict famous sculptural types of satyrs and Pan-related attributes such as syrinxes and *lagobola* (Meshorer 1984–85: 42–43, 44–46). In fact, the sanctuary at Caesarea Philippi seems to have been

one of the main Levantine centers for the worship of Pan (Hajjar 1990b: 2596–97; Lichtenberger 2003: 310; Aliquot 2008a: 100; Ovadiah and Mucznik 2009: 163–72). Multiple representations of Pan at the Temple of Mercury-Bacchus at Baalbek suggest that he may have been worshipped there as well, while literary sources also mention a sanctuary at Antioch, founded in the Hellenistic period.[5]

Another cult figure of the Paneion that was represented in three dimensions is a nymph, preserved in the life-size torso that served as a fountain figure (cat. 11). Epigraphic evidence also documents the worship of nymphs at the Paneion: one of the inscriptions associated with the Court of Pan and the Nymphs records the dedication of a statue of Hermes to "Pan and the nymphs" (Isaac in press: 1–2, no. 1a; Aliquot 2008a: 100–2, no. A/14). Although it is not possible to determine which nymph the sculpture represents, it is tempting to identify this fountain figure as Echo, since she is mentioned in two inscriptions from the site. The first, contemporaneous with the inscription mentioning Pan and the nymphs, dedicates a "Goddess" (perhaps a statue that may have represented Echo) to "the God Pan, lover of Echo" (Isaac in press: no. 2; Aliquot 2008a: 99–100, no. A/13). Another inscription, associated with the shrine to Nemesis and dated in its text to AD 221/2, records the dedication of a statue of the goddess Echo (Isaac in press: no. 5; Aliquot 2008a: 104–5, no. A/17). Though Isaac notes that Pan and Echo are not regularly found as a couple in inscriptions (Isaac in press: 2), and Aliquot mentions that the association of the nymphs with Pan is not part of the Arcadian cultic tradition (2008a: 101), Pan and the nymphs are intimately related and often share the same cult places, as at the Paneion, because they inhabit the same landscape (Borgeaud 1988: 107). These deities have similar powers, which allow them to overcome mortals with panic or panolepsy and nympholepsy, respectively (Borgeaud 1988: 107–8). Pan is often connected more specifically with Echo based on the legend, which appears in various sources from the Hellenistic period onward, of his unsuccessful love for the musician-nymph (Borgeaud 1988: 79).

In the Levant, the Paneion was one of several cult centers dedicated to the nymphs. Other sanctuaries dedicated to the nymphs are known in the Béqa' at Qsarnaba and Timnin el-Foqa (Krencker and Zschietzschmann 1938: 151, fig. 216 [Qsarnaba]; 138–40, figs. 191–96, pl. 65 [Timnin el-Foqa]). A cult of the nymphs is attested by two inscriptions from Abila dedicated by the theophore Nymphaios in the early first century AD (Hajjar 1990b: 2552–53, 2598). As well, public *nymphaea*, thought to be cult places to the nymphs, graced many large cities in the region, including Palmyra, Bosra, Gadara, Pella, Gerasa, Philadelphia/Amman, Beth Shean/Scythopolis, and perhaps even Aelia Capitolina (Lichtenberger 2003: 105 [Gadara], 130, 140, 155–56 [Beth Shean], 177–79 [Pella], 235 [Gerasa], 264 [Philadelphia], 308; Belayche 2001: 169 [Aelia Capitolina]).

If the life-size head of Zeus or Asklepios (cat. 4) represents Zeus, it could be counted among the sculptural representations of cult deities found at the sanctuary. Zeus is closely related to Pan, since he is recorded in the literary sources as both the father and foster-brother of the Arcadian god (Borgeaud 1988: 42–44; Aliquot 2008a: 99–100). Pan, in his role as brother of Zeus, is cited as an ally of the chief Olympian god in his battle against the Titans (Borgeaud 1988: 100–101). It was during this battle that the scene of the first panic occurred, when Pan caused the Titans to flee by creating a "Panic noise" (Borgeaud 1988: 113–15). If the Paneion head does represent Zeus, then Zeus, like Pan, is represented in the sculptural, epigraphic, and numismatic evidence from the site.

Three inscriptions from the Paneion record the worship of Zeus in several guises. One dedication on a tiny hexagonal altar preserves only the name Zeus Olybrios (Isaac in press: 16, no. 13). Two others are addressed to Heliopolitan Zeus, who was a favorite of soldiers and is related to the Syrian Hadad.[6] However, since the two most common sculptural types of Heliopolitan Zeus show the god unbearded and in a frontal pose, they are not comparable to the Paneion head of Zeus or Asklepios. Thus, it is unlikely that the Paneion head is associated with the worship of Heliopolitan Zeus.[7] Zeus appears on the coins of Caesarea Philippi from the time of Marcus Aurelius to that of Elagabalus and is shown either standing and holding a *patera* or standing within a tetrastyle temple

(Meshorer 1984–85: 42).[8] Zeus was worshipped widely throughout the Levant, both in his Graeco-Roman form and assimilated to many local deities under numerous guises, including Zeus Belos, Zeus Kataibates, Zeus Koryphaios, Zeus Philios, Zeus Kasios and Zeus Nikephorios (Ovadiah and Mucznik 2009: 201–18; Lichtenberger 2003: 279–82; Hajjar 1990a: 2255–57, 2263–68; Hajjar 1990b: 2535, 2559–61, 2572–73).

Although no portraits of Augustus or Augustan family members substantiate the literary evidence for the practice of the early imperial cult at the site, if the colossal helmeted head found at the site (cat. 1) does depict Roma, then this fragment would provide sculptural evidence for the imperial cult at Caesarea Philippi. The worship of Augustus and Roma in the Levant seems to be confined largely to the three Augustea dedicated by Herod at Caesarea Maritima, Samaria, and Panias (Bernett 2007a),[9] although there may have been a temple to Roma at Antioch dating as far back as the time of Julius Caesar (Mellor 1975: 94–95), and inscriptions from Apamea, Arados, and Gerasa attest to the imperial cult at these cities in the Augustan period as well (Kropp 2009: 100).

To date, no sculptural evidence for the worship of Nemesis has been found. However, epigraphic evidence suggests that this goddess was represented in three-dimensional form at the sanctuary: an inscription accompanying the niche at the back of the Court of Nemesis states that the donor of this court not only funded the construction of the shrine, but also erected a statue of Nemesis to be displayed in the niche (Isaac in press: 3, no. 4; Aliquot 2008a: 102–3, no. A/16). Nemesis, the goddess of vengeance and punishment, is known to have been worshipped throughout the Levant, including at numerous cities in Roman Syria, at Caesarea Maritima and Beth Guvrin/Eleutheropolis, at Gerasa, and perhaps at Abila (Rosenthal-Heginbottom 2010: 216–18; Ovadiah and Mucznik 2009: 146–55; Bru 2008; Lichtenberger 2003: 305; Linant de Bellefonds 1992; Hornum 1993: 282–85; Seyrig 1932). In addition to her many roles, she is associated also with the Roman military and with the ruler cult, both of which may explain her presence at the Sanctuary of Pan at Caesarea Philippi/Panias, which was home to an early imperial cult site (the Augusteum) and whose patrons' Roman names may associate them with the army. The goddess is often represented by a griffin with a wheel, an attribute particular to the eastern Roman provinces (Rosenthal-Heginbottom 2010: 216), which also appears on another sculptural fragment from the site (cat. 16, fragment of an Ephesian Artemis).

THE SCULPTURAL EVIDENCE FOR "VISITING DEITIES:" THE "CIRCLE OF PAN"

The sculptural fragments suggest that in addition to the five cult figures worshipped at the Paneion, at least nine other deities were honored and perhaps given *cultus* at the site. Because none of these deities is recorded in the epigraphic or numismatic evidence, the sculptural finds provide the only evidence for their worship or honor here. In the following discussion, I refer to these nine gods as "visiting deities," after B. Alroth, who coined this term to refer to the dedication of a representation of one deity to another (Alroth 1989: 7, 65–66). Epigraphic evidence from the Paneion preserves two such instances from the Sanctuary of Pan: the dedication of a statue of Hermes to Pan and the nymphs (Isaac in press: 1–2, no. 1a; Aliquot 2008a: 100–2, no. A/14), and the erection of a statue of Asklepios to Zeus (Isaac in press: 4–6, no. 6). Since none of the other sculptural fragments discovered at the sanctuary are accompanied by inscriptions (except for the Antinous [Appendix 4, fig. 95]), it is impossible to determine whether any of these statues were dedicated specifically to one of the cult deities or whether they were dedicated to gods who did not receive *cultus* at the sanctuary. Thus, I apply the term "visiting deity" broadly to mean all gods represented in sculptural form who are not currently identified as main cult figures of the Sanctuary of Pan.

The major Olympian "visiting deities" represented by the sculptural finds are Athena, Artemis, the Ephesian Artemis, Aphrodite, Apollo or a Muse, Eros, and Dionysos. All of these sculptures (except for the Eros, which is likely to have been a subsidiary figure) are life-size or just under life-size. The demi-gods depicted are Herakles, Kybele,

and perhaps Orpheus; all of these are carved in miniature. This correlation between scale and subject matter may suggest that the major Olympian deities played a more prominent role in the religious life of the sanctuary, whereas demi-gods were honored on a more individual, *ad hoc* basis. Epigraphic evidence shows that two other "visiting deities" were represented in sculptural form: the life-size statue of Hermes that was dedicated in one of the niches surrounding the Court of Pan and the Nymphs (Isaac in press: 1–2, no. 1a; Aliquot 2008a: 100–2, no. A/14), and the freestanding statue of Asklepios (Isaac in press: 4–6, no. 6), whose scale is not determinable, that was dedicated to Zeus.

Of the visiting deities represented in sculptural form at the Paneion, many may be understood as part of what I will call the "circle of Pan," the group of deities associated with the mythology of the Arcadian god. As will be shown, Artemis, Aphrodite, Eros, Dionysos, and Kybele all have close relationships with the god Pan. In fact, the sanctuary may even have served as a cult site for some of these deities, most of whom were known to have been worshipped at other sites in the Levant as well.

Artemis, depicted as goddess of the hunt in the marble Artemis Rospigliosi (cat. 15), shares the wooded landscapes of Pan and is thus at home in the rural setting of the sanctuary at Caesarea Philippi. She is also connected to Pan, since both deities are associated with Arcadia: Pan having his origins there and Artemis being one of the principle gods of Stymphalos (Borgeaud 1988: 17–19). Since there is no other evidence to suggest the worship of Artemis at the Paneion, this statue seems best understood as an individual dedication honoring the goddess at the city's major sanctuary. Artemis is known to have been worshipped at other sites in the Levant, where she was integrated into the traditional oriental pantheon and frequently assimilated to Astarte or Atargatis (Ovadiah and Mucznik 2009: 33–39; Lichtenberger 2003: 286–87; Weber 1993: 43). For example, at Gerasa, Artemis was the patron deity of the city (Sourdel 1952: 42). At Larissa on the Orontes, Artemis had an oracle, where she communicated her messages via dreams (Hajjar 1990a: 2285). Two torsos of the goddess from Petra (one bronze, the other marble) show that the goddess was important in this Nabataean city as well (Weber 1993: 44, pl. 8,2 [bronze], pl. 13,1–2 [marble]).

Although the worship of Ephesian Artemis is distinct from that of Artemis as huntress, the discovery of a fragment of a marble statue of the Ephesian Artemis at the sanctuary should be noted here (cat. 16). Representations of Artemis of Ephesos in marble and on coins are known from the Levant; however, there is little secure evidence for cult centers dedicated to the goddess in this region (Ovadiah and Mucznik 2009: 34). A marble statue of the goddess was discovered at Caesarea Maritima in a large cistern outside the theater (Frova 1966: 206–15, no. 11), and many scholars conclude that this life-size figure suggests the worship of the goddess in this city (Frova 1966: 213–15; Holum and Hohlfelder 1988: 145–47). Artemis of Ephesos was also shown on the city coins of Akko-Ptolemais in the pre-Roman period (Kadman 1961: 26, 71) and on those of Neapolis in the Antonine period (Hill 1914: 54–62, pl. VI, 5 and 65). Another marble torso of the Ephesian Artemis was discovered in the area of the Nymphaeum at Gadara (Weber 1990: 352, pl. I,1; 1993: 44; Bol et al. 1993: 204, fig. 9). However, in the absence of more conclusive evidence for well-established cult centers to the Ephesian Artemis in the Levant and at the Paneion in particular, the fragment of the *ependytes* of an Artemis of Ephesos from the Sanctuary of Pan is best understood as an individual dedication to the goddess at the city's major cult center, rather than evidence for an established cult of the deity at the site.

Aphrodite is depicted in the life-size left leg and support of the Capitoline/Medici Aphrodite (cat. 13) found at the sanctuary. According to Borgeaud, Aphrodite and Pan were related both because of their similar spheres of sexual influence and through "a contrast between Beauty and the Beast" (Borgeaud 1988: 75). He argues that this connection and contrast, which was represented in art of all media from the fifth century BC onward, may indicate that the cults of the two gods were related and sometimes celebrated jointly.[10] Thus, it is possible that Aphrodite was worshipped alongside Pan at the Paneion. Both the scale and the type of the Capitoline/Medici Aphrodite may indicate

that the piece served as a cult statue.[11] Furthermore, at least two, if not three, other representations of Aphrodite have been found in the vicinity of Caesarea Philippi: a small-scale torso and thighs of a nude Aphrodite was found in the fields of Kibbutz Snir, which lies over part of the territory of ancient Caesarea Philippi (Dar 1991: 117, pl. 16, B; Avida 1978: 64, no. 14); a lower torso of a nude Aphrodite was found in the Golan Heights (Dar 1991: 117, pl. 16, C–D); and a bronze *imago clipeata*, which may represent Aphrodite, was found in one of the tombs at Caesarea Philippi (Dar 1991: 116, fig. 1, pl. 16, A).[12]

Evidence for the worship of Aphrodite in the Levant is not abundant, though the goddess is noted in epigraphic sources and depicted in multiple media, including sculpture, coins, gems, and tesserae (Ovadiah and Mucznik 2009: 4–18; Lichtenberger 2003: 286). Often, it can be difficult to determine whether Aphrodite was worshipped publically or privately, as at Caesarea Maritima, where the goddess is represented in statuary as well as on coins, gems, and tesserae (Ovadiah and Mucznik 2009: 8–10, 13–18; Gersht 1996b: 319–22). The goddess, who was assimilated to the oriental Astarte, had a temple in northern Syria at Afqa, at the source of the Adonis River to the east of Byblos (Krencker and Zschietzschmann 1938: 56–64, pls. 27–30, figs. 81–88). This temple's rituals, which are described by Sozomen and Zosimos, involved the casting of objects into springs and are strikingly similar to those documented at the Paneion (Zosimos *New Hist.* 1. 1).[13] In addition, Lucian tells us that there was a temple to Aphrodite at Byblos (Lucian *Syr. D.* 6). The goddess' name is included on an inscription from Shohba, dedicated by a woman who acted in response to orders from Aphrodite herself (Hajjar 1990a: 2282). Literary sources indicate that Aphrodite was worshipped at Ascalon as early as the fifth century BC, at Gaza as late as the sixth century AD, and at Aelia Capitolina (Ovadiah and Mucznik 2009: 4–5; Belayche 2001: 142–54 [Aelia Capitolina])

The sculpture of Eros found at the Sanctuary of Pan (cat. 22) was probably associated with the worship of Aphrodite or Pan, since its scale and style indicate that it was likely to have been a subsidiary figure. Moreover, there are no true cults known to have been dedicated solely to Eros/Amor/Cupid in the Hellenistic and Roman worlds. It seems most likely that the Eros was associated with a statue of Aphrodite, whose honor and possible worship at the Paneion has just been discussed. Alternately, Eros and Pan have their own associations centered around their legendary struggle alluded to by Virgil in his tenth *Eclogue* (10.69; Borgeaud 1988: 219, n. 263) and shown on several Roman sarcophagi (Matz 1968: 128–29, nos. 36 and 41, pls. 30, 40–42).

Dionysos is depicted in fragments of two life-size heads (cats. 7 and 8), possibly in the life-size nude male torso (cat. 12), and perhaps in the fragment of a tree trunk (cat. 28) and the fragment of a base with human and animal feet (cat. 29). The discovery of so many sculptures with Dionysiac themes is not unusual, since the wine god was firmly connected with Pan from the Archaic period onward.[14] According to the Homeric Hymn to Pan, when Hermes presented Pan to the Olympians, Dionysos, of all of the gods, was especially delighted with the half-man/half-goat creature (*Hymn. Hom. Pan.* 40–47). A myth, which probably dates to the period of Alexander the Great's campaigns, has Pan allied with Dionysos in his conquest of the Indies (Polyaenus *Strat.* 1.2; Borgeaud 1988: 54, 100–101, 178). The associates of Dionysos, satyrs and Silenoi, were logical companions of Pan, since the Arcadian god was also half-goat/half-man and inhabited the same woods, grottoes, and countryside. Thus, based on these associations, Dionysos, his various consorts, and Pan were frequently represented together in the plastic arts.

It is not clear whether Dionysos was merely honored or received *cultus* at the Paneion. He is, however, known to have been worshipped throughout the Levant, where he was assimilated to local deities such as Mercury Heliopolitanus at Baalbek, Dusarès in the Hauran, Malakbel at Palmyra, Adonis-Eschmun at Byblos, Berytus, Sidon, and Tyre, and perhaps Yahweh at Jerusalem (Smith 1975; Ovadiah and Mucznik 2009: 84–93; Lichtenberger 2003: 290–92; Hajjar 1990b: 2588; Smith 1974: esp. 821–29 [Yahweh]). Dionysos is known to have been an important god at Antioch as early as the Seleucid era, when he appeared on coins minted in the city (Norris 1990: 2348). In addition, there is literary evidence for the erection or rebuilding of a temple of Dionysos in this city during the Augustan or Tiberian period (Norris 1990: 2348), and numerous Dionysiac mosaics discovered in the houses of Antioch may attest to the god's importance there in the private sphere of worship (Levi 1947; Kondoleon 2000; Becker and Kondoleon 2005; Çimak 2000). The small temple of Dionysos at Baalbek, which is decorated with Bacchic themes and is thought to have been used for the celebration of Dionysiac mysteries, attests to the worship of the deity at one of the region's largest religious centers (Sourdel 1952: 63). In the Hauran, the town of Soueida considered Dionysos to be its founder, as is evidenced by its Greek name, Dionysias, used from at least AD 231 onward, and by an inscription found at the site that commemorates the construction of a building "[at the inspiration of its lord-founder, Dionysos]" (Hajjar 1990a: 2285–86). In addition, many Latin and Greek writers considered Dionysos to be the founder of Beth Shean/Scythopolis in Palestine (Avi-Yonah 1962: 253). At Caesarea Maritima, Dionysos appears on the city coins of the first and third centuries AD (Hopfe 1990: 2387–90) and in several statues from the site (Gersht 1996b: 317).

Kybele, probably depicted in the miniature limestone votive found at the sanctuary (cat. 23), is also firmly connected to Pan, since she shares certain powers and inhabits the same landscape (one of her standard epithets is the Mother of Mountains) (Borgeaud 1988: 147). In the art historical record, this connection is borne out by the numerous dedications to Kybele that include attributes of Pan, such as pine trees or cones, syrinxes, *lagobola*, cymbals, and sometimes depictions of Pan and satyrs.[15] The small scale and local fabric of the Paneion Kybele, coupled with the absence of any other evidence for the worship of this goddess at the Sanctuary of Pan, suggests that this statue should be understood as evidence for the honor rather than the worship of Kybele at the site. In the Roman Levant, the worship of Kybele does not seem to have been widespread (Ovadiah and Mucznik 2009: 76–78; Belayche 2001: 155, 182). Though terracotta figurines representing the goddess have been found at Hellenistic Tel Dor, Maresha, and Akko, recent work shows that her presence in Palestine in this period was notable, since representations in Cyprus, Syria, and Egypt during the Hellenistic period are rare (Erlich 2009: 281*–82*). The lack of evidence for the worship of Kybele in the Roman Levant may be due to the fact that the Anatolian and Greek goddess' powers, functions, and attributes were embodied in and assumed by Dea Syria. Dea Syria, the Western name for the Syrian goddess Atargatis, had her main sanctuary at Hierapolis but was also worshipped throughout the Levant.[16] The most common representation of Dea Syria shows her in the manner of Kybele (enthroned, flanked by two lions, and holding various attributes in her hands) (Drijvers 1986: 358); however, three-dimensional limestone and marble representations of this type are rare in the Roman Levant.[17]

THE SCULPTURAL EVIDENCE FOR "VISITING DEITIES:" NON-PAN-RELATED FIGURES

Sculptures of several visiting deities who have no clear associations with Pan were also dedicated at the Paneion. It is difficult to determine whether the dedication of two life-size heads, one depicting Athena (cat. 2), the other representing either Apollo or a Muse (cat. 6), were honorary or represent cult activity to these deities at the site. We know, however, that Athena was worshipped widely in the Levant, where she was identified with the Arab goddess Allat and revered not only as a goddess of war but also as a nurturing divinity who provided springs and fertility (Friedland 2008; Ovadiah and Mucznik 2009: 60–66, 69; Lichtenberger 2003: 285–86; Sourdel 1952: 73). Temples to Athena were erected at many sites, including Raha (Sourdel 1952: 70, n. 8), Moushennef (Sourdel 1952: 71, n. 6.), and Palmyra (Sartre 1991: 492, n. 5; Gawlikowski 1977: 253–74).

Likewise, whichever deity the head of Apollo or a Muse represents, there are parallels for worship in the region. Apollo and the Muses were worshipped at various cities in the Levant. While the god is less common in the Decapolis cities (Lichtenberger 2003: 282–83), sanctuaries and dedications to Apollo are known at Ascalon and Gaza (Ovadiah and Mucznik 2009: 19–29), as well as at Daphnaios, Hadet, Baalbek, Palmyra, and

Hierapolis (Hajjar 1990b: 2586–88).[18] In addition, J. Magness has proposed that the Roman temple at Kedesh was an oracular shrine dedicated to Apollo (Magness 1990; Ovadiah et al. 1993). Evidence for the worship of the Muses in this region comes largely from Heliopolis (Hajjar 1990b: 2598),[19] though depictions of Muses are found throughout the region in the same cultural contexts (theaters, funerary contexts, and villas) in which they are known to have played a role in Italy and Greece (Weber 2007: 222, 230; Lichtenberger 2003: 309).

The statuettes of Herakles (cat. 21) and the possible Orpheus (cat. 25), because of their small scale and representation of semi-divine, personal deities, seem best interpreted as individual dedications to these gods at the Paneion. The statuettes may have been dedicated by donors who had special relationships to these gods and thus honored them at the local sanctuary, despite the fact that they were neither cult deities, nor associated with the primary cult figure of the site. This is certainly the case for the no-longer-extant statue of Asklepios, recorded in a dedicatory inscription on a freestanding pillar. Since the dedicator was a physician, it was natural for him to erect a statue of the healing god to Heliopolitan Zeus (Isaac in press: 4–6, no. 6). In Sidon, Asklepios was associated with the cult of the healing god Eschmun, the primary deity of the city, probably around the third century AD (Jidejian 1971: 59–62; Sartre 1991: 490). Dedications to Asklepios have also been found in the Hauran (Sourdel 1952: 46), at Amman, and at Hamat Gadar (Jalabert 1906: 157–61).

Herakles was by no means a stranger to the Roman-period pantheon of the Levant, where he was one of the more popular Graeco-Roman gods assimilated to the Semitic pantheon. The hero-god seems to have been introduced into the region during the Hellenistic period, perhaps via the armies of Alexander the Great, who were known devotees of Herakles (Downey 1969: 1). In light of the Seleucid control of Panias between 200 BC and the late first century BC, the well-attested Seleucid connections to Herakles should also be noted. Tyre had a sanctuary to Herakles,[20] and several towns in northern Syria were named for him, including Heraclea and Herakleion.[21] Representations of the hero-god appear on both public and religious buildings at Baalbek, and he is shown on a stele found at nearby Douris (Hajjar 1990b: 2598–99). His worship is also documented at Palmyra from the first century BC to the late third century AD (Downey 1969: 77–80) and at Dura Europos from the first century BC to at least the second and third centuries AD (Downey 1969: 71, 808–83). While there are no documented instances of his worship in Roman Palestine, Herakles was depicted in statuary, coins, gems, mosaics, and tesserae found at various sites in this region (Ovadiah and Mucznik 2009: 113–19).

If the forequarters of a bovine discovered at the sanctuary (cat. 25) are associated with a sculptural group of Herakles and the cattle of Geryon, the statue would emphasize Herakles' role as protector of herds and herdsmen, an aspect of the deity entirely appropriate to the Sanctuary of Pan. On the other hand, if it comes from a group depicting Orpheus charming the animals, it would also have associations with the bucolic setting of the sanctuary. Furthermore, since several statues of Orpheus charming the animals have been found in nymphaea and baths, this group seems to be associated with watery contexts such as the Paneion.[22]

THE SCULPTURAL EVIDENCE FOR THE IMPERIAL CULT

As noted above, there is clear evidence for the practice of the early imperial cult at the Paneion, as found in Josephus and supported by the colossal head that may have depicted Roma (cat. 1) discovered at the site. And, though there is no evidence for what became of the cult of Augustus and Roma after the Herodian era, literary and epigraphic sources provide evidence for imperial interest in or connections to the sanctuary and the city of Caesarea Philippi beyond the period of Augustus. Josephus tells us that in AD 61 Agrippa II refounded the city and renamed it Neronias, to honor his imperial patron Nero (*AJ* 20.211; Wilson 2004: 28). Shortly thereafter, Vespasian and Titus visited the site during the First Jewish War (Joseph. *BJ* 3.443–44). A marble plaque dated to AD 98–117 and associated with an altar mentioned in its inscription is dedicated "for the salvation of our lord Trajan Caesar" (Isaac in press: no. 8; Ma'oz 2007:

26–27). Finally, the inscription carved on the cliff face at the back of the Court of Nemesis dedicates a statue of the goddess erected in AD 178/9 for the "preservation of our Lords the Emperors" (Isaac in press: 3–4, no. 4; Aliquot 2008a: 102–3, no. A/16).

Still, no official portraits of emperors or imperial family members have been recovered from the sanctuary (that represented in cat. 24, if it does represent an emperor, is too cursorily worked to have been based on official imperial models). This absence of imperial portraits is not unusual in this region, where far fewer portraits of emperors and their families have been discovered (Skupinska-Løvset 1999: 60–78; 103–15).[23] The dearth of imperial portraiture is perhaps due to logistical issues, including the lack of native sources of marble, the absence or rarity of local sculptors trained to carve marble, and the mechanics of distribution of imperial portraiture in the eastern fringes of the empire. It may also be due to environmental, historical, and political conditions that caused the destruction of official (as well as private) portraiture (Skupinska-Løvset 1999: 34–35).

There is, however, one sculptural find from the Sanctuary of Pan that is tangentially related to the imperial cult: the over-life-size bust of Antinous, reportedly found at the site in the mid-1800s (Appendix 4, fig. 95). The over-life-size scale and high quality of the bust make it likely that this Antinous was a prominent, public dedication. To date, it is one of only two portraits of Antinous found in the Levant.[24] The discovery of this imperially-related portrait is significant, as it substantiates the literary and epigraphic evidence noted above that the site had imperial associations beyond the first century AD. Furthermore, it may suggest that in the high and later imperial periods, the worship of Augustus and Roma at the site was recast to encompass the more all-inclusive imperial cult.[25]

THE ABSENCE OF PRIVATE PORTRAITS AT THE SANCTUARY

The absence of private or non-imperial portraits in the sculptural fragments discovered at the Sanctuary of Pan is notable, since portraits of private patrons are common dedications at Roman period sanctuaries.[26] For example, at least six Roman portraits were found at the Sanctuary of Poseidon at Isthmia. These represent victorious athletes, officials of the games, and important citizens who may have been major donors to the sanctuary (Sturgeon 1987: 131–44). Likewise, at Cyrene, "most of the private portraits, where we know the exact findspots, can be associated with various temples... Some of [these]...were portraits of priests and priestesses; others may have been either votive statues or statues erected in honour of benefactors of the respective sanctuaries" (Rosenbaum 1960: 13). Thus, one might expect to find at least a few private portraits dedicated at the Sanctuary of Pan. However, no portrait heads, draped female figures, or togate male figures were discovered.

This lacuna in the sculptural dedications at the Paneion seems less anomalous, however, when compared with the number of marble portraits discovered in the Levant.[27] In general, far fewer marble, non-imperial, private portraits have been found in this region than in other provincial centers.[28] The small corpus includes two portraits of women from Ascalon, one bust (IAA S.894; Vermeule and Anderson 1981: 12, figs. 25–26; Fischer 1998: 139) and one head (IAA 31.324; Vermeule and Anderson 1981: 12; Iliffe 1933b: 14, pl. 4; Fischer 1998: 139; Skupinska-Løvset 1999: 125–26); the portrait of the bearded priest of the imperial cult from Jerusalem (Skupinska-Løvset 1999: 83–86); a late antique head of a woman from Beth Shean;[29] four portraits of women and one of a male official from Caesarea Maritima;[30] a head of a young boy who was perhaps a devotee of Isis from Samaria-Sebaste (Skupinska-Løvset 1999: 52–54); a head of a woman (IAA 45.3; Vermeule and Anderson 1981, 14, figs. 23–24; Fischer 1998: 154–55; Skupinska-Løvset 1999: 81–82; Weber 2002: 545, H 7), a head of a youthful boy (Weber 2002: 546, H 9) and a draped male (Weber 2002: 547, H 12), all from the "Jordan Valley;" two draped women (Weber 2002: 492–93, nos. C 18 and C19) and three *togati* (Weber 2002: 490–91, nos. C 11–13), all from Gerasa; a *togatus* (Weber 2002: 408–9, PL 20) and a draped female (Weber 2002: 409–10, PL 21) from Gadara; two portrait heads of bearded men from Philadelphia/Amman (Weber 2002: 510–11, D 10–11); a portrait head of a bearded man (Weber 2002: 523–24, G 14), a *togatus* (Weber 2002: 523, G 12), and two draped

females from Petra (Weber 2002: 524, G 15–16); the bust of a young man from Sidon (Skupinska-Løvset 1999: 50–52); the head of a young boy from Emesa (Skupinska-Løvset 1999: 54–57); two heads of men, one bearded, and a third head of a mature male, all from Berytus (Skupinska-Løvset 1999: 83, 121, 121–22, respectively); a head of a bearded male from Antarados (Skupinska-Løvset 1999: 87–90); a young bearded male from Seleukeia Pieria (Skupinska-Løvset 1999: 117–19); and the head of a male from Antioch (Skupinska-Løvset 1999: 119–21).

Although some may wish to explain the smaller number of private portraits in the Levant — and especially in Roman-period Palestine — with the general aniconic tendencies of several of the populations in the region (namely the Jews and the Nabataeans), current scholarship shies away from characterizing the region so monolithically and emphasizes instead the more complex world in which Jews and others negotiated the icon-filled pagan centers through which they had to move on a daily basis (Fine 2005: 82–123; Millar 1993: 12–14). Furthermore, this explanation for the absence of portraits would not be appropriate at a highly Hellenized center of pagan worship such as the Paneion, where patrons clearly had no qualms about dedicating marble "graven images" or "idols."

Others attribute the paucity of private portraits discovered in the Roman Levant to accident of survival, environmental factors that destroyed artifacts (the region was plagued by a series of severe earthquakes from the third century AD on), and religiously- and politically-motivated destruction of statues (Skupinska-Løvset 1999: 34–35). I would add that another explanation for the dearth of private portraits in this region is the absence of a native source of marble and the improbability of established sculptors' workshops whose artists were trained in the Graeco-Roman style.[31] The five portraits found at Caesarea Maritima, several of them carved in a non-Graeco-Roman style, may be explained by the possibility that a marble-carving workshop of locally-trained artists did exist at this site in conjunction with its role as a harbor and point of entry for imported marble artifacts and uncarved blocks (Gersht 1995a: 36; Gendelman and Gersht 2010). For example, the uncarved protome found at Caesarea Maritima and now on display in the courtyard of the S'dot Yam Museum supports this theory (Gersht 1995a: 36; Gendelman and Gersht 2010: 37). However, overall, the commissioning of marble portraits in the Levant may have been impeded by the lack of the materials and artists to create them. Thus, patrons and benefactors of the Sanctuary of Pan were less likely to have dedicated marble portraits of themselves. Furthermore, the predominance of marble in the sculptural dedications at the site makes it unlikely that, in the absence of marble, patrons would have substituted likenesses carved out of local limestone.

CONCLUSIONS

Thus, the sculptural fragments discovered at the Paneion provide invaluable information about the pantheon and religious life of the sanctuary. Of the five known cult figures of the Sanctuary of Pan (Pan, the nymphs, Zeus, Nemesis, and Augustus/ Roma), sculptural representations of at least two, and possibly four, survive. Of these sculptures, only one, the head of Roma or Athena (cat. 1), is clearly identifiable (due to its scale) as a cult statue. The life-size head of Zeus or Asklepios (cat. 4) may have served as a cult statue as well. More notable than these sculptural representations of the cult deities of the sanctuary are the representation of at least nine other "visiting deities." Some of these (Artemis, Aphrodite, Eros, Dionysos, and Kybele) are associated with the "circle of Pan" and thus with the worship of the primary cult figure of the sanctuary. Others (Athena, Apollo or a Muse, Herakles, and Orpheus) are unrelated to Pan and may suggest either that these deities were honored or received *cultus* at the site. Such a large number of visiting deities shows that in addition to offerings to its own cult figures, the Sanctuary of Pan attracted dedications to a variety of major Olympian deities and several semi-divine figures. The second-century AD portrait of Antinous may indicate that the late first-century AD worship of

Augustus and Roma was later transformed into the worship of the imperial cult.

The preceding analysis of the pantheon of the Sanctuary of Pan and the worship of its deities at other sites throughout the Levant offers a clearer understanding of the position of the Paneion within the broader practice of polytheism in this region. The site constitutes one of the primary centers for the worship of Pan and the nymphs in the Levant. Moreover, it is only one of three or four architecturally-attested Levantine centers for the practice of the cult of Augustus and Roma and one of only two sites in the region to preserve evidence for the honor or worship of Antinous. If Aphrodite was worshipped here alongside Pan, the site would constitute one of only a few known cult centers to the goddess in this region. The worship of Zeus and Nemesis here is, however, not unique. Furthermore, the honor and possible worship of Artemis, Artemis of Ephesos, Dionysos, Athena, Apollo or a Muse, Herakles, and Orpheus also have parallels in this region. The honor of Kybele via the dedication of a three-dimensional sculpture, on the other hand, is rare in the Levant.

Thus, the sculptural evidence from the Sanctuary of Pan provides a window onto the pantheon of the sanctuary that is not preserved in other evidence, a fact that several recent studies of the religious life of the sanctuary have acknowledged (Berlin 1999; Wilson 2004: 56–69; Burton 2010).[32] Furthermore, the most distinctive feature of the pantheon worshipped and/or honored at the Paneion, discernible in large part only from the sculptural evidence presented here, is its entirely Hellenistic, as opposed to Semitic or mixed, character. The epigraphic evidence, which is bereft of any trace of the worship of Semitic deities, suggests that these sculptures were not read by their patrons and viewers as Semitic deities dressed in Hellenistic iconography and style. Instead, they were mainstream Graeco-Roman gods. The broader implications of this conclusion are discussed in the following chapter.

NOTES

1   There is currently, to the best of my knowledge, no monograph on sculptural programs from sanctuaries parallel to those on the sculptural programs from theaters (Fuchs 1987), baths (Manderscheid 1981), and Italian villas (Neudecker 1988), thus I have created these categories to serve as a framework for analysis here.

2   Although the miniature votive of Kybele or Dea Syria (cat. 23) differs in that it is made of limestone and worked in a more geometric style, its iconography follows mainstream Hellenistic representations of the goddess.

3   It should be noted that this list of cult deities is based only on literary and epigraphic evidence, as depictions of gods and goddesses on coins do not necessarily provide secure evidence for the erection of cult statues and the worship of those deities at a site (Prayon 1982; Dumser 2006; Sobocinski in press). Other scholars have posited that the nymph Maia and the goddess Tyche were also worshipped at Panias, based solely on depictions of these deities on coins (Ma'oz 2007: 28; Wilson 2004: 66, 67–68; Tzaferis 1992a: 193). Because we lack other evidence for the worship of these deities at the site, I do not include either goddess in the list of established cult figures of the Paneion.

4   Mellor, who has surveyed the evidence for the worship of Roma, notes that "at least during the reigns of Augustus and Tiberius, Roma's presence was required in the provincial cults of the emperor" (1975: 26).

5   Pan is shown in three different areas of the temple at Baalbek: in the company of satyrs and maenads in the triangles and lozenges of the platform of the peristyle; alongside Amors, satyrs, and maenads on the decoration of the door to the cella; and in the scene of the chastisement of Lycourgos sculpted on the interior of the cella on the right socle of the podium of the adyton (Hajjar 1990b: 2596). For the sanctuary at Antioch, see Aliquot 2008a: 100 and n. 23.

6   Isaac in press: 4–6, no. 6 and 10–11, no. 8. Inscription no. 6, carved on a marble pillar, is dedicated to Heliopolitan Zeus "for the salvation of our lords the emperors" and is internally dated to AD 63/4. Inscription no. 8, carved on a marble plaque once attached to an altar, is dedicated to both Heliopolitan Zeus and Pan "for the salvation of our lord Trajan Caesar" and can be dated on the basis of the mention of the emperor Trajan to AD 98–117 (Ma'oz 2007:

26–27). On Heliopolitan Zeus, see Hajjar 1977; 1985; and 1988.

7   Although bronze representations of Heliopolitan Zeus are more common than those in imported marble (Hajjar 1988: 573–92), several three-dimensional marble statues of Heliopolitan Zeus have been found in the Levant: two from Beirut (Hajjar 1977, 1: 239–41, 241–43) and one from Byblos (Hajjar 1977, 1: 261–62).

8   Zeus standing and holding a patera: nos. 5, 5a, 8, 10, 10a, 10b, 11a, 15, 19, 28; Zeus standing in a tetrastyle temple: nos. 29, 37.

9   Note that Bernett does not agree that the building constructed in front of the natural cave at Panias was the site of Herod's Augusteum (2007a: 138–40); instead, she believes that the building on the elevated terrace west of the cave could have been constructed as Herod's temple to Augustus (2007a: 141–44).

10   For a list of representations of Pan and Aphrodite together found in classical through Hellenistic Greece, see Borgeaud 1988: 75, 138, 222, n. 15, 247, n. 77. For representations of Pan and Aphrodite in sculpture of the Hellenistic and Roman periods, see Marquardt 1995: 128–30, 227–44.

11   The original Knidian Aphrodite, from which the Capitoline and Medici types are thought to be derived, was erected as a cult statue, surrounded by its own shrine in the city of Knidos. For a discussion of the setting of the Aphrodite of Knidos, see Havelock 1995: 58–63.

12   Based on this *imago clipeata,* whose ideal female he identifies as Aphrodite, Dar argues that there was a cult of Aphrodite and a temple to the goddess in the vicinity of Caesarea Philippi. However, further evidence is needed to construct a persuasive argument that the female represented in the tondo is, in fact, Aphrodite and that the discovery of this bronze tondo at the site suggests that Aphrodite was worshipped and had a temple somewhere in or just outside of Caesarea Philippi.

13   The temple of Aphrodite at Afqa is renowned for its destruction by Constantine.

14   However, Dionysos and Pan do not seem to have had direct cultic relations until the end of the fourth century BC (Borgeaud 1988: 54, 100–101, 178).

15   Examples include: the altar to Kybele from the western slope of the Acropolis, which has two standing Pans carved on it (*CCCA* 2: no. 180); a marble relief from the western slope of the Acropolis, which

shows Kybele seated in a *naiskos* whose columns are carved with a nude Pan holding a syrinx and a *lagobolon* (*CCCA* 2: no. 182); a marble sculpture of Kybele seated on a rock from Corinth with a pine tree, syrinx, and *lagobolon* carved on one side of the rock (*CCCA* 2: no. 457); two marble altars from Phlya, which show Kybele seated with a consort on one side and pine trees, syrinxes, and cymbals on the others (*CCCA* 2: nos. 389 and 390); and several altars from Rome with similar arrays of Pan attributes (*CCCA* 3: nos. 239, 241a, 241b, and 357).

16 For a listing of places of worship of Dea Syria-Atargatis in the Levant, as well as in the rest of the Roman empire, see Hörig 1984.

17 Vermaseren in the *CCCA* 1 does not catalogue any three-dimensional representations of Kybele from the Levant; Drijvers 1986 lists one limestone statue from Tahtalıköyü (*LIMC* 3: Dea Syria no. 14) and one statuette from Hatra (*LIMC* 3: Dea Syria no. 17).

18 The evidence for large-scale worship of Apollo includes a temple at Hadet (a village to the west of Baalbek) and a sanctuary and sacred wood at Daphnaios. Individual dedications to the god come from Palmyra and from Baalbek, where he was honored in a dedication engraved on a fragment of an architrave found in the grand court of the Temple of Jupiter. At Hierapolis, the oracle of Apollo was celebrated.

19 Heliopolis was called the "city of the Muses" in the *Expositio totius mundi* 32. According to an epigram dated to AD 430–431 and engraved on the southern wall of the podium of the round temple that commemorated the construction of a canal, the city possessed an "enclosure of the Muses."

20 As cited in Vollkommer 1988: 105, see Hdt. 2, 44; Cass. Dio 42, 49; and Strab. 16, 2, 23.

21 As cited in Vollkommer 1988: 107. For Heraclea, see Strab. 16, 2, 7 and Pliny *HN* 5, 18; for Herakleion, see Strab. 16, 2, 8.

22 A table stand (?) was found in the baths at Lepcis Magna (*LIMC* 7: Orpheus no. 143b) and another was found in the Nymphaeum at Byblos and is now in the Beirut National Museum (*LIMC* 7: Orpheus no. 143a; Picard 1947: 266–68, fig. 2; Lauffray 1940: 29–30, pl. 5). In addition, a first-century BC rendition was found in the Tiber at Rome (*LIMC* 7: Orpheus no. 162).

23 Though see Albertson 1988 on a portrait of Marcus Aurelius and for a general discussion of the carving of imperial portraits in the Levant.

24 The other Antinous, which is far more poorly preserved, is from Caesarea Maritima (Meyer 1991: 91–92, no. I 70, pl. 82,1).

25 Some scholars suggest that the Augusteum was converted into a temple to Zeus at some point in the first century AD (Wilson 2004: 65), though there is no definitive evidence for this. For the early imperial cult in the Levant, see Kropp 2009; for the imperial cult in Roman Palestine, see Bernett 2007a; 2007b.

26 For the purposes of this discussion, I exclude the following sculptural types from the category of "non-imperial private portraits:" cuirassed statues, because they were likely to have represented emperors; philosophers, since they did not represent truly private individuals; and headless draped females, unless they are of the Large or Small Herculaneum types, since it is not always possible to determine whether these carried portrait or ideal heads. It should be noted that several portraits of philosophers have been found in Roman Israel: one from Hamat Gadar (now on view in the Haifa Museum); three from Caesarea Maritima, which represent Carneades, Olympiodoros, and Sophocles and may have been displayed in the niches or intercolumniations of the Caesarean Christian library (Gersht 1996d: 99–103, 102 n. 5; for Sophocles and Carneades, see also Skupinska-Løvset 1999: 58); one of Hermarchus from Samaria-Sebaste (IAA 35.3449; Vermeule and Anderson 1981: 12, fig. 21; Skupinska-Løvset 1999: 58); and one from Raphia (Skupinksa-Løvset 1999: 58). For this genre of portraiture in the Roman Levant in general, see Skupinska-Løvset 1999: 57–59.

27 For private portraiture in the Levant, see Skupinska-Løvset 1999: 15–128. Locally-produced funerary busts such as the limestone pieces from Beth Shean/Scythopolis (Skupinska-Løvset 1983; Gazda 1986) or those from Palmyra (Sadurska and Bounni 1994) constitute an entirely different body of portraiture than that considered here, since they are made of local material, carved by local craftsmen in local traditions, and served a funerary rather than religious function. For recent discussions of such funerary portraits from Syria, see Skupinska-Løvset 1999; 2003; for funerary portraits in local materials from Arabia, see Weber 2002: 414–45 [Gadara], 466–81 [Abila], 503–4 [Gerasa], 514 [Philadelphia/Amman], 537–39 [Arabia Petraea], 553–55 [Jordan Valley].

28 Vermeule and Anderson note that "Greek and Roman portraits from the Holy Land are, in a word, spotty as regards type and chronology" (1981: 12–15). More recently, see Skupinska-Løvset 1999: 22, 34–35.

29 Unpublished. I thank Gabi Mazor of the Israel Antiquities Authority for showing me this head.

30 For a fourth-century head of a woman, see Gersht 1995b: 110–13, figs. 5–8; for a Severan bust of a woman

(IAA 93.1009), see Gersht 1996d: 109–12, figs. 14–18; another head of a Severan woman is published in Hebrew only (Gersht 1987: 54–55, no. 55); I have been unable to locate a publication of the fourth female portrait from Caesarea Maritima. For the headless statue of an official (IAA 92.658), see Gersht 1996d: 103–7, figs. 6–13.

31 See Chapter 3 above and Friedland in press.

32 Because Tzaferis wrote his 1992 article before the discovery of the sculptures, he notes that the further archaeological work planned at the site should produce more information regarding the religious life of the sanctuary. His discussion is based necessarily only on literary, epigraphic, and numismatic evidence, and thus he refers only generally to "the attendant gods and deities associated with [Pan's] sanctuary" (1992a: 195). He is not able to offer much information beyond the five cult figures listed above and known to have been associated with the site, though he does reconstruct a cult of Tyche at the site (1992a: 198–99).

Chapter 5

The Function and Meaning of the Sculptures

The Sanctuary of Pan
as a Graeco-Roman Cult Center in the Levant

This study of the Roman marble sculptures from the Sanctuary of Pan at Caesarea Philippi documents a large group of statuary dedicated and displayed at a Roman-period sanctuary in the Levant: its origins, style, sculptural types, technical features, chronology, patrons, possible display contexts, and subjects. As material culture, the group is important on multiple levels: in and of itself, the assemblage constitutes an example of sculptural dedications in a major provincial Graeco-Roman sanctuary; regionally, the sculptures offer a window into Graeco-Roman worship in an otherwise largely Semitic context; and in the context of the larger Roman empire, the pieces shed light on cultural exchange between the eastern provinces and the imperial core. Thus, the study of these sculptures not only reveals new information on the character and function of the Sanctuary of Pan, it also has ramifications for our understanding of religious life in this largely Semitic region throughout the course of Roman rule from the Herodian period through the fourth century AD, and even into the early Christian period. Finally, the study also contributes to our understanding of the imperial marble trade and to the dialogue on cultural exchange or "Romanization" in the Near East. Here, I summarize the conclusions reached in the studies of the origins, patronage and display,

and pantheon of the statues, and then analyze these within the local, regional, and imperial contexts of the Sanctuary of Pan at Caesarea Philippi.

THE SCULPTURES
FROM THE SANCTUARY OF PAN:
ORIGINS, CHRONOLOGY, PATRONS,
DISPLAY, SUBJECTS

The group from the Paneion offers a rare opportunity to study the function and meaning of marble statuary in one specific context within the Levant — a Roman period sanctuary. Although the sculptures were found in a ninth-century AD deposit at the sanctuary, they may be clearly associated with the six religious buildings constructed there from 19 BC through AD 220. The nearly-complete excavation of these buildings and the well-studied architectural, epigraphic, numismatic, and ceramic evidence provide a fairly clear picture of the physical, historical, and cultural contexts in which the sculptures were dedicated and displayed. But it is the material, style, carving tradition, chronology of dedication, patronage, and subjects of these Roman marble sculptures that reveal the highly Hellenized and Romanized nature of worship at the Sanctuary of Pan.

Since there is no native source of marble in the Levant, nor a local tradition of carving marble, the Paneion sculptures (and indeed all other marble artifacts discovered in this region) had to be imported from one of the other marble-rich provinces of the empire. Isotopic analyses of marble samples from fifteen of the sculptures found at the sanctuary suggest that these sculptures were carved of marble primarily — if not exclusively — from Anatolian quarries (for three of the sculptures, the marble may be associated not only with several quarries in Turkey but also with a few quarries in Greece, and further petrographic testing is needed to narrow these possibilities). It is likely that the unsampled pieces are also made of marble from Anatolian quarries, since the marble of the Paneion sculptures is remarkably homogeneous in grain size, grain density, and the ability to take a high polish. These results correspond with a multi-method scientific analysis of imported white marble sarcophagi, sculpture, and architectural decoration found in Israel, which showed that sculptural marble was imported primarily from Anatolia (especially Aphrodisias and Dokimeion) and less frequently from Greece. Similar Anatolian and Greek quarry origins have been found for marble artifacts discovered in Roman Jordan and Syria. The Paneion sculptures, then, add further evidence to our growing knowledge of the participation of this region in the imperial marble trade.

All of the marble sculptures discovered at the sanctuary, except the tiny locally-worked male head (cat. 24), are carved in the Graeco-Roman tradition. Stylistic and technical analyses of the Paneion sculptures associate many of the pieces with the sculptural workshops of western Asia Minor, and more specifically with those of Asia and Caria (Ephesos and Aphrodisias). Iconographically, the Paneion sculptures follow Graeco-Roman conventions. Seven of the sculptures found at the sanctuary echo sculptural types thought to have been created in the fourth century BC and the Hellenistic period: a nymph based on the Aphrodite Anadyomene, a Capitoline/Medici Aphrodite, an Artemis Rospigliosi, an Artemis of Ephesos, a dancing satyr related to the Borghese Faun, a weary Herakles, and a Kybele or Dea Syria (cats. 11, 13, 15, 16, 20, 21, 23). In terms of carving technique, most

diagnostic are the neck struts found on four of the pieces (cats. 3–6), which are most commonly interpreted as a technical feature unique to the sculptural workshops of Asia Minor, although they are occasionally found on sculptures from other regions, such as North Africa. Also important are the close stylistic and technical comparisons of several of the Paneion sculptures to statues created in the workshops of Aphrodisias and Ephesos. For example, the head of Apollo or a Muse (cat. 6) is directly comparable to a head of a Caryatid (often identified as Aphrodite) from Aphrodisias; the torso of a nymph (cat. 11) recalls a similar statue from the Fountain of Trajan at Ephesos; and the linear rendering and idiosyncratic shape of the spine of the dancing satyr (cat. 20) may be found on two figures from Aphrodisias, the satyr from the small *spinario* group and the satyr from the small group of a satyr and young Dionysos. Thus, many of the Paneion sculptures seem to have been carved by sculptors trained in Anatolian workshops. The lack of evidence for sculptural workshops in the Levant that produced statuary in a Graeco-Roman style suggests that the Paneion sculptures were imported to this region fully-carved, and evidence from shipwrecks demonstrates that statuary was shipped in such a state. For Caesarea Philippi, the most likely port of entry was Tyre, since the sanctuary lies just 29 miles east of this port city along the Tyre–Damascus road. As recent research has detailed how expensive sea — and even more so land — transport was, patrons clearly undertook great financial burden to import and dedicate these mainstream Graeco-Roman sculptures.

Important to an exploration of the meaning of the sculptures are the identities of their patrons (gleaned from the literary and epigraphic evidence), the chronology of sculptural dedication at the sanctuary, and the display contexts in which the statues were erected. Clear patterns of sculptural dedication have been identified. Although there is no epigraphic or sculptural record for Herodian dedications of marble statuary at the sanctuary, architectural and numismatic evidence suggests that during the first century AD a large number of sculptures was erected by these royal patrons as part of their architectural elaboration of the site. In the second and early third centuries AD, epigraphic and sculptural evidence demonstrates that the dedication of statuary constituted one of the main means of patronizing the sanctuary; however, now the patrons were not Herodian client kings, but local Romanized religious and civic officials: all patrons have Roman names, but the names of their fathers (one Roman, one Greek, and one Semitic) suggest their identities or at least their paternal affiliations. Although the majority of epigraphic and architectural evidence from this period suggests that sculptural dedications were associated primarily with the architectural elaboration of the sanctuary, numerous sculptural fragments datable to this period — but not associated with any architectural context — show that there were also statues that were not programmatic, but dedicated individually and erected on pedestals throughout the buildings and courts of the sanctuary. This dedication of programmatic and cult statues in aediculated interiors and on pedestals erected on porches, in cellas, and in open air courts represents a standard mode of sculptural display at Roman sanctuaries. After the late third century AD, the sanctuary saw fewer and smaller sculptural offerings. Only two (or perhaps three) late fourth- or early fifth-century AD miniature marble sculptures were discovered at the site. In contrast to the large-scale, often architecturally-related dedications of the second century AD, these were probably the result of individual votive offerings layered onto the sanctuary's existing sculptural program and other *ad hoc* dedications. These late antique sculptural dedications show that the pagan sanctuary continued to function during the time when Christianity was already well-established in the city below. Their small scale and sparse numbers, however, indicate that imported marble statuary was no longer the primary vehicle for patronage of the sanctuary. The absence of epigraphic material from this period makes it difficult to know anything about the patrons of these votives. Thus the patrons of the Paneion were, from the outset of the architectural and sculptural elaboration of the sanctuary, focused on connecting the site to the imperial core and participating in Roman religious, cultural, and political realms. In fact, the height of sculptural dedication at the site and the evidence for Romanized patrons occur during the Antonine

and Severan periods, a period of heightened imperial interest and presence in the Near East.

What deities were the Herodian dynasts and later the Romanized local civic and religious officials worshipping and honoring at the Paneion? Literary, epigraphic, and numismatic evidence suggests that there were at least five main cult deities worshipped at the Sanctuary of Pan — all mainstream Graeco-Roman gods — and the subject matter and iconography of the sculptures substantiate the worship of these and extend the pantheon of the Paneion to other standard Graeco-Roman deities. In addition to representing at least two and perhaps four of the main cult figures of the sanctuary (Pan, a nymph, probably Roma, and perhaps Zeus), the sculptural fragments show that at least nine other Olympian and semi-divine deities were worshipped at the sanctuary. Because of their close mythological relationship with the god Pan, some of these deities (Artemis, Aphrodite, Eros, Dionysos, and Kybele) may be seen as part of the "circle of Pan," which may have been honored at the site alongside its original and primary cult figure. The dedication of life-size representations of Athena and Apollo or a Muse are less easily explained, since these two deities are not often related to Pan. That of a miniature Herakles may represent a dedication by an individual who had a special devotion to this semi-divine figure; that of a possible Orpheus charming the animals is certainly appropriate to the pastoral setting of the sanctuary and may be related to the Paneion's watery context, since other representations of this demi-god have been found in nymphaea. The presence of the imperial-related portrait of Antinous at the sanctuary (Appendix 4, fig. 95) may indicate that the worship of Augustus and Roma established at the site by Herod the Great in 19 BC was later reconfigured to encompass a broader imperial cult. That the sculptures depict only Olympian and semi-divine deities and that one imperially-related portrait is also associated with the site demonstrates the Graeco-Roman nature of worship conducted at the Sanctuary of Pan at Caesarea Philippi. Indeed, though some have argued that in the deep, Canaanite history of Mount Hermon, Aliyan, son of Ba'al and the god of sources, may have been worshipped at the site (Wilson 2004: 2; Dussaud 1936: 283, 295), from the pantheon preserved in the Roman epigraphic record and sculptural dedications, Semitic deities never seem to have held sway at Caesarea Philippi — or were long forgotten by the Hellenistic period (Aliquot 2008b: 85).

Thus, the sculptures discovered at Caesarea Philippi shed light on the character and function of the Sanctuary of Pan: the Anatolian marble and style, Hellenistic sculptural types, Romanized patrons, and Graeco-Roman subject matter of the sculptures from the Paneion suggest that our Levantine sanctuary was both Hellenized and Romanized.

LOCAL CONTEXT: FUNCTION AND MEANING OF THE SCULPTURES

Sculptures such as those discovered at the Paneion played a central role in religious experience (Elsner 2000: 52) and, as I have discussed elsewhere (Friedland 2008), the ancients' "visualizations" of their deities resulted from selections of format, material, iconography, and style. Sculptural patrons must have known, at least at some level, that the choices that they made (and paid for) had a profound effect on the "look" and therefore the identity of the deities to whom they were making their dedications. Thus, the format, material, style, sculptural types, iconography, and subjects of the Paneion sculptures all contributed to their highly Hellenized and Romanized function and meaning for both their patrons and viewers.[1]

First, in terms of format, all statues and sculptural fragments discovered at the sanctuary were three-dimensional as opposed to relief. This is significant, because in Arabia and Syria, reliefs were quite common, and they were not only dedicated as votive offerings, but often served as the object of cult itself (Downey 2008). The wholly three-dimensional format of the statuary discovered at the Paneion is more in line with traditional Graeco-Roman cult statues and votive dedications in temples and sanctuaries. Second, the material of these sculptural fragments, white marble imported from Anatolia and perhaps also from Greece, would have provided a stark contrast to statuary in local materials of white limestone, yellow or red-

dish sandstone, and black basalt. Even when awash in their original polychromy (see cat. 2), the gleaming, crystalline, non-native stone — and the high polish and fine details it could take — would have been apparent to viewers and would have emphasized the participation of patrons of the Paneion in this mainstream, Mediterranean-wide worship of marble-made deities. Third, the style, iconography, and subject matter of the sculptures (except for cat. 24) echo standard Graeco-Roman patterns for depicting Olympian deities and semi-divine mythological figures. Because many of the statues dedicated at the Paneion were based on sculptural types developed in the fourth century BC and the Hellenistic period but adopted and adapted by the Romans, and because all represented standard Graeco-Roman deities and mythological figures, they had no visual relation to local Semitic deities. Instead, the Paneion sculptures could have been readily recognized by a visitor to the sanctuary from Rome, Athens, or Ephesos.

Finally, the scale and placement of many of the pieces — in niches that lined the interior *cella* walls or served as the focal points of *cellae* and courts — suggest that many of the pieces discovered were used as cult statues, while others functioned as votive offerings. Recent research on the hierarchy of statues set up in Roman temples and sanctuaries (cult statues, votive offerings, and programmatic pieces, sometimes referred to as *ornamenta*) demonstrates that, at sanctuaries, "statues set up among the *ornamenta* of a temple… as property given to the gods,…participated also in the sacrality of the shrine, which sheltered them" (Estienne 2010: 270–71). In other words, visitors to a sanctuary would have honored not only the main deities to whom the temples were dedicated, but also the "visiting deities" who were represented by the numerous other images of gods and goddesses dedicated within the temples of the main deities. Thus, the highly Hellenized and Romanized nature of the Paneion sculptures provides critical information about the character and the nature of ritual at the sanctuary. Clearly a major portion of the cult and ritual here was dedicated to Graeco-Roman deities and followed standard Graeco-Roman practices of propitiating the gods via interactions with three-dimensional marble representations of them. Here, it is important to recall that for the Greeks and the Romans the visualizations of their deities — the three-dimensional statues depicting them — were animated, powerful objects. The gods were thought to inhabit these statues of themselves, which had been "activated" by certain rituals and religious rites, and ancient authors describe statues of the gods sweating, bleeding, weeping, turning, and moving.[2] Thus, the sculptures dedicated at the Paneion were not merely euergetistic veneer; they functioned as a central part of the Graeco-Roman rituals at the sanctuary, and they stood in their niches and on their pedestals awaiting propitiation and offerings (Mylonopoulos 2010). Their very presence characterized the Paneion as a Graeco-Roman cult center.

REGIONAL CONTEXT: A GRAECO-ROMAN SANCTUARY IN A SEMITIC MILIEU

The highly Hellenized and Romanized character of the Sanctuary of Pan is especially noteworthy in comparison to other sanctuaries in both the immediate region of Mount Hermon and in the broader regions of Syria and Arabia (Aliquot 2008b; Dar 1993; Tzaferis 1992b). Panias does share some architectural features with other Hermonian cult places and sanctuaries, such as the niches cut into cliff faces of the mountainside (Aliquot 2008b: 78). The chronology of sculptural dedication at the Paneion also parallels a similar chronological pattern for the construction of sanctuaries noted at neighboring Hermonian cult places (Aliquot 2008b: 85–95). However, no other cult site on Mount Hermon is nearly so Hellenized through and through, that is, in respect to its architecture, sculptural presence of deities, and cults worshipped. For example, at cult sites such as the High Place at Tel Dan and the Roman Temple at Kedesh, though we lack the sculptural evidence to know whether the local gods were ever conflated with or subsumed by Graeco-Roman deities, we have epigraphic evidence for the worship of archaic Semitic deities.

Similarly, the highly Hellenized and Romanized nature of the Sanctuary of Pan at Caesarea Philippi/Panias stands in direct contrast to other religious centers in the broader region of the Levant, where Semitic deities such as Eschmun and Allat were, in the Roman period, conflated with classical gods such as Asklepios and Athena, and where a similar correlation between the character of worship and the types of sculptural dedication may be seen. Since there is no other sanctuary in the Decapolis for which we have recovered the complete extant sculptural assemblage, here I provide two brief examples from Syria Coele and Syria Phoenicia, though the comparative study of sculptural dedications at sanctuaries in the Roman Near East merits fuller treatment in a separate venue. For example, in the northwestern sector of Palmyra, the Palmyrenes worshipped the Arab pastoralist and warrior goddess Allat, whose cult was established in Syria around the end of the Hellenistic period and continued into the Roman and Islamic eras. Archaeological evidence shows that the temple was built as early as the first century BC, received additions in the first century AD, and was renovated in the middle of the second century (Gawlikowski 2008: 397–401). The temple was partially destroyed during the Roman sack of Palmyra in AD 272, then repaired with the establishment of the so-called Camp of Diocletian. It seems to have gone out of use entirely in the fourth century. Allat was clearly the main deity of this sanctuary, though other Arab deities, such as Shamash and Rahim, were worshipped here as well. Though as early as AD 64, Allat is identified with the Greek goddess Athena in both the epigraphic record (Drijvers 1978: 341–42; Kaizer 2002: 99–108) and, as we will see, to a certain extent in her sculptural representations, the sculptural visualizations of the deity remain largely local — until the renovation of the temple in the second century AD.

The format, material, style, sculptural types, and iconography of the majority of fragmentary statues published from the Temple of Allat echo the primarily Semitic nature of the sanctuary's main deity and contrast sharply with the group from Caesarea Philippi. First, the majority of statues discovered in the sanctuary are reliefs more common to Palmyra and the Palmyrene steppe, as opposed to the three-dimensional representations found at Caesarea Philippi. In contrast to the wholly marble assemblage at Panias, the majority of the sculptures found in the Temple of Allat were made of local limestone. Rather than the Graeco-Roman style and deities of the Paneion sculptures, those from this temple are carved in typical Palmyrene style and depict common Palmyrene subject matter (Gawlikowski 2008: 401). The relief style is characterized by frontal figures arrayed in a single line, unnaturalistic proportions, and an interest in pattern as opposed to realistic depiction of anatomy or drapery. The reliefs often depict gods in characteristic Palmyrene military costume and several feature the camel, ship of the desert, as emblematic of the geographic location of the city and the caravan trade so central to Palmyra's livelihood. As opposed to the varied backgrounds of the patrons at the Paneion, the published epigraphic record from the Temple of Allat, which spans from AD 62 to the 240s, documents the largely Semitic character of her patrons: the majority of the inscriptions are in Aramaic (only two are bilingual in Greek and Aramaic), the names of the patrons are all Semitic, and most were dedicated by specific tribes (Drijvers 1995; Hillers and Cussini 1996).

Several of these reliefs, however, do provide some hint of the religious syncretism manifested in the Greek and Aramaic bilingual inscriptions — mostly through the visualization of native deities via standard elements of Graeco-Roman iconography. For example, on one famous relief from the temple, which at first seems to represent a typical Palmyrene scene of a dedicant offering incense to a row of four deities, the goddess on the far right side, opposite the dedicant, stands out, because her iconography is distinctly non-Palmyrene (Friedland 2008: 348, no. 45; Drijvers 1978: 338p, pl. 73; Starcky 1981: 565, no. 13; *PAT* 1128). Though carved in traditional Palmyrene style, this depiction of Allat represents the goddess with the Graeco-Roman iconography of Athena: a flounced *peplos* with scales to allude to an ægis, a spear in her right hand, and a crested helmet. Indeed, such representations of Allat as Athena occur here from the first century AD onwards and, though carved in local materials and local styles, may be taken to indicate at least some degree of religious syncretism and cultural assimilation. However, the dedication of two other statues, around the middle of the second century AD, sends a far clearer message of cultural assimilation.

Two marble statues, a colossal version of a Pheidian-influenced Athena and a small head of an Athena Giustiniani, were found in the *cella* of the Temple of Allat. They are thought to have been erected sometime around the middle of the second century AD in conjunction with the construction of a Graeco-Roman *cella* over the archaic temple (Gawlikowski 1977: 269; Gawlikowski 1983: 188; Gawlikowski 1996).[3] These two statues provide a stark contrast to the rest of the sculptural assemblage from the Temple of Allat. First, both pieces are carved in imported white marble. Though we do not know who paid for the importation of these sculptures, it is clear that their dedication was a concerted and costly act: not only would the material and workmanship have been costly — for the colossal piece in particular — but, as noted in Chapter 2, the expense of transporting marble statuary from a Levantine port of entry (perhaps Tyre) over land and deep into the Syrian desert would have been staggering. Thus, whoever dedicated these two pieces was determined to erect sculptures of imported material. The patron or patrons of these pieces must also have been interested in importing Graeco-Roman sculptural types and styles: the colossal Athena is a Roman creation influenced by several fifth-century BC Pheidian Athenas, including the Parthenos, and the small Giustiniani head echoes a type created in the fourth century BC.

There is much debate over the function of the colossal Pheidian-influenced Athena in the temple at Palmyra. The piece has been dated by the excavator, first on the basis of stratigraphy to the middle of the second century AD, and then on the basis of style to the late Hadrianic or early Antonine periods (Gawlikowski 1996). Whatever its function, its findspot within the *cella* of the temple suggests that from the mid-second century AD on, when a Palmyrene entered the Temple of Allat, he or she would be confronted with a colossal, three-dimensional, white marble, foreign-carved, Graeco-Roman image of the temple's deity. The stark contrast to the surrounding local Palmyrene statuary cannot have been lost on the worshipper. Thus, the sculptural assemblage on view in the Temple of Allat at Palmyra from the second century AD onwards was varied in terms of format, material, style, sculptural types, and subject matter — and this mixed sculptural assemblage seems to reflect the mixed character of the deity worshipped there.

Also instructive is a comparison to the sculptural assemblage discovered at the Sanctuary of Eschmun in Sidon. This sanctuary was founded in the first half of the sixth century BC by the Sidonian king Eschmunazor II some 3 km north of Sidon on the southern bank of the river Bostrenus and was dedicated from the start to the Phoenician god of vegetation, Eschmun, whose myth of death and resurrection made him an important symbol of life and health. However, as early as the fifth century BC, the Phoenician deity seems to have been associated with the Greek god Asklepios. The temple to Eschmun was built, destroyed, rebuilt, renovated, and augmented with other buildings (including the so-called Basin of Astarte) from the fifth century BC through the third century AD.

While this sanctuary has been studied largely to understand the Hellenization of the Phoenician population of Sidon, and indeed most of the sculptural finds date from the fifth through the second century BC, worship and even major architectural elaboration did continue through the imperial and late Roman periods. This Roman-period worship is commemorated by eight marble statues found in various areas surrounding the temple podium. The finds include three representations of Hygieia, one at one-third life-size, two at two-thirds life-size, and all associated with the Broadlands type (Stucky 1993: 26–27, 76–77, cats. 73, 74/75, 76); a two-thirds life-size Dionysos, associated with the Jacobsen type (Stucky 1993: 28, 79–80, cats. 85–87); a fragment of a dolphin that must have served as a statue support, probably for a piece depicting Aphrodite (Stucky 1993: 52, 106, cat. 235); a late Trajanic or early Hadrianic portrait head, associated stylistically with the workshops of Asia Minor (Stucky 1993: 52, 96, cat. 179); a draped man wearing a himation, now missing its portrait head (Stucky 1993: 52, 96–97, cat. 180); and a headless togate man, which also would have carried a portrait (Stucky 1993: 52, 97, cat. 181). Like the Caesarea Philippi pieces, these three-dimensional pieces, which date from the second through third centuries AD, are characterized by their carving in imported marble (though quarry origins are unknown),[4]

representation of mainstream Graeco-Roman subject matter and iconography, reproduction of Hellenistic sculptural types, and carving in Greek, Hellenistic, and Roman style, and in some cases in foreign workshops.

At Sidon, which was highly Hellenized even as early as the fifth century BC, the worship or honor of the sanctuary's deities via such imported statuary may seem no surprise. In fact, Stucky notes that even in the sanctuary's high classical period, Eschmun was never represented in Phoenician style or iconography, but always as the Greek god Asklepios (Stucky 1993: 26). However, Stucky does note several distinctly Phoenician aspects of the sanctuary's sculptural dedications from the Greek and Hellenistic periods. First, he notes that the numerous dedications of so-called "Temple Boys," though carved in Greek style, did not represent standard Greek subjects and were accompanied by Phoenician dedicatory inscriptions recording votives by Phoenician parents on behalf of the health of their children (Stucky 1993: 135–37). Second, he argues that the Throne to Astarte would have served as an aniconic cult statue, even in the face of so many figurative votive dedications (Stucky 1993: 137). He concludes, then, that "Hellenization had manifested itself without profoundly penetrating Phoenician culture" (Stucky 1993: 137). It should also be noted here that from the Roman period there is no evidence for any statue large enough to be interpreted as a possible figurative cult image. Stucky does not comment on the cultural affiliations of those worshipping at the sanctuary in the Roman period, but certainly the willingness of the patrons to dedicate votive statues in which they visualize their deities in anthropomorphic, Graeco-Roman fashion suggests their assimilation of and participation in more mainstream Graeco-Roman religion. However, the mixed nature of this Hellenistic sculptural assemblage reveals the Semitic origins of the deity worshipped at the Temple of Eschmun.

Correspondingly, one might argue that if Semitic deities were worshipped at the Paneion, traces of this might have been more visible in the sculptural record from the sanctuary along the lines of the evidence from Palmyra and Sidon. Thus the entirely Graeco-Roman nature of the sculptural assemblage from the Paneion demonstrates that the Sanctuary of Pan seems to have been from its inception a center of Graeco-Roman worship situated within the Semitic Levant.

ROMAN IMPERIAL CONTEXT: THE PANEION SCULPTURES AND "ROMANIZATION"

Connections have long been known between the seemingly remote, mountainside, eastern site of Panias and Rome: first, from epigraphic sources that list sculptural patrons with Roman and Romanized names, and second, from literary sources that document Herod's connection of the sanctuary to Rome by the construction of a major temple to the imperial cult and his successor's further overtures to Roman emperors via renaming the city and the hosting of emperors (or soon-to-be-emperors) at the site. Thus, from its earliest architectural elaboration by Herod the Great to its foundation as the capital of Herodian dynasts, the sanctuary and its nearby city became a venue where these client-kings expressed their connection to the imperial core via mainstream Graeco-Roman architecture and sculptural dedications. In the second century AD, when the city and its territory had become part of the Roman province of Syria, local Romanized elites adopted these patterns and continued to patronize the sanctuary in like manner — their focus was westward, toward Rome, rather than in their local eastern milieu. As Aliquot has recently noted, this interest in the imperial core may well have been not only historical (associated with the interests of Herodian client-kings) but also related to "the role possibly assigned by Rome to the cities which had definitely taken over from the…Herodian rulers" (2008b: 94).

The sculptures discovered at the Sanctuary of Pan substantiate and extend these connections, demonstrating that the originally Hellenistic cult became Romanized during the first through the fourth centuries AD. As discussed in Chapter 4, in addition to the standard Graeco-Roman subjects of the statuary, the association of the site with the imperial cult is substantiated and extended by the discovery there of a head that probably depicts Roma (cat. 1) and the bust of Antinous (Appendix 4, fig. 95). Furthermore, as noted in Chapter 3, the manner of display of the statues in ædiculated interiors is distinctly Roman. Most importantly, as shown in Chapter 2, the Anatolian (and perhaps Greek) marble out of which the statues were carved provides further important evidence for the incorporation of the Levant — even its interior cities, such as Caesarea Philippi — into the Roman imperial marble trade. The large number of statues and sculptural fragments discovered is also important, as it demonstrates (alongside the large numbers of marble statuary discovered at such sites as Caesarea Maritima, Beth Shean/Scythopolis, Gadara/Umm Qais, and Gerasa/Jerash) that the region's import of marble statuary was not sporadic and occasional, but occurred on a large scale and throughout the high imperial and late antique periods.

Thus, the sculptural finds from this Levantine sanctuary provide important evidence to further the dialogue on cultural exchange or "Romanization" in the Near East.[5] This sculptural assemblage is particularly informative regarding cultural exchange due to its display context: it does not come from an imperial-style bath building, nymphaeum, theater, hippodrome, or other public venue that represents a clear Roman or Graeco-Roman cultural institution that was adopted by local populations. Instead, it comes from a religious context. In negotiating the adoption, assimilation, or denial of foreign cultural norms, religion plays a key role. More importantly, religion is also one of the more conservative aspects of a society's culture. To date, in order to study cultural exchange within the religious sphere of the Roman Near East, archaeologists have often focused on the architecture of sanctuaries (Gawlikowski 1989; 1998; Dentzer 1991). The sanctuaries and temples in which these deities were worshipped, however, were merely the architectural skeletons that housed these deities and their rituals. I argue that to witness the shifting ideas and beliefs of the indigenous Semitic worshippers as they reconciled their local mythologies with those of their Roman occupiers, we must turn to the contents of these sanctuaries — the visualizations of their deities, the statues of gods to whom suppliants appealed for divine intervention with their problems, needs, and hopes (Elsner 1996; Gordon 1979). At the Sanctuary of

Pan at Caesarea Philippi, through the sculptural dedications made from the first through the fourth centuries AD, we are able to witness those shifting beliefs, as we learn that the patrons, some of whom were of Semitic origin, were not only interested in adopting Roman names, but also in adopting Roman modes of worshipping Olympian deities and demi-gods and the Roman custom of honoring them by dedicating three-dimensional, marble, Hellenistic visualizations of Pan, his cohorts, and other visiting deities.

CONCLUSION

This study, I hope, has not only documented a newly-discovered sculptural group from a Roman-period sanctuary but has also entered the Sanctuary of Pan at Caesarea Philippi into the broader discourse on Hellenism and Romanization in the ancient Near East. It indicates that further insight into this phenomenon could be gained from a more thorough comparative study of the sculptural assemblages of various sanctuaries in this region. Likewise, a study of the distribution of marble statuary in all contexts in the Levant could reveal what factors affected the patronage and display of these expensive imported elements of mainstream Graeco-Roman material culture. For now, it is hoped that the preceding pages have shown that not only was there a market for marble statuary in the Levant, but that finds of such sculptures in this region offer a rare opportunity to learn more about the function and meaning of Roman marble statuary in its varied physical, historical, and cultural contexts.

NOTES

1   Similarly, it has been documented that the price of a sculpture was affected by its size, quality, age, condition, and the reputation of its maker (Bartman 1992: 30).

2   Sweating (Appianus, *Bellum civile* 2.5.36.13; 4.1.4.11); bleeding (Appianus, *Bellum civile* 4.1.4.11); weeping Apollo (Augustine, *City* 3.11, 1.1); turning east (Suetonius, *Lives* 8.5); moving (Lucian, *Lover of Lies* Harmon 3: 347–53).

3   Note that Gawlikowski, the excavator, states that he was incorrect in his first identification of the sculptural type and association of this marble cult statue with the Pheidian Parthenos (2008: 410–11); he also rescinds his initial assignment of the piece (dated stylistically to the second century AD) to the new Roman-style *cella* erected in the second century AD. Instead, Gawlikowski now believes that the marble cult statue was erected in the sanctuary when it was rebuilt in the third century AD, in consort with the new Roman legionary camp. However, because Gawlikowski does not provide enough evidence to support this new, later display context, I have chosen to maintain his initial dating and association of the piece with the *cella* of the second century AD.

4   Though Stucky (1993: 76, n. 498) declares that the marble may be identified as Cycladic or Pentelic based on the color, crystal-size, and patina of the surfaces, he also notes that marble analyses were not possible. His identifications of the marble sources should therefore be disregarded, as it is impossible to identify quarry origins of white marbles by eye.

5   Though current scholarship has exposed the serious weaknesses of the term and concomitant paradigm of "Romanization" established by F. Haverfield and elaborated on since the early twentieth century, and though some have suggested that scholars cease using this term at all (e.g., Mattingly 2011; Webster 2001), I have chosen to employ the term here for want of a clearer word to express the adoption and adaptation by native populations of certain aspects of Roman culture and religion. By using this term, I do not mean to suggest that this cultural exchange was unidirectional or uniform throughout the Near East — quite the opposite. I also employ the term here with full understanding that the sort of evidence that I study (expensive imported marble statues) provides only the elite perspective on and response to Roman imperial domination (as opposed to other sorts of material culture, such as the thousands of coarse-ware saucer lamps dedicated in the Tripartite Building of the Paneion in the third century AD [Berlin 1999: 36–40]).

Catalogue of Sculptures

INTRODUCTION

The following catalogue describes and identifies the twenty-nine identifiable sculptures found in the excavations of the Sanctuary of Pan at Caesarea Philippi/Panias between 1989 and 1993. The remaining two-hundred and seventeen fragments that may have belonged to these pieces or others, no longer preserved, are listed by category in Appendix 3, and the over-life-size bust of Antinous reportedly found at Caesarea Philippi in the mid-1800s is presented in Appendix 4. The primary aim of the catalogue is to document this body of previously unpublished material and, in doing so, to identify the subject of each piece. Where possible, entries provide comparanda, workshop associations, and dates of production, though in some cases pieces are too small or damaged to allow any reliable conclusions.

Each entry begins with basic data, including the catalogue number and title of the piece; its excavation number; its maximum preserved height, width, and depth, followed by its reconstructed height/scale; a description of its material; a note on the condition of the statue; and a brief discussion of carving techniques. The excavation numbers include the following information in the order listed:

permit number/year of excavation/locus number/basket number/item number (if one was issued). The main portion of each entry includes sections on description and reconstruction ("right" and "left" refer to the statue's proper right and proper left); identification; and comparanda, workshop, and date.

The catalogue entries are arranged according to the scale of the pieces, with the single surviving colossal piece presented first, near life-size to life-size pieces second, statuettes third, and small-scale statuettes last.[1] Colossal scale is defined as any sculpture over 1.65 m in height; near life-size to life-size as any sculpture between 1.15 and 1.45 m tall; statuette as any sculpture between 1 and 0.5 m tall; and small-scale statuette (or miniature) as anything below 0.5 m.[2] This order was chosen primarily because in a sanctuary, the scale of a piece is more often related to its function than in other contexts, with colossal sculptures more likely to have served as cult statues and small-scale statuettes functioning as individual votive dedications rather than part of the sanctuary's liturgical furnishings or programmatic decoration.

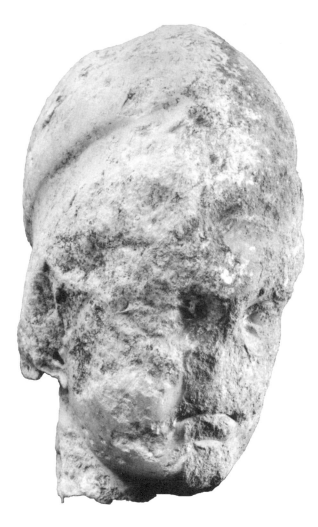

*Fig. 6   Cat. 1: Head of Roma or Athena, three-
              quarter. Photo IAA, by permission.*

*Fig. 7   Cat. 1: Head of Roma or Athena,
              front. Photo IAA, by permission.*

COLOSSAL STATUE

1 — HEAD OF ROMA OR ATHENA

Exc. no. 85/92/156/7865/1 (figs. 6–9)

Preservation and Material

H. 0.50 m; 0.25 m (face); W. 0.23 m; D. 0.33 m; reconstructed H. 2.75 m/colossal.

White marble; large, highly translucent crystals; isotopic analyses show that the marble is of Turkish origin, probably from Mylasa, Afyon, or Aphrodisias.

The piece is broken at top of neck, and the entire face is badly abraded. Missing are the rim of the Corinthian helmet, part of the right side of the helmet, most of the left eye, lower lid of the right eye, nose, lips, and part of the ear lobes. Two struts are preserved on the back of the helmet: one on the crown (irregularly shaped: H. 4.5 cm; W. 3.0 cm), the other on the neck guard (rectangular: H. 3.0 cm; W. 1.5 cm). There is a raised, square, broken area preserved at the back of the neck beneath the helmet (H. 6.0 cm; W. 8.0 cm). The lower right cheek preserves the original surface. Dark brown accretions cover the center of the face and the entire left side of the head.

Technique

Chisel lines create the upper and lower eyelids. Drillwork indicates the separation between the lips as well as the ear wells. Deep drill holes mark the corners of the mouth. The face and the front of the helmet were polished, while the sides and back of helmet were smoothed.

Description and Reconstruction

The figure wears a Corinthian helmet that is pushed up and rests atop the head. The face has an oval shape and rounded cheeks. Little of the features or modeling is preserved. The large eyes (W. 7.0 cm) were deeply inset, especially at their inner corners; however, there is no indication of tear ducts or drilled pupils. The upper lids are thick (W. 1.0 cm). The depression below the lower lip would have added to the three-dimensional quality of the mouth. The area beneath the broad chin is plump, and the neck is thick. The Corinthian helmet (H. 25.0 cm) consists of a bulbous crown with a wide band encircling it, meant to represent both the visor and the neck-guard. On the sides, this band arcs outward, and at the back it extends down the neck into a point, so that the guard protects the back of the neck, but not its sides. The front of this band is damaged, thus no evidence of eye-openings or the nose piece is preserved. Nor is there evidence on the sides of the band for slits through which leather straps could be inserted to hold the helmet in place. Below the neck guard, there is an irregularly-shaped raised area, whose surface is now broken. Little of the hair-style is preserved, though a raised, abraded and encrusted area on the left side of the head, running from the temple along the side of the head, across the upper third of the ear, and behind the ear, may be understood as locks of hair. A damaged area on the right side of the neck behind the ear may indicate that side-locks fell along the neck. Because little of the neck is preserved, it is difficult to determine how the head was held; however, the relative symmetry of the face and the helmet may indicate that the head was frontal. Because the head is fully worked on all sides, it was meant to be viewed from all angles.

It is difficult to reconstruct details of hairstyle, posture, gesture, costume, and attributes, because this head is badly damaged and none of its body is preserved. The square area preserved at the nape of the neck, below the helmet, may represent a ponytail commonly depicted on heads of Athena or Roma beneath the Corinthian helmet. The two struts remaining on the back of the helmet

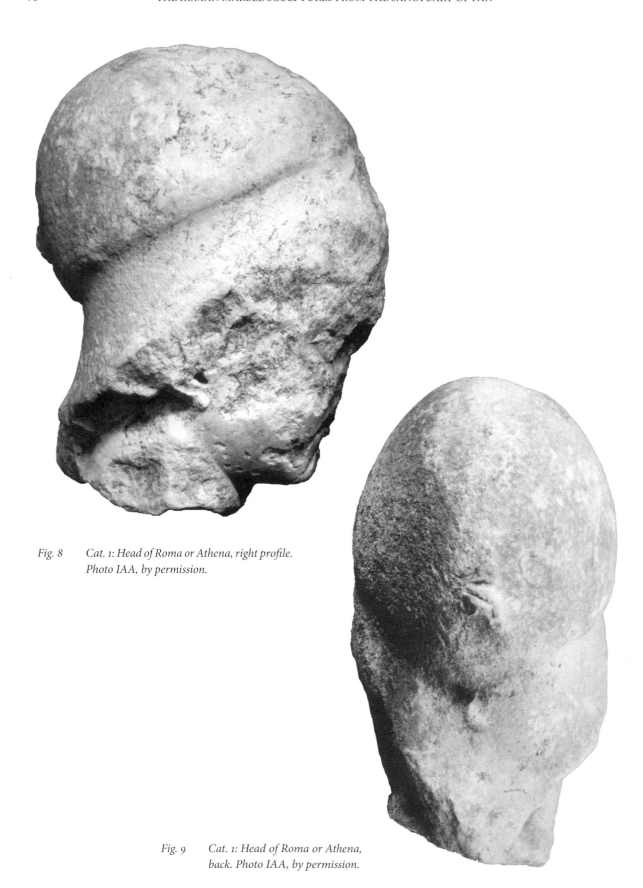

Fig. 8   *Cat. 1: Head of Roma or Athena, right profile.*
            Photo IAA, by permission.

Fig. 9   *Cat. 1: Head of Roma or Athena,*
            back. Photo IAA, by permission.

could be attachment points for a crest, although these are usually attached to the top of the helmet. Alternately, they may have played a role in anchoring the colossal piece to its display context.

Identification

From the single attribute preserved on the sculpture (the Corinthian helmet), the piece may be identified either as Athena or Roma, the two ideal figures most commonly shown wearing Corinthian helmets.[3] It seems more likely that the piece represents Roma, because its scale and association with a sanctuary make it likely to have served as a cult statue, and because Herod the Great is known to have dedicated a temple to Augustus at Panias, which is likely to have included the worship of this goddess. Thus, this head could have been part of a group of cult statues representing Augustus and Roma.[4] Furthermore, there is no evidence that Athena received *cultus* at the Paneion, though she appears at the sanctuary in at least one if not two other life-size marble heads (cats. 2 and 3). This is the only colossal sculpture discovered at the Paneion, and although not all colossal sculptures functioned as cult statues, it is likely that this piece did, because of its association with a sanctuary site and its distinction in scale from the rest of the Paneion sculptural group.

Comparanda, Workshop, and Date

This head of Roma or Athena is comparable to the colossal head of Athena found at Tel Naharon (near Beth Shean) (Vitto 1991).[5] Noteworthy are the similarities in scale and the rendering of the Corinthian helmet (Vitto 1991: 33–36). Although the helmet of the Paneion Athena or Roma preserves fewer details than that of the Tel Naharon example, both helmets are represented in an unrealistic fashion. In both cases, the sculptor represented the visor as a continuation of the neck guard, rather than as a protective covering that would fit over and cover the face. Other similarities between the two heads, which may be due largely to their colossal scale, include the oval shape of the face, the rounded cheeks, the thick neck, the depression below the lower lip, the broad chin, and the polished facial surface contrasting with an unpolished helmet (Vitto 1991: 33–34).

Because the Paneion Roma or Athena is so badly damaged, it is difficult to assign a date or workshop association based on stylistic and technical characteristics. If the sculpture served as a cult statue for the Herodian Augusteum and was dedicated contemporaneously with the construction of the building, it would date to the late first century BC or the early first century AD.

Fig. 10   Cat. 2: Head of Athena wearing an Attic helmet, front.

Fig. 11   Cat. 2: Head of Athena wearing an Attic helmet, back.

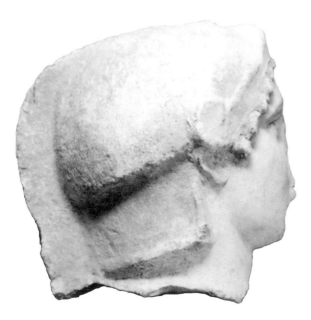

Fig. 12   Cat. 2: Head of Athena wearing an Attic helmet, right profile.

Fig. 13   Cat. 2: Head of Athena wearing an Attic helmet, left profile.

LIFE-SIZE STATUES

2 — HEAD OF ATHENA WEARING AN ATTIC HELMET

Exc. no. 85/92/192/7157/1 (figs. 10–13)

Preservation and Material

H. 0.23 m; W. 0.17 m; D. 0.22 m; reconstructed H. 1.26 m/life-size.

White marble; small crystals. Isotopic analyses show that the marble may come from one of two quarries in Greece (Paros/Lychnites and Thasos/Cape Vathy — if the marble is dolomitic) or from a quarry at Afyon in Turkey.

The piece is broken at the base of neck. It is missing the crest of the helmet, the pointed ridge of the helmet's forehead guard, the nose, the right half of the upper lip, and the chin. There is damage to the surface of the helmet, the curls, and the cheeks. The crown of the helmet is pitted overall. Paint is preserved overall: dark yellow on the helmet and red on the back of the helmet, the sides of the back portion of the crest, the snail-shell curls, the left cheek in front of the ear, the lips, and the inner edges of the eyelids.[6] Brownish/blackish accretions cover the left side of the back of the head.

Technique

The crest was carved separately and attached to the top of the helmet, which is leveled and keyed.[7] A small metal tenon (W. 0.6 cm), preserved at the center of this attachment area, and plaster, removed during cleaning, effected the join. There is little drillwork on this piece. Instead, a chisel was used to carve a recessed area in the forehead guard of the helmet, the concentric circles of the snail-shell curls, the edges of the band on which the snail-shell curls sit, the upper and lower eyelids, and the separation between the lips. Tiny drill holes mark the tear ducts and the left corner of the mouth. The face, eyeballs, and neck were polished.

Description and Reconstruction

The head is turned to the left and tilts slightly toward the side. The oval-shaped face is framed by a painted Attic helmet. On top of the head, a rectangular attachment area for the separately-carved crest runs the entire depth of the head, beginning behind the forehead guard (L. 13.2 cm; W. 7.5 cm). The portion of the crest that runs down the back of the helmet was sculpted as part of the head and is painted red (this red pigment could also be bole for gilding). The golden-colored forehead guard of the helmet is pushed up to rest above the forehead, where its triangular peak is aligned with the central axis of the face. The guard is bordered by a narrow, raised rim (W. 0.5 cm). On each side, it has rounded ear flaps that cover the top halves of the cursorily indicated ears. The gold helmet follows the round contour of the head until just above the neck. At the base of the head, the helmet becomes more snugly fitted and extends straight down to protect the back and sides of the neck. Like the forehead guard, this neck guard has a narrow raised border (W. 0.4 cm).

From beneath the forehead guard, a single row of dark red snail-shell curls frames the forehead, one curl aligned above the central axis of the head. While only one of these curls is well-preserved, it indicates that the individual curls were not carved in great detail, but consisted of two concentric circles. These curls are carved within a band whose top edge is clearly delineated and whose lower edge is visible only below the four central curls.

The face is composed of stark features. The forehead is broad and planar. The arch of the eyebrows extends to form the side lines of the nose. The eyes are deeply set with tear ducts indicated at their inner corners. The heavy upper eyelids (W. 0.4 cm) form small shelves above the rounded eyeballs and extend beyond the lower lids, which are thin. The small, closed mouth contrasts with the large, heavy-lidded eyes. On the sides of the head, the lower halves of the ears are outlined in relief below the ear guards; however, no ear wells are indicated. The tilted head has a strong diagonal axis, emphasized by the alignment of the now-missing crest, the triangular peak of the helmet guard, the central snail-shell curl, and the nose. Other than the turn and tilt of the head, there is little indication of an expression.

The face and neck are highly modeled. The forehead has two bulges just above the inner corners of the eyebrows. In accordance with the inset eyes, the temples dip inward, the left one more so than the right because of the turn of the head. The smooth cheeks are rounded, while the back of the jaw is squared. To further effect the turn of the head, the right cheekbone and jawbone are modeled more prominently than the left, and a chisel line delineates the curved edge of the left side of the face from the neck. The neck is also delicately modeled to indicate a stretched muscle on its right side and an Adam's apple at its front.

The piece was meant to be viewed from the front or in three-quarters view only to appreciate the modeling that emphasizes the leftward turn of the head. The sides and back of the head are less finished than the front, and the profile views reveal the rectangular, unnatural shape of the helmet and head.

A marble crest would have been attached to the top of the Attic helmet by means of a metal tenon and plaster adhesive.[8] It is likely that this crest would have been painted red in accordance with the color preserved on the back crest and in contrast to the gold color of the helmet (though, as noted above, this red pigment could have served as bole for gilding). In addition to the row of snail-shell curls, sidelocks may have been added in paint as indicated by the line of red paint (L. 1.0 cm) descending directly from the outermost curl down the left cheek and ending below the earlobe.[9] The eyes were probably given further detail in paint as well. This statue and the crest of an Attic helmet (cat. 10) are the only two sculptures found at the sanctuary that preserve large amounts of paint.

Identification

This head may be identified as Athena based on the Attic helmet and archaizing features (Fullerton 1990: 198). While Attic helmets are most commonly worn by Athena, Ares, and Amazons, only Athena is commonly given archaizing features.[10] Despite this one archaistic feature, overall the head appears quite classicizing.[11] The tilt of the head, deeply inset eyes, soft modeling of the face, and the Parthenonian proportions (such as the broad forehead) all recall the Hellenistic- and Roman-period reinterpretation of classical form, common throughout the Mediterranean, but especially in Greece and Asia Minor. This classicizing style differentiates the head of Athena from the remainder of the sculptures discovered at the sanctuary, which recall Hellenistic forms, proportions, and sculptural types. Since only the head of this sculpture is preserved, it is difficult to associate the piece with any specific Athena type.

This head of Athena is the only securely identifiable representation of the goddess from the site, though two other heads, one colossal (cat. 1) and one life-size (cat. 3), may represent either Athena or Roma. Representations of Athena influenced by Graeco-Roman iconography and sculptural types are known from sites throughout the Levant in a variety of media (Friedland 2008). The Paneion Athena is one of the few representations of the goddess from this region that incorporates an archaizing feature.[12]

Comparanda, Workshop, and Date

The eclectic nature of the piece precludes association with any comparable sculpture or assigning a date based on style. Stylistically, the ridge below and above the band of snail-shell curls can be found on a portrait head of an unknown Roman woman now in the Ny Carlsberg Glyptothek (Hekler 1912: 41, fig. 303). The archaizing snail-shell curls are comparable to those carved on several of the female heads from the Mausoleum of Halikarnassos (Waywell 1978: 103–5, pl. 13; 106–7, pl. 16); therefore, the Paneion head may be associated with an Anatolian workshop.

3 — HEAD OF ATHENA OR ROMA

Exc. no. 85/92/705/7825/1 (figs. 14–7)

Preservation and Material

H. 0.22 m; W. 0.09 m; reconstructed H. not determinable/life-size.

White marble; large, densely-packed, glittering crystals.

The piece is broken at base of the neck and vertically through the center of the head. Missing are the crown of head and most of the hair, which would have been carved separately and joined, and the left two-thirds of the face, including forehead, left eye, most of right eye, nose, mouth, and chin. There is damage to the hair above right eye, helmet strap above the right ear, right ear, and left side of the ponytail. There are brownish/reddish stains overall and brown accretions on the abraded portion of the hair above the right eye and on the back of the head. Red paint (10R 4/6; removed during cleaning) was preserved on the left side of neck, throughout the hair, on the helmet strap, and on the right side of the ponytail. Plaster, removed during cleaning, was preserved on the right top of the head, near the helmet strap, and in the lower right corner of the keyed area above the ledge in the ponytail.

Technique

The piece is characterized by the absence of drill-work. Chiselwork defines the locks of hair, the upper and lower eyelids, and the ear well. While

Fig. 14   *Cat. 3: Head of Athena or Roma, front.*   *Fig. 15*   *Cat. 3: Head of Athena or Roma, right profile.*

Fig. 16   Cat. 3: Head of Athena or Roma, back.

Fig. 17   Cat. 3: Head of Athena or Roma, back three-quarter.

the face was polished, the hair was only smoothed. The crown of the head and upper portion of the ponytail were carved separately and joined to the main portion of the head. To effect the join, the sculptor carved the top portion of the head as a convex curve. At the crest of the skull, the back of the head is carved as a flat, steeply sloping plane. Two large rectangular sockets preserved on the back of the head effected the join. One side of the top socket (3.0 × 3.3 cm; D. 2.5–3.0 cm) is lined with plaster. The lower socket (3.0 × 3.5 cm) contains a large metal tenon surrounded by brownish/grayish cement. Plaster was spread across the convex and planed areas to further strengthen the join. On top of the ponytail, the sculptor created a small ledge (L. 5.6 cm; D. 1.0 cm) to receive the joining crown and to allow gravity to assist in securing the join. A small ledge was cut into the locks of hair along the right side of the head (L. 13.5 cm; W. 0.5 cm), perhaps to make the line of the join less visible.

Description and Reconstruction

This piece preserves the right third of a life-size female head whose back would have been completed by an adjoining fragment. The head turns to the left, so that the right eye is centered over the neck. The shape of the attachment area for the adjoining crown of the head left only a narrow band of hair carved around the forehead and side of the face. The hair is drawn along the right side of the head in elongated waves and at the back of the head is gathered into a ponytail. The locks on the sides of the ponytail flow diagonally, while those on the back fold into a central part, which runs down the middle of the ponytail. Because they are chiseled rather than drilled, the unpolished locks, which lie close to the head, appear broad and flat. There are no wisps of hair in front of the ear, nor locks cascading down the sides of the neck. Above the right ear, a raised rectangular area (now-broken) is carved atop the locks. While the majority of the surface of this rectangular area is broken, its top end preserves a shallow, slightly arced ledge leading to an inset planed area.

It is difficult to discuss the rendering of facial details, because most of the face is missing. The top eyelids extended beyond the lower ones. The ear is cursorily rendered with only a small crescent-shaped depression indicating the ear well. The remaining portions of the face suggest that it was delicately modeled. The right brow is indicated by two planes. The front of the neck contains a bulge, showing the Adam's apple. The transition from the jaw line to the neck is modeled gradually rather than emphasized by a chisel line. The piece is carved equally on all sides and was meant to be viewed from all angles.

Identification

Based on its hairstyle, this head depicted either Athena or Roma wearing a Corinthian helmet.[13] The hairstyle preserved on this head, in which the locks are drawn along the side of the head in elongated waves and at the back into a ponytail parted at its center, is unique to representations of Athena and (by association) Roma, and most often appears on those depictions that show the goddesses wearing Corinthian helmets. The shape of the attachment area, which leaves only a small band of hair encircling the forehead and side of the face, but exposes the lower portion of the ponytail, also suits the attachment of a Corinthian helmet. As well, an adjoining Corinthian helmet would be sufficiently heavy to merit the large sockets and tenons preserved in this piece. The now-broken rectangular area above the right ear may be identified as a helmet strap, and the ledge and inset plane at the top of this broken rectangular area show that the helmet straps were looped up under the helmet, like those shown on the Ince Athena (Ashmole 1929: no. 8, pls. 10–11), rather than left trailing down the sides of the head.

Other marble representations of both Athena (cat. 2) and Roma or Athena (cat. 1) have been found at the Paneion; thus, whichever goddess this piece represents, it has parallels at the Paneion itself. Roma is thought to have been one of the major cult deities of the site in conjunction with Augustus, while Athena was probably only honored at the sanctuary with votive offerings.

Comparanda, Workshop, and Date

Because so little of this head remains, and because the chiseled rendering of the hair seems related to the sculptural type as opposed to chronological factors, it is impossible to determine a date or workshop origin for this piece.

4 — HEAD OF ZEUS OR ASKLEPIOS

Exc. nos. 85/92/705/7805/1; 78/93/712/7951 (crown) (figs. 18–21)

Preservation and Material

H. 0.26 m; W. 0.16 m; D. 0.20 m; reconstructed H. 1.43 m/life-size.

White marble; medium, glittering, flaky crystals. Isotopic analyses suggest that the marble comes from one of several quarries in Turkey: Uşak, Marmara, Mylasa, or Afyon.

The piece is broken above the clavicles. The right side of the crown was found separately and joined. The head is missing the nose, most of the mustache, part of the right side of the crown, and the back of the head. There is damage to the forehead, the brows and eyes, the beard, the hair, and the neck strut. Brownish encrustations cover the piece, especially on the joining fragment and the lower locks on the left side of the head. Traces of red paint are preserved on the hair and the beard. The original

Fig. 18   Cat. 4: Head of Zeus or Asklepios, front.

Fig. 19   Cat. 4: Head of Zeus or Asklepios, right profile.

Fig. 20   Cat. 4: Head of Zeus or Asklepios, left profile.

Fig. 21   Cat. 4: Head of Zeus or Asklepios, back.

highly-polished surface remains on the forehead, the left eyeball, the cheeks, the lower lip and the area beneath it, the undersides of some locks of the hair on the left side of the face, and the neck and tops of the shoulders.

Technique

Drill channels define the locks of hair, encircle the curls of the beard, and separate the lips. A drill hole pierces the center of each curl of the beard. Chisel lines delineate individual strands of hair within the locks, the upper and lower eyelids, and the tear ducts. The entire piece was highly polished.

Description and Reconstruction

The head turns three-quarters to the right and tilts downward slightly. The oval shape of the face is accentuated by a frame of long, doughy locks and a short, curly beard. At the center of the forehead, two rows of curls curve upward and outward from a central part, resembling a double *anastole*. Those on the right side rise higher off the head than those on the left. Longer, corkscrew locks frame the sides of the face. On the right side, the locks stand farther out from the face and contain more drill work, while on the left the curls are longer, lie flatter against the side of the head, and are punctuated by fewer drill holes. On the left, a deep drill channel runs from mid-forehead along the side of the face to separate the hood of hair from the face. On the right side, a shorter, shallower drill channel runs from the temple to the beginning of the beard. The snail-shaped curls of the beard spring from the cheeks just above the jaw-line. As in the hair, there is more drill work on the right side of the beard than on the left. The mustache covers the entire area between the nose and upper lip and curves softly into the beard at the corners of the mouth.

The high forehead is distinguished by two wrinkles, which are accentuated by surface modeling. The narrow eyes, with deeply-set inner corners and tear ducts, have slightly arced upper lids and straight lower lids. Both eyelids appear thin. The undrilled eyeballs are flat planes that angle downward due to the tilt of the head. The rounded lips form a small, slightly open mouth. The face is delicately modeled with the slight indication of cheekbones, heightened naso-labial lines, and a depression below the lower lip. Similarly, the neck is modeled with an Adam's apple beneath the beard, a depression between the clavicles, and a flexed muscle on its left side. The expression is created by the turn and tilt of the head, the movement in the locks of hair, and the parted lips.

The sides and back of the head are not as fully carved as the front. Behind the three-dimensional locks of hair that frame the face, a thin fillet (W. 0.7 cm) encircles the crown of the head. On the crown, the hair is cursorily carved as flat locks that lie close to the skull and radiate out from an uneven central part. On the sides of the neck, behind the ears, several locks are outlined by drill channels as unnaturalistic S-curls. Behind these, the marble is only roughly shaped as a mass of hair. At the nape of the neck, there is a large rectangular neck strut that was shaped with a pick. This neck strut has no relationship to the anatomy of the head, since it is not aligned with the true center of the back of the head but is positioned to the right of the central part in the hair. The head was meant to be seen from the front or from the right side in three-quarters view.

Identification

This head may be identified as either Zeus or Asklepios based on the style of its hair and beard.[14] Because the two locks resembling an *anastole* above the center of the forehead are common on both gods, it is difficult to determine which of the two this piece represents without further attributes. A representation of either deity would be appropriate at the Paneion. Zeus is thought to have been one of the main cult figures of the site (Ma'oz 2007: 26–27), while an inscription found at the sanctuary shows that a statue of Asklepios was erected at the sanctuary in the second half of the first century AD (Isaac in press: no. 6).

Comparanda, Workshop, and Date

The Paneion head of Zeus or Asklepios is most comparable to the head of Asklepios (or Zeus) found at Gerasa, now in the National Museum in Amman, Jordan (Stemmer 1976: 33–36; Weber 1999: 449; Weber 2002: 487, pl. 123b).[15] Similarities include the turn of the head, the elongated, oval-shaped face, the delicate modeling of the face, the contrast between smooth skin and drilled hair, and the use of the drill to create the locks of hair and the beard. As well, the two heads have similar hairstyles, which include the deep drill lines running from the lower forehead along the sides of the face that separate hoods of hair from the temples. The eyes of the Paneion head, however, do not have drilled irises or pupils and are much narrower than those of the Gerasa head. Furthermore, the Paneion head has a large rectangular neck strut, not included on the Gerasa head.

The Paneion piece may be dated stylistically to the Antonine or Severan period by the manner in which the drill was used in the hair and the beard, the contrast between the smooth surface of the face and the drilled curls of the hair and beard, and the delicate modeling of the face. The narrow eyes may be related to the distinctive shape of those of Lucius Verus.[16] It was not uncommon for ideal sculptors to include portrait features in their representations of deities. Because the drilling of eyes is frequently omitted on ideal heads, the lack of drilled pupils and irises on the Paneion head does not necessarily associate it with the Hadrianic or pre-Hadrianic period.

As noted above, the rectangular neck strut is most commonly associated with the sculptural workshops of Asia Minor. This link with Asia Minor through sculptural technique is reinforced by the isotopic analyses noted above.

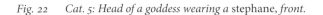

Fig. 22   Cat. 5: Head of a goddess wearing a stephane, *front.*

Fig. 23   Cat. 5: Head of a goddess wearing a stephane, *back.*

5 — HEAD OF A GODDESS WEARING A *STEPHANE* (HERA, HYGIEIA, OR APHRODITE)

Exc. no. 85/92/705/7829/1 (figs. 22–25)

Preservation and Material

H. 0.25 m; 0.12 m (from hairline to break at bottom of chin); W. 0.16 m; D. 0.19 m; reconstructed H. 1.37 m/life-size.

White marble; large, coarse, glittering crystals. Isotopic analyses show that the marble from this piece comes from one of two quarries in Turkey: Afyon or Uşak.

The piece is broken at the base of the neck. Missing are the right side of the face, left eyebrow and portion of the forehead above it, back of the left ear, nose from the bridge down, entire lower half of the face, upper crest of the *stephane*, lower portion of the right sidelock, right and left sides of the chignon, and locks of hair around both of the ears. The hair is abraded overall. Dark brown accretions cover the back of the head, chignon, and neck strut. Brownish/reddish stains cover areas of the face. A reddish hue appears on the chignon and curls at the back on the right side.

Technique

The piece is characterized by an almost complete absence of drill work. Flat or curved chisels were used to carve the eyes and the strands of hair on the crown, the chignon, and the front and sides of the head. Chisel work also divides the flat hair on the crown from the more three-dimensional hair along the sides of the head. Drill work separates the shoulder locks from the neck and from the three-dimensional hair above them and delineates the neck strut from the chignon and neck. A drill was used to pierce the earlobes. The neck strut was worked with a point. The face, neck, and *stephane* were highly polished, while the hair and shoulder locks were only smoothed.

Description and Reconstruction

The head turns to the right and tilts downward. The egg-shape of the face is created by the peaked headdress, full hairstyle, and inward slope of the cheeks. Atop the forehead, the wavy hair is parted at the center and drawn back along the sides of the head to cover two-thirds of the ears. At the back of the head, the hair is pulled into a chignon represented as a square block (8.0 × 5.0 × 3.5 cm). From the sides of the chignon, long, three-dimensional, curling shoulder locks fall onto the neck. The front of the *stephane* (H. 4.0 cm), which is parallel and even with the plane of the figure's forehead, is highly polished; however, there is no evidence that it was further enhanced with relief or painted decoration. The right side of the *stephane* preserves an outward curve and shows that the headpiece flared toward the viewer along its top edge. Behind the *stephane* the hair is cursorily rendered as locks lying flat on the crown radiating out from a central part.

The highly-polished forehead is delicately modeled. The eyes are deeply-set, especially at their inner corners, and have thick lids. The upper lid is formed by two chisel lines, the lower by one. Modeling of the lower lids makes them appear thick and somewhat puffy. The eyeballs are notably flat with no indication of tear ducts, although the inner corner of the left eyeball is more deeply inset than the right. While the outer edges of both eyes are abraded, that of the left eye indicates that the upper lid extended beyond the lower. On the preserved right eye, the arch of the brow continues to form the sideline of the nose. The preserved left side of the face shows that the tapering cheeks were smooth with little undulation. The pierced earlobes must have been ornamented by added earrings, perhaps of metal. The transition between the cheeks and neck is smoothly modeled, although there is now a ridge where the lower portion of the face has broken away from the neck. The oval shape,

Fig. 24   Cat. 5: Head of a goddess wearing a stephane, *right profile.*

Fig. 25   Cat. 5: Head of a goddess wearing a stephane, *left profile.*

highly-polished skin, and *sfumato* treatment of the face give this head a youthful appearance.

It is clear that the piece was meant to be seen from the front or in three-quarters view. Beneath the chignon, the excess marble was never carved away from the back of the neck. Consequently, an elongated neck strut makes for an unnaturalistic profile view. In addition, the shoulder locks are detailed with individual strands of hair mainly on their front sides, so that their profile views show only areas of smoothed marble.

Identification

This figure is identifiable as an ideal type based on the *stephane*, the hairstyle with chignon and sidelocks, and the turn and tilt of the head. Some Aphrodite types (Aphrodite Anadyomene, Venus Marina, and Venus Felix; Delivorrias et al. 1984: 55, 66, 79, Aphrodite nos. 430, 554, 696, respectively), several Roman-period renditions of Hygieia (Sobel

1990: 16, n. 85; Hygieia in the Ostia Museum: Helbig 1963–72: 4: no. 3039; Hygieia from Seville in the Casa de Pilatos: Sobel 1990: 94; and Hygieia from the House of the Europa Mosaic on Kos: Davaris n.d.: 15, 22, no. 98), and some representations of Hera/Juno (Kossatz-Deissmann 1988: 674–75, Hera no. 131; La Rocca 1990: 842–43, Iuno nos. 229–32) are shown with sidelocks and a *stephane*. However, because of the absence of other attributes, it is impossible to identify this head as any one of these three goddesses.[17]

The display of a representation of Hera or Hygieia at the Sanctuary of Pan would complement the sculpture of Zeus or Asklepios discovered at the site (cat. 4); however, if the Paneion head represents Hera/Juno, it would be unique among the corpus of marble sculpture from the Levant, since to date, no other representations of this goddess are known from the region. Although Aphrodite is not known to have been worshipped at the sanctuary, it is possible that she was honored here by the dedication of a sculpture, especially because a life-size sculpture representing the Capitoline/Medici Aphrodite was recovered from the site (cat. 13).

Comparanda, Workshop, and Date

The Paneion head is comparable to a female head discovered at Gaza (Avida 1978: 60, cat. 8; IAA no. 39.10) in terms of the *stephane*, hairstyle (although the Gaza head lacks sidelocks), and neck strut. In terms of style, several features of the Paneion head, including the shape of its eyes, the fullness of its eyelids, and the presence of a neck strut, are noted on pieces carved throughout the eastern Mediterranean. Similar narrow, puffy-lidded eyes are found on an Aphrodite in the Ephesus Museum from the Fountain of G. Laecanius Bassus (Erdemgil 1989: 51, Ephesos [Selçuk] Museum no. 1582; Fleischer 1972–75: 425, pl. 6) and on several pieces displayed in the Thessaloniki Museum, including a water-bearer from the northwestern area of the Agora (Thessaloniki Museum no. 895; Despinis et al. 1997: cat. 98, 128–29). The shape and workmanship of the neck strut on the Paneion head and the clear delineation of the chignon and the sidelocks from the neck strut are most comparable to that on a figure of Hygieia from Kos found in the House of the Europa Mosaic (Davaris n.d.: Kos Museum no. 98). Thus, the piece may be associated with the workshops of the eastern Mediterranean based on the rendering of its eyes and more specifically with those of western Anatolia due to the neck strut. Isotopic analyses confirm this association with Asia Minor.

Because this head is so fragmentary and lacks any chronologically distinctive stylistic or technical features, it is not possible to assign a date.

6 — HEAD OF APOLLO KITHARODE OR A MUSE

Exc. no. 85/92/705/7803/1 (figs. 26–29)

Preservation and Material

H. 0.25 m; 0.16 m (face); W. 0.19 m; D. 0.24 m; reconstructed H. 1.37 m/life-size.

White marble; large, coarse, glittering crystals. Isotopic analyses show that the marble of this piece comes from one of three quarries in Turkey: Marmara, Denizli, or Uşak.

The piece is broken at the middle of the neck. Missing are the headdress, hair on the right front of the head, right side of the forehead, most of the right eye, left eyebrow, part of the left eyelid, nose, lips, bottom of the chin, front of the neck, earlobes, and sidelocks. There is damage to the locks of hair and the circular area on the left side of the crown. Dark brown encrustations cover the right ear, wisp of hair on the right cheek, chin, and hair on the crown. A thin layer of brown encrustation covers the right side of the face. There are brownish/reddish stains on the face.

Technique

A headdress was carved separately and attached using a large socket atop the head (W. 2.0 cm; D. 2.0 cm) and the chisel-marked attachment band encircling the top half of the head (W. 2.0 to 2.5 cm; Circum. 28.0 cm). Deep drill channels give the locks their plastic form, divide the back of the neck from the chignon on the left side of the head, and create the separation between the lips. Single drill holes indicate tear ducts at the inner corners of the eyes. Chisel lines indicate two to three strands of hair within each lock, create the central part and thin locks carved flat onto the crown, and delineate the eyelids. The face, neck, and hair surrounding the face were highly polished.

Fig. 26   Cat. 6: Head of Apollo Kitharode or a Muse (?), front.

Fig. 27   Cat. 6: Head of Apollo Kitharode or a Muse (?), back.

Fig. 28   Cat. 6: Head of Apollo Kitharode or a Muse (?), right profile.

Fig. 29   Cat. 6: Head of Apollo Kitharode or a Muse (?), top.

Description and Reconstruction

The head turns to the left and tilts sideways slightly. The oval shape of the head is framed by the wavy, highly plastic hair. The hair is parted at the center and drawn along the sides of the head in several thick, three-dimensional waves, which cover the top halves of the ears and are gathered into a chignon at the back of the head. These locks do not emerge naturalistically from the sides of the head, but begin abruptly at the hair line. On both sides of the head, small wisps of hair escape and lie on the cheeks in front of the ears. Two strands of hair are indicated in the curl on the right cheek, and both wisps are highly polished. On the right side of the chignon, the hair is gathered into a sidelock, now broken away. Similarly, on the left, at the base of the chignon on the nape of the neck there is a raised elliptical broken area where another sidelock was apparently located. On one edge of this raised broken area, two chisel lines mark strands of hair.

Four cm back from the forehead, the three-dimensional locks are cut into abruptly to form a ledge that encircles the top half of the head (approximate H. 1.0 cm; approximate circum. 28.0 to 29.0 cm). Below this ledge, a wide semicircular band is chiseled around the upper half of the head (W. 2.0 to 2.5 cm; circum. 28.0 cm).[18] In this band, a large socket is preserved just to the left of its center (W. 2.0 cm; D. 2.0 cm). Behind this semicircular band, a second, smoother band (W. 1.0 to 1.8 cm) encircles the entire head. On the back of the head, thinner locks of hair are rendered flat on the crown, radiating out from a central part.

The large, square chignon serves as a neck strut and is therefore cursorily delineated. Its top and back are carved with five strands of hair, while each side is marked with a triangle to indicate a knot of hair. This chignon/neck strut is not carved in line with the central part, but is unnaturalistically positioned to its left, so that it is centered on the back of the sculpture and appears unrelated to the anatomy and movement of the head.

The eyes are deeply-set and have tear ducts indicated at their inner corners. Both eyelids form shallow arcs, the upper lid extending slightly beyond the lower one. The upper eyelids are heavy and wide (up to 0.5 cm), forming small ledges over the flat eyeballs. There is no evidence of drilled pupils.

The face is evenly modeled. The forehead is smooth and unwrinkled, the cheekbones are shown delicately, and the face appears rounded and plump. The muscles on the right side of the neck are stretched by the turn of the head, and those on the left side are contracted. The face is separated from the neck by a chisel line, which runs beneath the chin and along the right jaw-line, emphasizing the turn of the head. The lips are parted slightly. What little expression the piece conveyed would have been created by the turn and tilt of the head and the slightly opened mouth. The smooth face is framed by the play of dark and light created by the deeply-drilled locks of hair. The piece was meant to be seen from the front or in three-quarters view, since the chignon is only roughly worked and unnaturalistically positioned.

The confluence of locks on the right side of the head and the broken raised area between the nape of the neck and the chignon on the left side suggest that the figure had sidelocks, which cascaded down the sides of its neck and onto its shoulders. In addition, the large socket and semicircular band encircling the top of the head suggest that the sculpture was crowned with a headdress or wreath, which was made separately and attached by means of a socket and tenon join.[19] The attached headdress was probably made of marble rather than metal, since the attachment of a heavier marble piece is characterized by a single, larger socket like that carved in the top of this head, whereas the attachment of a lighter metal addition required multiple, small sockets arrayed along the attachment area.[20] Because the attachment area on this piece is only a semicircular band carved into the otherwise finished top of the head, the headdress was probably not larger than a half-circle and covered little more than the area delineated by this band. Both the ledge carved into the hair and the rough surface on the attachment band behind it helped to secure the join. Not only did the ledge disguise the join, it prevented the headdress from slipping off the head toward the front. This ledge continues down the left side of the head, but not down the right, presumably to accommodate the tilt of the head to the left, which might have caused the headdress to slide more readily in this direction. Chisel marks may have been left on the attachment band either to create a rough surface for the application of adhesive or because the sculptor knew that this area would never be seen. The second, smoother band, was clearly meant to be seen, because it is fully finished, encircles the entire head, and is carved naturalistically. It may represent either part of the headdress or some sort of headband.

Identification

This head may represent one of the Muses or Apollo Kitharode based on its face-shape, headdress, and hairstyle, which includes a chignon at the back of the head and locks that cascade down the sides of the neck and onto the shoulders (Apollo Kitharode: Lambrinudakis et al. 1984; Simon and Bauchhenss 1984a; Deubner 1934: 7–8, 17–20, 31–33; Pinkwart 1965: 152–57; Muses: Queyrel 1992; Faedo 1994; Lancha and Faedo 1994; Pinkwart 1965: 128–52, 174–82, 187–215; Lippold 1918: 64–102). Both of these mythological figures often wear wreaths, usually of laurel, encircling the top half or two-thirds of their heads. If this head does represent either an Apollo or a Muse, it would be one of the handful of representations of these deities found in the Levant.

Comparanda, Workshop, and Date

Stylistically and technically, the Paneion head is most comparable to a head from Aphrodisias often identified as Aphrodite but now believed to depict a Caryatid, which is dated to the second century AD (excavation inv. no. 66-269; Smith 2007: 212–13, 224 no. A18, fig. 16). Similarities include the shape of the face and chin, the shape of the eyes, the shape and expression of the mouth, the drilling of the inner ears, the technical approach to the hair, and the contrast between the highly-polished skin and the shadows of the heavily-drilled hair. In particular, the deep drilling of the hair to create broad S-curving locks seems to be unique to Aphrodisias (Friedland 1999: 14–15, figs. 7–10). These many shared stylistic and technical features suggest that the Paneion head is likely to be a product of the same workshop and period. In addition to these stylistic similarities, the technical feature of the neck strut, although not common at Aphrodisias, also associates this piece with the sculptural workshops of Asia Minor, and isotopic analyses confirm this association with Turkey.

Fig. 30   Cat. 7: Fragment of a head of Dionysos, right profile.

Fig. 31   Cat. 7: Fragment of a head of Dionysos, back.

7 — FRAGMENT OF A HEAD OF DIONYSOS

Exc. no. 78/93/716/8093/1 (figs. 30–31)

Preservation and Material

H. 0.19 m; W. 0.12 m; reconstructed H. not determinable/life-size.

White marble; large, chunky, glittering crystals.

The piece is broken at the top of the neck and vertically through the head, preserving only the outermost corner of the right eye, half of the right cheek, five locks of hair, a portion of the wreath, the right ear lobe, and the right side of the neck. There is some damage to the wreath and the right cheek. Remains of plaster cover the join surface, especially behind the mid-ear. Dark brown accretions cover the join surface, areas of the wreath, and the bottom break.

Technique

The back of the head was carved separately and attached. The back of this fragment is leveled to an almost vertical plane that is partially keyed and has a small socket at its center to receive the joining fragment, which was attached with a metal tenon and plaster. To keep the joining fragment in position, a small ledge is carved along the edges of the join surface beginning at the middle of the ear and encircling the lower half of the head. Chisel lines delineate the locks of hair, individual strands within them, the eyelids, and the separation of the cheek from the neck. Drill channels outline and punctuate the flowers or berries, leaves, and fruits of the wreath. The face was highly polished, but the hair was only smoothed.

Description and Reconstruction

This fragment preserves the front right half of a life-size head of Dionysos, including portions of the hairstyle and wreath. Four long wavy locks of hair are pulled back from the forehead, so that they flow horizontally along the side of the head. A fifth lock runs down along the side of the face to the ear. Below the ear more locks spill onto the neck. On top of the locks, a wreath runs from the crown of the head down its right side and covers two-thirds of the cursorily-rendered right ear. From the top down, this wreath consists of a rosette with six rounded petals (perhaps representing a cluster of berries), half of an ivy leaf, and several ovoid, grape-shaped objects, which cluster around the ear.

In profile view, the smooth face is framed by the textured, three-dimensional locks of hair and the bulbous elements of the wreath. The hairline and the incised jawline, which separates the right cheek from the upper neck, intersect at the ear to create a triangular frame for this side of the face. The cheek is evenly modeled and flat. The preserved portion of the neck bulges out beyond the plane of the cheek above it. These bulging neck muscles suggest that the head was turned sharply to the right and tilted downward. Further details of expression, posture, gesture, costume, and attributes are impossible to reconstruct, because so little of the piece is preserved.

Identification

This piece may be identified as a head of Dionysos based on the hairstyle and the wreath composed of ivy leaves, rosettes/berries, and grape-clusters (Augé and De Bellefonds 1986a). It is not possible to assign this piece to a specific sculptural type, because so little of the head and none of the body are preserved and because multiple sculptural types of the god bear this hairstyle and wreath. The dedication of a statue of Dionysos at the Sanctuary of Pan is appropriate, since the god of wine is so closely related to Pan and his consorts.

Comparanda, Workshop, and Date

Because this head of Dionysos is so fragmentary, it is not possible to identify any stylistic comparanda for it, and therefore it is not possible to associate it with any particular workshop or date.

8 — FRAGMENT OF A HEAD WEARING A WREATH (DIONYSOS?)

Exc. no. 78/93/714/8214/1 (figs. 32–33)

Preservation and Material

H. 0.16 m; W. 0.09 m; reconstructed H. not determinable/life-size.

White marble; large, chunky, glittering crystals. Isotopic analyses show that the marble is of Turkish origins, probably from Aphrodisias, Afyon, Miletos, Ephesus, or Uşak.

Fig. 32   Cat. 8: Fragment of a head wearing a wreath (probably Dionysos), top.

Fig. 33   Cat. 8: Fragment of a head wearing a wreath (probably Dionysos), break in side.

The piece is broken through the center, preserving the right half of the crown, a portion of the wreath, and half of the socket. Dark brownish/reddish accretions cover the lower two-thirds of the piece.

Technique

The fragment was meant to be joined to the main portion of a head. The join surface is leveled, pitted, and scored, and contains a deep cubic socket (D. 3.3 cm; W. 0.9 cm). Chisel lines delineate the waves of hair and the elements of the wreath. Drill holes separate the petals of the rosette or individual berries.

Description and Reconstruction

This fragment preserves the right side of the crown of a head meant to be joined to a life-size head wearing a wreath. The waves of hair are chiseled flat on the crown of the head as though radiating out from a central part. Along the outer edge of the crown, several elements of a wreath are preserved, including (from front to back) the front half of an ivy leaf, a portion of a rosette or berry cluster, and a larger tri-foliate leaf.

Identification

The ivy and rosette or berry wreath makes it likely that this fragment was meant to complete a head of

Dionysos (Augé and De Bellefonds 1986a). This piece has many similarities to cat. 7, including the join surfaces (which are leveled at a similar angles), comparable wreaths, and the delineation of the hair with a chisel as opposed to a drill. However, these two pieces were not part of the same head, because they differ in scale, positioning of sockets, and shape of tenons. Like the other head of Dionysos, this fragment is one of five sculptures found at the Paneion that were not carved of a single block of marble, but relied on the techniques of marble joining.

This fragment of a head wearing a wreath indicates that there were probably two, life-size representations of Dionysos displayed at the Sanctuary of Pan at Caesarea Philippi (this one and cat. 7).

Comparanda, Workshop, and Date

Because this piece is so fragmentary, it is not possible to identify comparable pieces or to determine a date or workshop based on stylistic or technical details.

9 — FRAGMENT OF A FACE OF A GODDESS

Exc. no. 85/92/705/7830/1 (figs. 34–35)

Preservation and Material

H. 0.17 m; W. 0.13 m; reconstructed H. not determinable/life-size.

White marble; medium, glittering, closely-packed crystals.

This piece preserves the lower half of a face, including the bottom of the right eye, both cheeks, lower half of the nose, lips, chin, part of the right side of the neck, and a ringlet of hair on the right cheek. There is some damage to the eyeball, nose, right side of the mouth, left side of the upper lip, center of the lower lip, and chin. Dark brown accretions cover the center and right side. After initial study, dark brown accretions were removed by bathing the piece in acid solution (3–5 % EDTA) and scraping with a scalpel and toothbrush. The entire piece was coated with Hagesan ("HG") to "restore" a smooth, shiny surface.

Technique

Because so little of the piece is preserved, few technical characteristics survive. Chisel lines denote the

bottom eyelid and two delicate strands of hair in the ringlet. A drill channel separates the lips, and drill holes punctuate both corners of the mouth. The face was highly polished.

Description and Reconstruction

This fragment preserves the lower half of a face broken away from a life-size, three-dimensional head. The preserved fragment shows that the face was fleshy and rounded. Although not much remains of the right eye, a deep depression beneath it makes the lower lid seem puffy. All that remains of the hairstyle is a single ringlet of hair, positioned in front of the now-missing ear on the right cheek. This ringlet is not carved in high relief, but is only slightly raised above the plane of the cheek.

The face is modeled to show full, exaggerated forms. The cheeks are smooth and voluminous, with the left cheek more rounded and protruding than the right. The fleshy appearance is heightened by clearly-defined naso-labial lines and by a depression running from the inner corner of the right eye diagonally into the right cheek. In addition to the indentation below the right eye, there are exaggerated depressions around both nostrils, above the

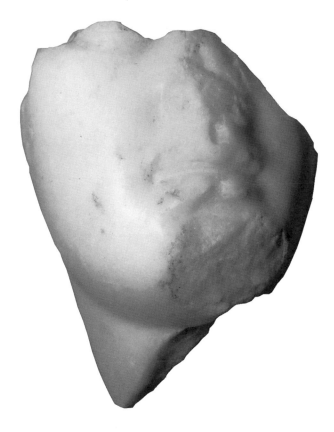

Fig. 34   Cat. 9: Fragment of a face of a goddess, front.

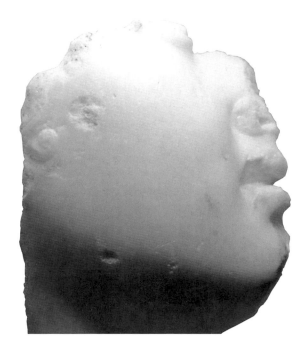

Fig. 35   Cat. 9: Fragment of a face of a goddess, right profile.

center of the upper lip, and beneath the lower lip. The parted lips are curvaceous and full. The more rounded, protruding left side of the face may indicate that the head was turned slightly to the right.

Identification

Because so little of this face is preserved, it is difficult to determine whether it comes from a portrait or an ideal sculpture. The ringlet of hair, positioned in front of the now-missing ear on the right cheek and carved in low relief, is most comparable to the ringlets found on the portrait of a young girl from Cyrene, dated to the Trajanic era (Rosenbaum 1960: 50–51, no. 32, pls. 23–24). However, the rounded, non-descript facial form and the parted lips, which were uncommon in portraits, make it likely that this fragment comes from an ideal sculpture that had been given some portrait features specific to its era of carving. The stylistic technique of adopting a portrait feature in the representation of an ideal subject may also be found in the head of Zeus or Asklepios from the Paneion (cat. 4), in which the god is given narrow eyes that resemble those of Lucius Verus.

Comparanda, Workshop, and Date

Because the piece is so fragmentary, it is difficult to identify comparanda for it or to associate it with a specific workshop; because the ringlet of hair is best understood as a chronological indicator, the comparison of the ringlet on the Paneion piece to that on the head from Cyrene should not be taken as an argument that both pieces are associated with the same workshop.

The Paneion fragment may be tentatively dated to the late first or early second century AD, based on the Trajanic comparison cited above. The erection of a marble sculpture at the sanctuary during the Trajanic era is plausible for two reasons. The Temple of Zeus is known to have been constructed in the late first or early second century A D. As well, another statue found at the Sanctuary of Pan, the torso of a nymph (cat. 11), is conjecturally dated to the Trajanic period based on its stylistic and tech-

nical characteristics and comparison to a similar nymph discovered in the excavations of Fountain of Trajan at Ephesus. Thus, if this piece is dated to the Trajanic era, it would be one of the two earliest sculptural fragments discovered at the sanctuary.

10 — CREST OF AN ATTIC HELMET

Exc. no. 78/93/712/7953 (figs. 36–37)

Preservation and Material

H. 0.11 m; L. 0.14 m; W. 0.06 m; reconstructed H. not determinable/life-size.

White marble; fine, compact, glittering crystals.

There is damage to the tops of the back three plumes. The piece is abraded and has dark brown accretions overall, especially on the back half of the top. Red paint is preserved on all surfaces except the bottom.

Technique

This crest was meant to be attached to the main part of a helmet. The bottom join surface is leveled

and contains a small socket (Diam. 0.6 cm); the attachment area is too large for the Paneion head of Athena wearing an Attic helmet (cat. 2). Chisel lines indicate the plumes.

Description and Reconstruction

This fragment preserves the marble crest of an Attic helmet that was carved separately to be attached to a life-size or just over life-size head. As preserved, the crest consists of some six "plumes," graduated in size from thin and short at the front, to wider and taller at the center, to thinnest and shortest at the back. Because the tops of the back plumes are no longer preserved, it is difficult to determine the original height of the crest or the original number of plumes (perhaps seven or eight). The divisions

Fig. 36   Cat. 10: Crest of an Attic helmet, right profile.

Fig. 37   Cat. 10: Crest of an Attic helmet, left profile.

between plumes are not carved symmetrically on both sides of the crest, so that the right side has one more plume than the left. Divisions between plumes are also indicated on the top and front of the crest. The bottom join-surface is not flat but arcs slightly.

The arced bottom of the crest was meant to accommodate the curved top of a helmet. This crest would have been joined to a sculpted head by means of a metal tenon inserted into the small socket on its bottom (Claridge 1990: 135–62). The socket and tenon join may have been aided by the addition of some sort of adhesive. Because the attachment area of this crest is larger than that atop the Paneion head of Athena wearing an Attic helmet (cat. 2), the crest does not seem to have been carved to complete that particular head. However, this crest and the head of Athena wearing an Attic helmet (cat. 2) are unique among the sculptures discovered at the sanctuary in that they retain a large amount of paint.

Identification

Crested Attic helmets are worn primarily by the mythological figures Athena, Ares, and Amazons, and rarely appear in three-dimensional portrait sculpture. This crest, with its six preserved plumes, probably belonged originally to a marble representation of either Athena or Ares, for several reasons. First, representations of deities, rather than mythological figures such as Amazons, are more likely to have been dedicated or displayed at a Sanctuary of Pan. Second, both Athena and Ares were worshipped throughout the Levant. Finally, other three-dimensional marble representations of both of these gods have been discovered in this region, whereas the representation of Amazons is limited to stock scenes on sarcophagi.[21] If this crest of an Attic helmet was associated with a representation of Athena, it would add a second or perhaps third marble statue of the goddess to the sculptural display at the Sanctuary of Pan (cat. 2 and possibly cat. 3 represent Athena as well).

Comparanda, Workshop, and Date

Because so little of this piece remains, it is impossible to determine a date or associate it with any particular workshop based on stylistic and technical features.

11 — TORSO OF A NYMPH

Exc. nos. 85/92/705/7814/1 (torso); 78/93/712/7954/1, 85/92/156/7866/1, 78/93/712/7745, 78/93/705/7902/7, 78/93/712/7946/1, 78/93/712/7938/1 (joining drapery fragments) (figs. 38–41)

Preservation and Material

H. 0.75 m; W. 0.29 m; D. 0.20 m; reconstructed H. not determinable/life-size.

White marble; large, coarse, glittering crystals. Isotopic analyses show that the marble of this piece may be associated with two quarries in Turkey (Uşak and Marmara) or, if the marble is dolomitic, with a quarry on Thasos in Greece.

The piece is broken through the torso at the waist and the lower thighs. It is missing the head, upper torso, arms, legs, and most of the shell or bowl. Drapery fragments, discovered separately, join at the center of the front. There is damage to two areas of the abdomen, the edges of the drapery, and the shell or bowl. Light brown stains cover the piece. There is dark brown encrustation on the inner wall of the shell or bowl, the drapery folds, and the buttocks. White cement-like deposits (removed during cleaning) were preserved on the broken left side of the shell or bowl and in the crevice between the buttocks. The original high polish is preserved on the torso.

Technique

This statue served as a fountain figure. A hole to accommodate a pipe (W. 1.5 cm at front; D. 17.0 cm) was carved in the back wall of the shell or bowl (which covers the front of the pubic region) and runs through the entire depth of the piece emerging below the buttocks. Deep drill channels create concentric folds of drapery that have rounded edges. Single, narrow drill channels create a fold of flesh between the lower abdomen and the right thigh and the separation between the buttocks. The navel is indicated by a shallow oval-shaped depression. The skin was highly polished and the drapery smoothed. The figure is fully-worked on all sides.

Description and Reconstruction

These joining fragments preserve the life-size torso of a semi-draped woman that served as a fountain figure. The drapery, wrapped around the thighs, reveals the contour of the legs and thus the stance of the figure. The figure stands in a contrapposto pose bearing its weight on the right leg, which is positioned slightly behind the free left leg. The outward thrust of the right hip is balanced by the leftward sway of the middle torso.

A wide roll of drapery is drawn horizontally across the back of the figure below the buttocks. One end of this drapery falls in vertical folds down the back of the right leg. From between the legs and below the horizontal roll, the other end of the cloth fans out around the back of the left leg. The roll of drapery is drawn around the sides of the lower hips to the front of the figure, where it is tied in a knot in front of the pubes. This knot is covered by a shell or bowl. Similarly, the lower folds of the drapery wrap around the sides of the thighs and are drawn up into the knot. From this knot, the ends of the drapery cascade downward

Fig. 38   Cat. 11: Torso of a nymph, front.

Fig. 39   Cat. 11: Torso of a nymph, back.

between the figure's legs. The joining fragments of drapery are too broken to discern the pattern of this cascade. At its bottom, two curved or hook-like ends overlap and point in opposite directions.

The drapery highlights the focal point of the torso, the fountain fixture covering the pubic region. From the front, the roll of drapery crosses the lower abdomen on a diagonal that slopes from the left side downward to the right, appearing to slip off of the figure's lower hips. The left side of the roll follows the diagonal line of the pubic region, and the right reveals a delicate fold of flesh between the lower abdomen and the right thigh. The knot peeks above the rim of the shell or bowl to cover the center of the pubes. All folds converge at this knot beneath the shell or bowl to make this, and ultimately the pubic region, the focal point of the torso.

The highly-polished and smoothly-modeled torso contrasts the textured ridges and drill channels of the drapery. Emphasized areas include the depression above the navel, the bulging abdomen,

the hip bones, the triangle of the upper pubic region, the muscles of the lower back, and the full buttocks, which protrude beyond the plane of the horizontal drapery roll. Modeling indicates ripples in the taut fabric between the drapery folds. The drill channel between the buttocks curves slightly toward the right in accordance with the asymmetry of the figure's hips.

Because the piece is finished and polished on all sides, it was probably meant to be viewed in the round, perhaps displayed in the middle of a court or building rather than within a niche or up against a wall.

The position of the right thigh behind the left reveals the figure's posture. The thighs and part of the lower legs are pressed tightly together. The feet were positioned slightly apart, with the right foot resting flat and the left foot barely touching the base with its toes. The ends of the drapery fall from the knot beneath the bowl and cascade down the center of the legs in a zigzag pattern. The two hook-like

Fig. 40   Cat. 11: Torso of a nymph, right profile.

Fig. 41   Cat. 11: Torso of a nymph, left profile.

ends, which overlap and point in opposite directions, represent the hem line of the drapery, which, when it reaches the base, folds back on itself to expose the toes and rest atop the feet. Because the lower legs of the Paneion figure are not preserved, it is not possible to determine whether the sculpture included a support on one side of this figure.[22]

The fountain attachment was part of the initial design of the figure, rather than a later alteration, since the area beneath the buttocks was designed to accommodate it. The hole for the pipe is not carved into either of the two buttocks, but exactly below them, and the drill line that creates the separation between the buttocks runs directly into the sloping wall of this hole. As well, the top of the horizontal drapery roll, which runs immediately beneath the hole, is positioned well below it and is fully finished.

Identification

Although the posture and drapery of the figure compare to several half-draped Aphrodite types, this piece may be identified as a nymph due to the shell or bowl and its use as a fountain. More than twenty-five versions of this type of half-draped nymph with a shell or bowl have been discovered throughout the Roman world in Italy, Gaul, Spain, Greece, and Asia Minor. They were displayed in a wide variety of contexts, including nymphaea (Gortyn, Corinth, and Ephesos), bath buildings (Tralles, Saint Columbe [Vienne], and Timgad), and private gardens (Pompeii).[23] Thus, the Paneion nymph may be understood as another example of the adaptation of the half-draped Aphrodite Anadyomene to represent a nymph (Havelock 1995: 86–93; Brinkerhoff 1978: 58–62; Prittwitz und Gaffron 1988: 117–24; Kapossy 1969: 12; Halm-Tisserant and Siebert 1997: 901). As such, it constitutes one of seven sculptures discovered at the Sanctuary of Pan that may be associated with sculptural types thought to have been created in the Hellenistic period.

Comparisons with other half-draped females whose pubic regions are covered by shells or bowls suggest two possible gestures for the Paneion nymph. The figure might have extended both arms downward to grasp the sides of the shell or bowl as do the nymphs in the Vatican Museum (inv. 4035; Kapossy 1969: 13, fig. 3) and the Istanbul Archaeological Museum from Selsébil, Crete (Mendel 1914 II: 303, no. 577). This posture may explain the damage to the sides of the shell or bowl, which would have been broken away along with the now-missing hands. Alternately, the figure may have assumed the gesture of the Aphrodite Anadyomene, who extends both arms upward above her shoulders to wring out her wet locks (Brinkerhoff 1978: 56).

Because the nymphs were worshipped as main cult figures of the site along with Pan, and, in fact, nymphs were a constant companion of Pan, it is not surprising to find a life-size, three-dimensional representation of one at the sanctuary (Larson 2001: 96–98, 234–36). Furthermore, because of the sanctuary's setting just above the rushing springs that form one of the sources of the Jordan River, the function of this figure as a fountain is appropriate to its setting. Despite the figure's rigging as a fountain, however, there is no evidence for running water on the sanctuary terrace or slope. Furthermore, the aqueduct, which runs above the cliff face, has no outlet in this area, and finds of pipes are few and scattered.[24]

Comparanda, Workshop, and Date

Though one other nymph of this type has been found in the Levant in a bath building at Beth Shean (Tsafrir and Foerster 1997: 129, fig. 38), the Paneion nymph is more comparable to the Kassel Aphrodite in compositional features such as drapery configuration, the placement of the drapery roll diagonally along the lower abdomen, and the size of the attached shell or bowl (Bieber 1915: 24–25, no. 30, pl. 22). However, in terms of technical features, the Paneion nymph is most comparable to the Aphrodite or nymph found in the excavations of the Fountain of Trajan at Ephesos (Ephesos Museum no. 768; Miltner 1959: 339, pl. 183; Longfellow 2011: 92–93). Similarities include the highly-polished skin, smoothed drapery surfaces, the carving of the drapery with deep drill channels to create concentric drapery folds with rounded edges, the modeling of small ripples in the drapery on the sides of the thighs, and the rolled hem-line above the feet. The Ephesos Aphrodite or nymph is dated to the early second century AD on the basis of its inclusion in the Trajanic monument (Miltner 1959: 331). Another Anatolian parallel to the Paneion nymph may be found in the nymph from Claros, now on display in the Izmir Museum, whose drapery knot also projects above the rim of its shell or bowl (Izmir Museum no. 3709).

The technical similarities of this sculpture to the nymph from the Fountain of Trajan at Ephesos and the nymph from Claros suggest that the Paneion nymph may be dated to the early second century AD and associated with a western Anatolian sculptural workshop, perhaps at Ephesos itself. As such, this piece is one of the two earliest sculptural fragments discovered at the sanctuary (the other is the fragment of a face of a goddess, cat. 9).

12 — TORSO OF A YOUTHFUL NUDE GOD (DIONYSOS?)

Exc. nos. 85/92/705/7816/1 (torso); 78/93/705/7910/1 (left shoulder);
78/93/712/7930, 78/93/712/7976/2 (fragments joining on back);
85/92/192/7206/2 (fragment joining at front of left thigh) (figs. 42–43)

Preservation and Material

H. 0.43 m; W. 0.29 m; D. 0.14 m; reconstructed H. 1.16 m/near life-size.

White marble; fine, glittering crystals. Isotopic analyses show that the marble of this piece may be associated with one of three quarries in Asia Minor (Denizli, Marmara, or Afyon) or with a quarry in Greece (Paros/Chorodaki).

The piece is broken at the base of the neck and below the buttocks. Joining fragments comprising the left shoulder, scapula, and upper arm were found separately. Missing are the head, right arm, left arm from above elbow, genitalia, and both legs. There is damage to the front of the torso above the navel on the right. There are brownish/reddish stains overall.

Technique

Drill channels divide the left upper arm from the back of the torso, set off the pubes from the upper thighs (the right drill line is longer and more carefully done than the left), and create the separation between the buttocks. A chisel line separates the left upper arm from the front of the torso. The entire torso was highly polished.

Description and Reconstruction

These joining fragments preserve the torso of a life-size youthful nude figure. The mostly-missing right arm reaches laterally at approximately a ninety-degree angle to the torso, causing the upper body to shift toward the right. The axis of the shoulders, however, remains horizontal. The left upper arm is held against the side of the torso. The right buttock is tensed and rounded with a dimple in the musculature on its outer side. The left buttock is relaxed, elongated, and extended diagonally toward the left. The remaining inner side of the left leg is carved in three dimensions and polished.

The subtle modeling and highly-polished surface portray a youthful, unmuscular, male adolescent with soft breasts and a bulging abdomen. Various areas of the torso were delicately modeled to catch the light and create soft shadows. At the base of the neck, a depression between the clavicles is indicated. Both breasts swell to peak in tiny nipples, the right one pulled toward the side in accordance with the gesture. Modeling also emphasizes the hip bones. A depression across the lower abdomen demarcates the top of the triangular pubic region, which swells gradually into the pubes. The drilled separation between the pubic region and the legs creates two delicate folds of flesh that lie atop the thighs. No pubic hair is indicated.

The back of this piece is as subtly modeled and highly polished as the front. The right trapezius muscle forms a taut ridge running from the neck along the back of the shoulder, emphasizing the reach of the right arm. In contrast, the left trapezius bulges due to the relaxed state of the left shoulder. The spine is shown as a delicate depression that runs down the length of the back. Depressions also mark the transition from the lower back to the buttocks.

There are no attachment points or damaged areas anywhere on the preserved torso, thus precluding the possibility that attributes, clothing, or hair were attached to the body. The high polish and delicate modeling on all sides indicate that the piece was meant to be seen at close range and from all sides.

The preserved musculature and limbs suggest possible reconstructions for the figure's posture and gesture. The rounded, tensed right buttock and the dimple in the musculature on its outer side indicate that the figure stood with its weight on a straight, right leg. Since the inner side of the left thigh is highly polished, the upper thighs were not held together tightly. In reconstructing the position of the left leg, three details must be considered: the elongated left buttock, which stretches diagonally to the side; the upper left thigh, which curves outward; and the drill channel separating the buttocks, which begins as a vertical line but curves toward the left at the lower buttocks. Two positions are possible for the non-weight-bearing left leg. The leg may have extended outward diagonally from the left side, or it may have been crossed in front of the right, a more common and therefore more likely stance.

In terms of gesture, the pulled muscles in the right breast, the extended scapula, and the shift of the neck and upper torso toward the right all suggest that the right arm reached purposefully outward and away from the body. This position would have balanced the opposing, extended left leg. The absence of attributes, however, makes it difficult to know why the figure made this gesture. Nor does enough remain to determine what position the lower left arm assumed. The absence of struts or damaged areas on the torso makes it clear that neither arm touched the torso, and that neither was held close enough to the torso to be steadied by struts attached to it.

It is difficult to determine the position of the head. The absence of ripples of musculature on the front and back of the neck suggests that the head may not have turned to one side, but may have faced the front; however, so little remains of the neck that modulations of musculature indicating a turned head may have been lost.

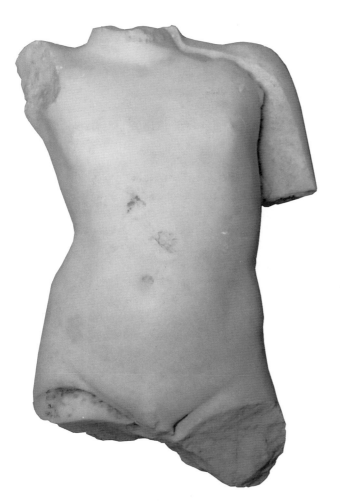

Fig. 42   Cat. 12: Torso of a youthful nude god (Dionysos?), front.

Identification

Though the fragmentary nature and absence of attributes make it difficult to identify this figure securely, the piece may possibly have represented Dionysos, based on the youthful, unmuscular rendering of the torso, the complete nudity, the absence of any locks of hair on the torso, the absence of pubic hair, and the gesture and posture, in which the youth stands with his weight on a straight right leg and the left leg either extended outward diagonally from the left side or crossed in front of the right. According to E. Bartman, "the youthful male figure characterized by a soft, pre-pubescent physique and a relaxed soignée pose…was limited to particular subjects: mythic for-

eigners (usually Eastern in origin) such as Paris, Ganymede or Adonis, and android creatures such as satyrs" (Bartman 1996: 389); however several Apollo and Dionysos types also employ this Praxitelean body type and posture. Distinctions in posture, gesture, and degree of nudity make it unlikely that the Paneion youthful nude represents Paris, Ganymede, Adonis, a satyr, the Apollo Sauroktonos, or the Apollo or Dionysos Lykeios.[25] In terms of the soft modeling of the torso and the Praxitelean body type and posture, this figure is most comparable to the Dionysos who holds grapes in front of his face, an example of which is housed in the Palazzo Aldobrandini (*DAIR* Fiche no. 28, A6). The fragmentary nature of the Paneion piece, however, requires that this identification remain hypothetical.

Comparanda, Workshop, and Date

This figure and the torso of the nymph (cat. 11) are the only two pieces found at the Paneion that are fully-modeled and polished on all sides and thus meant to be displayed in the center of a court or temple *cella*. Both sculptures are also comparable in their technical characteristics; for example, all tool marks were removed from the body surfaces of both pieces and the division between the buttocks is created with a single, continuous drill channel. Thus, it seems possible that these two pieces were created in the same sculptural milieu and perhaps the same workshop. Their disparate scales and unrelated subject matter, however, make it unlikely that they were initially part of a single sculptural group. The torso of a youthful nude god (Dionysos?) may be tentatively dated to the second century AD and associated with the sculptural workshops of Asia Minor, based on its comparison with the torso of a nymph (cat. 11). Isotopic analyses also associate the marble with three different quarries in Asia Minor (as noted above), though it could also have come from a quarry in Greece.

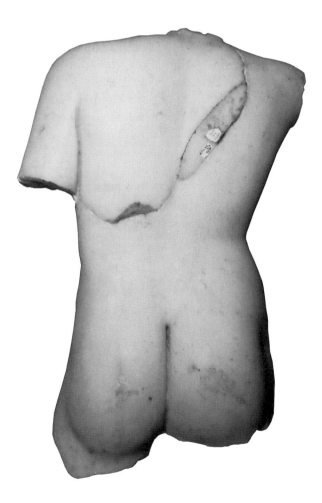

Fig. 43   Cat. 12: Torso of a youthful nude god (Dionysos?), back.

13 — LEFT LEG AND SUPPORT OF A CAPITOLINE/MEDICI APHRODITE

Exc. nos. 85/92/705/7826/2 (leg and support); 78/93/714/8191/1 (heels of both feet atop part of base); 78/93/726/8246/1 (front of right foot and wedge); 78/93/714/8271/3 (front of lower right leg); 85/92/195/1684/2 (back of lower right leg) (figs. 44–47)

Preservation and Material

H. 0.60 m; W. 0.24 m; D. 0.20 m, 0.13 m (of thigh); reconstructed H. not determinable/over-life- to life-size.

White marble; small, closely packed, glittering crystals. Isotopic analyses show that the marble of this piece may be associated either with Pentelikon in Greece or with İznik in Turkey.

The piece is broken at the upper left thigh, lower left calf, and right side of the base, preserving only the support, most of the left leg, the left heel, the right ankle and foot except the toes, and the back of the base. There are broken areas along the inner side of the left leg on the thigh and on the center of the calf. The base is damaged on its back, bottom of the left side, left half of the front, and smoothed area of the front. Small areas of dark brown encrustations cover the entire piece, while large areas of dark

*Fig. 44   Cat. 13: Left leg and support of a Capitoline/
Medici Aphrodite, front.*

*Fig. 45   Cat. 13: Left leg and support of a Capitoline/
Medici Aphrodite, back.*

brown accretions appear on the left side and the front of the right ankle. Light brown stains appear on the leg. The back and left side of the support are unfinished and worked unnaturalistically.

Technique

On the front, a chisel line divides the thigh from the support, and a drill channel divides the lower thigh and calf from the support. On the back, a chisel line separates the entire leg from the support. The chiselwork used to model the inner side of the lower thigh, knee, and calf was never smoothed away. Thin drill channels separate the sides of the *loutrophoros* from the drapery that flows around it. Both chiselwork and drill channels create the folds of the drapery on the front and right side of the support. The folds on the left are roughly carved with chisel lines. The front of the leg is polished, while the support, front of the drapery, back and inner side of the leg are smoothed only. The outer side of the right foot is polished, distinguishing it from the smoothed wedge beneath it. The inner sides and backs of both feet are not polished. The underside of the base is leveled with point.

Description and Reconstruction

These joining fragments preserve part of the left leg, support, and base of an over-life- or life-size nude figure. The remaining part of the base preserves the figure's right foot and left heel and thus something of the figure's stance. The left foot (L. 2.0 cm; H. 3.8 cm) stands directly atop the base only 1.0 cm away from the support, while the right foot (L. 4.0 cm; H. 6.0 cm; H. of wedge: 3.0 cm) rests

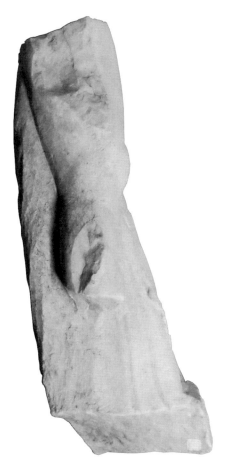

Fig. 46   Cat. 13: Left leg and support of a Capitoline/ Medici Aphrodite, right profile.

Fig. 47   Cat. 13: Left leg and support of a Capitoline/ Medici Aphrodite, left profile.

atop a wedge and is turned outward. The feet were positioned close together, the right foot only 2.0 cm away from the left.

The left side of the leg is attached to the support from mid-thigh to lower calf. There are two broken areas along the leg's inner (right) side. In the middle of the thigh one broken area bulges outward as though something had been attached to the leg at this point. In the center of the calf, another almond-shaped break with ridges surrounding it indicates that something was attached to the calf at this point as well. Where the inner side of the leg is not broken, it is fully carved in three dimensions. The front of the leg is carefully modeled to emphasize the knee, the ridge of the shin, and the calf muscles.

The breaks along the inner side of the left leg and the position of the heels preserved atop the base reveal the stance of the figure. The protruding broken areas encompassed by chisel lines show that the upper thighs and mid-calves were held tightly together. However, because the lower thigh, knee, and lower calf are carved in three dimensions, the legs must not have touched one another at these points. The figure, therefore, stood with its weight on a straight left leg, while it held its bent non-weight-bearing right leg against the left one, except at the knee, lower calf, and ankle. The right knee protruded in front of the left one, and the right foot rested on its ball and was turned slightly outward. This unstable stance was balanced by the *loutrophoros*-shaped support.

The support is an elongated, stylized *loutrophoros* with a drape piled on top of it and flowing down its sides and back.[26] The vessel has a wide mouth and a narrower neck that is encircled by a band (W. 0.8 cm). The lower body swells slightly before it narrows to stand atop a two-tiered base. The *loutrophoros* is set back from the front edge of the base (2.5 cm at sides; 1.5 cm at center) and is not carved in three dimensions; rather, it is enveloped by the flowing cloth. The cloth rests atop the *loutrophoros* in S-shaped folds. Within the vertical folds that flow straight down the outer sides of the vase, elongated zigzag folds frame the vessel. The bottom of the *loutrophoros* is flanked by two folds projecting outward from its sides toward the edges of the base. Beneath the *loutrophoros* and drapery,

the front edge of the base is highly polished. The left side of the support is concave. Here, along the front edge of the support, the folds form a pointed ridge that frames the left side of the *loutrophoros*. Although the left side of the base is now broken, a chisel line dividing the bottom of the drapery folds from the base indicates that the left side of the base was also concave.

The back of the piece is not fully worked and is covered with tool marks. Here, the leg is not carved in three dimensions. While the right half is fully worked, the left side of the leg melds into the drapery, which covers the back of the support. The back of the support is worked with four broad V-shaped grooves, stacked on top of one another to suggest the folds of the cloth draped across the back of the vase. The unfinished and unnaturalistic working of the back and left side of the support suggest that the figure was meant to be seen from the front.

Identification

This piece may be identified as either a Capitoline or Medici Aphrodite based on its nudity, its *loutrophoros*-shaped support with a drape piled on top, and its posture, in which the figure stands with its weight on a straight left leg and its bent, right leg held tightly against the left one, except at the knee, lower calf, and ankle. Because both the Capitoline and Medici types belong to a series of "*pudica* types," thought to be derived from the fourth-century BC Knidian Aphrodite of Praxiteles (Havelock 1995: 1–37; Brinkerhoff 1978: 100–107; Felletti Maj 1951: 61–62, 62–65) and have such similar posture, gesture, hair style, and position of the head, it can be difficult to distinguish the types from one another (Havelock 1995: 78).

Based on this identification, the gesture of the Paneion sculpture may be reconstructed. The figure would have assumed the characteristic *pudica* pose with her right arm drawn across her chest below or in front of her breasts and her left arm covering her pubes. Her head would have been turned to the left, perhaps more sharply if she was a Medici Aphrodite type. Her hair would have been parted at the center and drawn along the sides of her head into a chignon at the back. She may have had a bow

STATUETTES

15 — ARTEMIS ROSPIGLIOSI

Exc. nos. 85/92/702/7767/1 (torso); 85/92/705/7802/1 (right leg and base); 78/93/712/7978/1 (end of mantle joining under right arm); 85/92/709/7860/1 (left elbow wrapped in mantle); 714/8279/1 (left lower arm joining left elbow); 78/93/712/7955, 78/93/712/7955, 78/93/712/7962 (fragments of end of mantle joining behind left shoulder) (figs. 50–51)

PRESERVATION AND MATERIAL

H. 0.79 m; D. 0.34 m; reconstructed H. 0.94 m/ two-thirds life-size.

White marble; small to medium glittering crystals. Isotopic analysis suggests that the marble originated in Asia Minor at the quarries of Afyon or Marmara.

The piece is broken at the neck, mid-arms, and calf of the left leg. Missing are the head, most of the right arm, the left lower arm, the left leg from mid-calf, the lower right side of the chiton, the left half of the base, the hare's face, and the top of the quiver. There is damage to the left side of the neckline on the chiton, the folds of the chiton and mantle, the omega-folds on the hem of the *apoptygma* and chiton, and the edges of the base. Dark brown accretions cover the front, especially on and around the joining surfaces. High polish is preserved on the neck, right knee, and calf. Dull polish is preserved on the front of the drapery.

Technique

A combination of deep and shallow chisel lines depicts the drapery on the breasts. On the figure's torso and abdomen, chisel lines, which become drill channels at their lower ends, create the folds of the chiton. Drill channels emphasize the neckline of the chiton, the outer sides of the breasts, the separation between the breasts, and the outer sides of the torso. Deep drill channels create the omega-folds of the *apoptygma* and the hem line, the swirls of drapery around the right thigh, and

the folds of the mantle. Deep diagonal drill channels, whose edges were smoothed away, create the appearance that the chiton was pulled taut across the top of the left thigh. The lower third of the sculpture is carved in less detail and is less worked than the torso and the drapery. Rasp and tooth scraper marks were left on the lower folds of the chiton above the hem line. From the knee down, the figure's left leg is worked in high relief against the back folds of the chiton. The hound and the hare are carved in high relief. The hound's back leg is only cursorily delineated against a point-marked mound of marble, and the animal's underside is left in a point-worked state. Chisel work indicates the anatomical details of both animals. The sides and back of the piece are worked summarily with a chisel and a point. The top and right side of the base are left in a point-worked state. The skin was highly polished; the drapery was smoothed.

Description and Reconstruction

These fragments preserve a two-thirds life-size statue of a draped, booted, female figure running toward the right. The right leg is bent and turned outward, while the left leg is straight and extended behind the body. Despite this rightward motion, the upper torso remains frontal. The right arm extends outward horizontally at a ninety-degree angle to the side of the body, while the left arm trails downward at a forty-five-degree angle to the left side. This gesture creates a diagonal axis from the right arm through the chest and down the left arm. Beneath the swelling folds of the figure's chiton, a tree stump is carved against the right leg. To the right of this stump, a hound wraps his body around the side of the figure. A hare is nestled between the forelegs of this hound. The entire composition was carved in one piece on top of a "rusticated" base with unevenly shaped sides.

The figure wears a sleeveless chiton, which is fastened at her shoulders so that it falls onto her upper chest in a V-shaped neckline.[28] A rope-like belt passes below the breasts and is tied in a bow at the front, creating folds in the drapery above it. This belt also catches a portion of the chiton so that it bulges out over the band beneath the left underarm. The chiton hugs the body of the figure closely to reveal her breasts, swaying torso, navel, and bulging lower abdomen. The folds accentuate the form of the torso and its posture. A second, concealed belt, tied around the hips, shortens the

long chiton by folding the garment up under itself. The bottom of this *apoptygma* falls onto the hips in three-dimensional, omega-shaped folds. The remainder of the chiton flows downward from the waist to cover the figure's thighs. On the left leg, the folds run diagonally across the thigh, lying flat on top of it. On the right leg, they flow from the top of the thigh down both sides to swell into three-dimensional omega-folds between the legs and on the outer side of the leg. The drapery of the chiton is masterfully carved using a combination of the chisel and drill, so that the garment highlights the anatomy of the figure and creates a sense of rapid motion toward the right. In accordance with the figure's rightward motion, the right neckline of the chiton has a wider, thicker ridge, the drapery atop

Fig. 50   Cat. 15: Artemis Rospigliosi, front.

Fig. 51   Cat. 15: Torso of the Artemis Rospigliosi, back.

the right breast has deeper chiselwork, and the end of the mantle on the right is larger and more heavily drilled.

The figure wears a mantle, whose ends flutter outward from her body, whipped up by her rapid movement. While this mantle appears to fall logically around the figure's shoulders in the front, it is not naturalistically rendered on the back; thus the drapery appears to be more of a decorative flourish than a realistic garment. The right end of the mantle falls in front of the figure's right shoulder, loops under her arm, is caught at her side in the tie that runs below her breasts, and then flutters outward from the right side of her torso, its end flowing into a knobbed point. From the top of the right shoulder, the mantle arcs behind the right arm and disappears around the back. The left side of the floating mantle emerges from the back at waist level, where it crosses between the torso and the left arm, loops over the elbow, flows up the outer side of the upper arm, and flutters up behind the figure's left shoulder.

On her preserved right leg, the figure wears an *embas*, a closed boot characterized by its knee-high length and overhanging *piloi*, or boot liners.[29] As is common with *embades*, "the top edge is secured around the leg by a band...pulled so tight as to cause the top to swell into a single...[bulge]."[30] The three V-shaped flaps hanging from this band represent the unevenly-cut ends of the *piloi*. The band, which runs down the front of the boot shaft and onto the top of the foot, depicts the laced opening that allowed the wearer to step into the boot. At the back, a heel guard is depicted.[31]

Because the head and neck of the figure are not preserved, it is difficult to assess the degree to which the surface was originally modeled. The preserved area of the lower neck, however, is subtly modeled to show the clavicles and the depression between them. The preserved musculature on the right side of the neck makes it likely that the head was not turned to the right in the direction of the figure's motion, but remained frontal in line with the axis that runs through the left breast and thigh.[32]

The back of the figure is carved into the general form of a chiton, including an indication of the *apoptygma* and the omega-folds of the hem lines. The mantle is shown as a roughly-shaped swath of drapery, which runs diagonally from the right shoulder down and across the back continuing the line of the extended left arm. Behind the figure's right shoulder, above this mantle, there is a circular broken surface. At this same point, but underneath the mantle, a cylindrical "strut" (W. 6.3 cm; L. 4.0 cm) projects vertically down the back. At its end, the strut has a bulging rim (W. 1.5 cm).

In contrast to the care taken in rendering the figure's torso and drapery, little attention was given to the elements of the base. The dog is carved in relief against the side of the figure so that only its right side is shown. Rough modeling indicates toe and leg joints, the muscles of both legs, the back and front hips, the ribs, the neck muscles, a rectangular snout, a long mouth, and the right eye and nostril. Fur is indicated on the face, and the hound wears a thick collar around its neck (W. 1.4 cm), punctuated by three circular studs. The hound is disproportionately long and seems stretched to wrap around the entire side of the sculpture, its front and back legs over-extended in opposing directions, and its exaggerated snout and mouth craning to reach around to the front of the figure.

The hare is even more summarily treated than the dog. The rounded form of the creature seems dictated more by the shape of the space between the hound and the figure than by a desire to depict the animal realistically. The hare's sides are modeled to indicate shoulders. The front feet, now somewhat abraded, are wide. Two elongated ears point straight upward from the hare's head, the right one disappearing beneath the jaw of the hound, the left tickling his chin. Between the hare and the right side of the figure, there is a tree stump with a cropped branch arcing out of its right side. This stump is the most cursorily-rendered element on the base.

The piece was carved to be seen primarily from the front, since the front of the figure's chiton and the face of the dog are more detailed than their sides, and since the back of the group is not fully worked.

Identification

This figure may be identified as Artemis by the shortened chiton with *apoptygma*, the *embas*, the running pose, the rusticated base and support carved to represent a tree stump and an attendant hound with a hare nestled between its forelegs. The posture, drapery configuration with chiton folded to create an *apoptygma* falling onto the hips in three-dimensional, omega-shaped folds, and the mantle, whose ends flutter outward from the body, whipped up by the figure's rapid movement, identify this Artemis as an example of the "Rospigliosi type," probably created in the second century BC and known in more than twenty-eight replicas (Kahil 1984: 646, Artemis 274–83; Beschi 1959: 264–68; Fleischer 1971; Egilmez 1980: 132–34, 196–98 [K31–32], 372–76). The Paneion Artemis is most comparable to Beschi's Group C, the true Rospigliosi type (Beschi 1959: 270, 271, 272). Thus, the Paneion Artemis Rospigliosi constitutes one of seven sculptures from the Sanctuary of Pan that echo a sculptural type thought to have been created in the Hellenistic period. In addition, it is one of a handful of known Rospigliosi types from the Levant, including a head from Pella (Weber 1993: 39–44, pl. 3) and a fragment from Gerasa (Weber 1993: 42; Fisher 1938: 269, pl. 54c).

The original narrative context of this sculptural group is unknown. The running Artemis, carrying a bow and quiver and accompanied by a hound, may be associated with any number of battles in which the goddess participated, including the slaughter of Actaeon, the slaughter of the Niobids, the Gigantomachy, or the general hunt.[33] The inclusion, in several examples (Samos, Cyrene, and Caesarea Philippi), of the hunting companion (the hound) as well as the game (the hare) argues that the goddess is engaged in a general hunt (Simon and Bauchhenss 1984b: 809).

The identification of this Paneion statue as an Artemis Rospigliosi allows further details of gesture and dress to be reconstructed. The goddess probably held a bow in her lowered left hand and was reaching for an arrow from her quiver with her extended right hand.[34] Indeed, the circular broken surface behind the figure's right shoulder and the cylindrical "strut" carved on the back of the torso suggest that the Paneion Artemis wore a quiver, which projected above the right shoulder

and would have been visible from the front. The absence of a strap to hold the quiver in place, which should cross the front of the torso between the figure's breasts, is a common omission.[35] Finally, the figure's left leg continued behind, so that her foot was placed flat on top of the base, ready to propel the goddess to the right.[36]

Comparanda, Workshop, and Date

The Paneion Artemis is most comparable to two running Artemis figures classified as examples of the true Rospigliosi type. First, the Paneion piece echoes the Samos Artemis in posture, gesture, fullness of anatomical forms, and some details of drapery, including the sleeveless chiton, the tie directly beneath the breasts, the transverse folds across the left thigh, the positioning of the hem line of the chiton above both knees, and the mantle billowing out at the right side of the torso and crossing the left upper arm (Wiegand 1900: 156, no. 11). None of the publications of this piece give an archaeological or stylistic date for it. Second, the Paneion Artemis is comparable to the Cyrene Artemis in terms of the placement, number, and identity of accompanying figures, and in terms of drapery features such as the numerous omega-shaped folds along the hem line of the *apoptygma* and the manner in which the chiton falls straight along the sides of the torso (Beschi 1959: 255). Beschi dates the Cyrene example after the second half of the second century AD, based on the use of combined chisel and drill work; however, it is not clear that this is a chronologically diagnostic feature, and thus this date should not be taken as accurate (Pernier 1931: 228; Beschi 1959: 260). The Paneion Artemis' highly elongated torso and the formal rather than naturalistic rendering of the drapery, especially visible in the omega-folds along the hem lines of the chiton, may suggest a late second- or early third-century AD date for the piece. Since none of the stylistic or technical features of the piece are unique to any particular workshop, it is difficult to associate the Paneion Artemis Rospigliosi with a particular workshop tradition, though isotopic analyses associate the marble with two quarries in Turkey.

16 — FRAGMENT OF THE *EPENDYTES* OF AN ARTEMIS OF EPHESOS

Exc. nos. 78/93/716/8157/1; 78/93/726/8242/1 (figs. 52–55)

Preservation and Material

H. 0.12 m; W. 0.12 m; half circum. 0.23 m.

White marble.

This piece preserves two joining fragments. A drill channel with a metal tenon is preserved in the top break on the left side. There is damage to the reliefs on the front, and there are raised, broken areas at the center and on the left side just below the top break and on the right side just above the bottom break. Dark brown accretions cover the front of the piece except for the lower right side. The original polish is preserved on the lower left background.

Technique

Chisel lines create the low relief figures and the borders of the bands. No evidence of drillwork is preserved. The relief background was polished.

Description and Reconstruction

These fragments preserve a half-cylindrical object carved with low relief figures on its rounded front and summarily worked on its flat back. The front is divided into rectangular fields by evenly-spaced bands carved in low relief (W. 1.0 to 1.2 cm). One horizontal and three vertical bands remain. The bands have narrow borders on each side (approximate W. 0.2 cm), and their intersections are punctuated by oval depressions (H. 1.0 to 2.0 cm; W. 0.6 to 1.6 cm; D. 0.2 cm). Similar oval, square, or rectangular depressions are carved along the bands at regular intervals.

Seven rectangular fields are preserved, within which small figures are carved in low relief. Three of these relief figures are legible. In the lower right field, there is a bust of a human that includes details of the hair, eyes, mouth, and a cloak encircling the neck. In the lower left field, a damaged relief of the head of another human is preserved. The upper

Fig. 52 Cat. 16: Fragment of the ependytes *of an Artemis of Ephesos, front.*

Fig. 53 Cat. 16: Fragment of the ependytes *of an Artemis of Ephesos, back.*

far left field is the best-preserved. Here a rampant four-legged creature faces right, rearing up on its back legs to place its front left paw on top of a spoked wheel. The animal has a slit for its left eye, a hooked beak, three teats, and a tail. The wheel has four spokes.

In addition to relief figures, the fields contain oval depressions similar to those carved along the bands. In the lower right field, there is an oval depression to the right of the bust, and in the lower left field, there is another to the left of the head. Both the middle upper right and left fields contain three oval depressions each. Centered between these six oval depressions in the top fields, a broken, raised area overlaps the central vertical band. In the far left upper field, there is a broken, abraded semicircular area, which fills the space above the

rampant animal. In the far right lower field, there is another small, broken, semicircular raised area.

The back of the piece is flat. Here, the vertical bands are not indicated, so the back is not divided into rectangular fields. The single preserved horizontal band is continued onto the back without its borders. Above this horizontal band, an indiscernible figure or design is carved in very low relief. The figure is shaped like an abstracted horse shown in profile with a sagging belly and a sway back. Above the "horse's back" an unevenly-shaped band follows the curve of the sway. In the concave area above this band a circle is carved in low relief.

Of the three partially-preserved relief figures, only the four-legged animal is identifiable. The mythological creature represents the griffin of Nemesis, recognizable largely because of its ram-

Fig. 54   *Cat. 16: Fragment of the* ependytes *of an Artemis of Ephesos, right profile.*

Fig. 55   *Cat. 16: Fragment of the* ependytes *of an Artemis of Ephesos, left profile, enlarged to show detail of griffin of Nemesis.*

pant position and left foot placed on the spoked wheel, but also because of its vulture's beak and prominent teats.[37] The three raised broken areas, preserved in the two central upper fields, in the far left upper field above the griffin, and in the far right lower field, indicate that other relief figures were carved in these areas.

The numerous oval, rectangular, and square depressions carved along the bands and within the fields were probably filled with some sort of inlay, either glass paste or cut gems. Although there are few examples of inlay of marble statuary with precious stones, extensive archaeological evidence for the use of cut gems in the decoration of architectural elements, frescoes, and furniture has been found at the imperial residences of the Horti Lamiani.[38] Here, a wide variety of precious stones were found in shapes and sizes comparable to the depressions carved in the Paneion statuette.[39] Literary sources note that the Orient, including Arabia, was the primary supplier of these precious stones to the Roman empire.[40] Thus, the discovery, in the Levant, of a sculpture that makes extensive use of the decorative art of gem inlay is not surprising, since the luxury goods essential to the technique were readily available.

Because the Paneion example is so fragmentary, it is impossible to reconstruct its original scale.

Identification

In the *koiné* of Graeco-Roman sculptural iconography, the division by low relief bands of a semi-cylindrical shaft into rectangular fields, which are carved with relief figures, is reserved largely for the representation of the *ependytes* (or overgarment) of the Artemis of Ephesos, the Aphrodite of Aphrodisias, Jupiter Heliopolitanus, and related figures (Fleischer 1973; Fleischer 1984: 755–63). The Paneion fragment may be associated with the lower portion of the *ependytes* of an Artemis of Ephesos because of the number, regular shape, and placement of the registers (Fleischer 1973: 90, 170, 348), their placement on the front only (Fleischer 1973: 91, 346), and the inclusion of the griffin of Nemesis, which appears most commonly on the *ependytes* of the Artemis of Ephesos (Fleischer 1973: 90).[41] The identification of this fragment as part of a statue

of an Artemis of Ephesos makes it one of seven discovered at the sanctuary that may be associated with sculptural types thought to have been created in the Hellenistic period.

The Paneion Artemis fragment has several features that are not common to representations of this type. The multiple oval, rectangular, and square depressions, perhaps meant for the inlay of precious stones or glass paste, do not appear on any other example catalogued by Fleischer. Furthermore, this fragment does not have vertical bands on each side, which appear on most other examples to provide a clear division between the segmented front and sides of the skirt and the cursorily-rendered back. Finally, the griffin on the Paneion figure differs from those shown on most Artemeis of Ephesos in two important ways: it is represented in profile rather than as a protome, and it includes a spoked wheel, an unusual reference to the goddess Nemesis.[42]

The first two deviations from the normal Artemis of Ephesos type are difficult to explain; however, the inclusion of a griffin specific to Nemesis may be related to several factors. The chthonic origins of the goddess of just measure mean that she is often associated with Artemis, who represents the life force of nature. Consequently, in the Roman period, Nemesis and Artemis are often connected in both epigraphic and iconographic material (Hornum 1993: 7, 66–69, 71–72, 80–81). This reference to Nemesis may also be due to the open air court and cult site dedicated to her at the Sanctuary of Pan, where perhaps the dedicant of this statue of the Ephesian Artemis wanted to acknowledge the goddess of just measure although the primary honoree must have been Artemis. Moreover, epigraphic and iconographic evidence shows that Nemesis was widely worshipped in the Levant, so that a reference to the goddess in this region is neither unexpected nor extraordinary (Rosenthal-Heginbottom 2010: 216–18; Hajjar 1990b: 2593–94; Seyrig 1932).

Comparanda, Workshop, and Date

The iconography of the griffin represented on the Paneion fragment is comparable to that of a three-dimensional marble griffin of Nemesis discovered at Erez in Gaza (Leibovitch 1958; Metropolitan Museum of Art 1986: 234–35; Rosenthal-Heginbottom 2010: 213–14). However, because so little remains of the Paneion Artemis of Ephesos and because of the anomalous characteristics listed above, it is difficult to conclude much about its date or workshop association on the basis of stylistic and technical characteristics or by comparison to other representations of the goddess.

17 — FRAGMENT OF A BASE WITH TREE TRUNK AND RIGHT FOOT

Exc. nos. 85/92/705/7811/1 (two joining fragments of base with same number);
78/93/714/8277/2 (non-joining fragment of left foot and base) (fig. 56)

Preservation and Material

H. 0.19 m; 0.16 m (tree trunk); W. 0.27 m; L. 0.12 m (of foot); D. 0.18 m; reconstructed H. 1.08 m/ under life-size.

White marble; medium to large, chunky, glittering crystals.

The piece is broken at the right through the side of the tree trunk, at the left between the two feet, and at the back through the tree trunk and right foot, preserving part of the base, the bottom of the trunk, and the right foot from the toes to the beginning of the heel. A non-joining fragment, preserving two and a half toes of the left foot and a fragment of the base, is associable with the larger fragment because of similarities in scale, surface finish, and articulation of the toes. Sockets and metal tenons are preserved in the break on the left side of the large fragment and on the underside of the base in the small fragment. There is damage to all toes. Dark brown accretions cover the top of the base, the bottom of the tree trunk, the right foot, and the inner side of the left foot.

Technique

Drill channels separate the side of the right foot and ankle from the tree trunk as well as the big toe from the second toe on both feet. Tiny drill holes punctuate the ends of the divisions between the toes on the right foot. Chisel lines indicate the toe nail on the left foot. The feet were highly polished.

Fig. 56   Cat. 17: Fragment of a base with a tree trunk and a right foot, front.

Description and Reconstruction

These fragments preserve part of the base of an under life-size sculpture that represented a figure standing beside a tree trunk. The tree trunk has a broad base with a large hole in its front (H. 7.5 cm; W. 4.5 cm at base; D. 2.0 cm). On the trunk's right side, the bottom of an oblong gnarl is preserved (H. 4.5 cm; W. 2.5 cm). The surface of the trunk is modeled to show the uneven texture of bark. The left side of the tree extends outward to meet the back of the right foot and so does not curve as sharply as the right.

The unshod right foot is attached to the left side of the trunk at the ankle and heel, but the front of the foot extends beyond the trunk. The foot is carefully modeled to indicate the joints of the toes, the arch, and the ankles. A non-joining fragment with a left foot should be associated with this base, because it is the same scale, the surface of the foot is similarly finished, and the toes are articulated similarly to those on the right foot. The first toe of the left foot is the best-preserved and retains a clearly articulated toe nail.

The orientation of the statue is unclear, because the preserved edges show that the base may have been irregularly shaped. The curved edge of the base to the left of the right foot may have been the original front of the sculpture. Since none of the back of the piece remains, it is difficult to determine from which vantage point the sculpture was meant to be seen.

Identification

The bare feet indicate that the piece is more likely to have represented an ideal figure than a portrait. The attention lavished on the feet, both in terms of the high polish and the careful depiction of toe nails, is noteworthy.

Comparanda, Workshop, and Date

Because this piece is so fragmentary, it is impossible to locate comparanda, determine a date, or associate it with a particular workshop based on stylistic and technical characteristics.

18 — FRAGMENT OF A TREE TRUNK WITH A HANGING SYRINX

Exc. nos. 85/92/702/7796/1 (top fragment); 78/93/716/8137/1 (lower fragment) (figs. 57–60)

Preservation and Material

H. 0.31 m; 0.08 m (of syrinx); W. 0.09 m; 0.05 m (of syrinx); D. 0.07 m; 0.01 m (of syrinx); reconstructed H. not determinable/possibly under life-size.

White marble; medium, closely packed, translucent crystals.

The piece is broken at the top and bottom of the trunk. Missing are four branches on the upper half, a large branch that forked off the main trunk at the bottom, and the lower half and left side of the syrinx. There is damage to the leather strap, the cropped branch on which the syrinx hangs, and the *lagobolon*. Dark brown accretions cover the back, left side, and crevices.

Technique

Chisel lines separate the pipes of the syrinx. Drill channels outline the right side of the syrinx, the strap from which it hangs, and the *lagobolon*. There is a single drill hole at the point where the strap crosses itself, below the cropped branch. The surface was softly polished.

Description and Reconstruction

These two fragments preserve part of a gnarled, arching tree trunk, which has groups of pine needles growing on its upper half and a syrinx and cylindrical band hanging from two separate nodules on its lower half. Above the bottom break, a large branch, now mostly missing, forks off to the right of the main trunk.

Above the cropped branch on which the syrinx hangs, there is a rounded, striated group of pine needles growing out of the trunk. On the upper half of the trunk, three broken areas of similar shape and size suggest that more clusters of pine needles were depicted. In fact, six other groups of pine needles, broken away from their original trunks, were found at the sanctuary (see Appendix 3). One of these includes a pine cone. It is likely that these six fragments belong to this trunk, although no joins were found. On the right side of the up-per fragment of the trunk, there is an inverted V-shaped break, which may be the base of another branch that forked off of the main trunk or may have accommodated another group of these pine needles and cones.

On the lower portion of the trunk, a syrinx hangs on a leather strap, which is looped around a cropped branch that protrudes from the center of the trunk. The right side of the syrinx and the leather band are carved in high relief against the trunk (strap: W. 1.0 cm; D. 0.5 cm). The syrinx preserves the ends of six pipes and a horizontal band (W. 0.5 cm) that holds these pipes together. One end of the leather strap connects to the right side of the syrinx, crosses the trunk diagonally, loops around the cropped branch, and extends diagonally back down the trunk. Although the portion of the strap that connected to the left side of the instrument is now missing, its path shows that the syrinx was initially wider than its preserved state suggests.

Fig. 57 Cat. 18: Fragment of a tree trunk with a hanging syrinx, front.

Fig. 58 Cat. 18: Fragment of a tree trunk with a hanging syrinx, back.

Fig. 59 Cat. 18: Fragment of a tree trunk with a hanging syrinx, right profile.

The syrinx must have extended beyond the left side of the tree trunk. Thus, although its right side is shown in high relief, its left side would have been carved in three dimensions.

A cylindrical band runs beneath the syrinx. The lower preserved portion of this band is visible on the front of the trunk, beneath the middle pipes of the syrinx. The band is not evenly shaped or smoothed and has three nodules around its center. The top part of the band runs behind the syrinx, diagonally upward and around the left side of the trunk, toward its back. Although the cylindrical band is abraded and covered with accretions, three raised rings are visible encircling its upper shaft. Where the cylindrical object curves toward the back of the trunk, it is broken; however, a leather

Fig. 60   *Cat. 18: Fragment of a tree trunk with a hanging syrinx, enlarged to show detail of syrinx and* lagobolon.

strap, similar to that holding the syrinx, extends from this point to loop around a cropped branch, which is centered on the back of the trunk.

This cylindrical band may be identified as a *lagobolon*, a hunting stick thrown at hares to kill them (Borgeaud 1988: 64). After the syrinx, the *lagobolon* is Pan's most frequent attribute, and it was commonly carried by or shown next to Pans and satyrs. These sticks are usually represented hanging upside down on tree trunks alongside, under, or near syrinxes.[43] The unsmoothed, irregular surface and the three nodules on the lower portion of the Paneion example are in keeping with the convention of showing *lagobola* as knotted wooden sticks. The three bands encircling the lower end of the Paneion *lagobolon* are probably meant to depict a leather strap wrapped around the bottom of the stick. More commonly, a leather band is passed through a hole at the base of the *lagobolon* to create a short strap, which is then used to hang the stick on a trunk. On the Paneion example, the leather strap must have been fed through a hole in the now-missing bottom of the stick. Indeed, a leather strap does emerge from the broken end of the stick to wrap around a knot on the back of the trunk and suspend the *lagobolon* from the tree.

The front and right surfaces of the trunk are mostly smoothed but occasionally modeled with depressions to indicate gnarled bark. On the back, some ridges of chisel strokes were left unsmoothed. The upper portion of the back of the trunk also contains a small round protuberance and an elongated nodule. The trunk may have been meant to be viewed from all angles.

Identification

Tree trunk supports with hanging syrinxes and *lagobola* are most commonly represented with satyrs, the consorts of Pan. Sculptural types that have both of these attributes hanging on their supports include the young satyr holding the infant Dionysos (Gercke 1968; Pozzi 1989: 156–57, no. 19), the resting satyr (Vierneisel-Schlörb 1979: 353–69), the flute-playing satyr (Glaukler 1895), and the satyr from the "invitation to dance" (Mansuelli 1958: 80–82, no. 51). Thus, the Paneion tree trunk must have served as a support for the representation of a satyr, either alone or in a group. The display of three-dimensional marble sculpture with such Pan-related attributes and subject matter is to be expected at a sanctuary of Pan. In addition, multiple issues of the coinage minted at Caesarea Philippi depict the famous sculptural type of the flute-playing satyr, which some argue may have commemorated a sculpture or sculptures erected at the sanctuary (Meshorer 1984–85: 41, 42–43, 45–46; Ma'oz 1994–99: 95–97) or which may have served as a symbol of the city. In fact, some of these numismatic representations clearly record the tree trunk support with a syrinx and *lagobolon* hanging on it (Meshorer 1984–85: 51, pl. 10, no. 17a; 55, pl. 14, no. 43; 55–56, pl. 14, no. 48; 56, pl. 15, no. 54). This is one of three Pan-related sculptures found at the sanctuary.

Comparanda, Workshop, and Date

Because this piece is so fragmentary, it is impossible to locate comparanda, determine its date, or associate it with a specific workshop on the basis of stylistic and technical characteristics.

19 — LEFT HAND HOLDING A SYRINX

Exc. nos. 85/92/192/7212/1 (fingers and syrinx); 85/92/192/7213/1 (palm); 78/93/714/8189/1 (lower arm) (figs. 61–63)

Preservation and Material

L. 0.16 m; 0.10 m (from wrist to end of third finger); W. 0.08 m; D. 0.04 m; circum. of wrist 0.12 m; reconstructed H. not determinable/half life-size.

White marble; large, chunky, highly-translucent crystals.

The piece is missing the tips of its index and second fingers, the nail of the third finger, the end of the syrinx, which projected beyond the outer side of the hand, two pipes of the syrinx from the end on the inner side of the hand, and the underside of the arm. There is damage to the tips of the pipes. Dark brown accretions cover the underside of the syrinx, thumb, and lower arm. The back of the hand and the syrinx are not carved in as much detail as the front, and the instrument is only summarily differentiated from the palm.

Technique

Narrow drill channels separate the four fingers from one another, the thumb from the palm of the hand, and the hand from the syrinx. Shallow drill holes create the hollows in the pipes. Chisel lines separate the pipes, indicate the outlines of the finger and thumb nails, and create the skin folds at the knuckles. A toothed scraper was used to smooth the back of the instrument. There is a shallow drill hole on the back of the syrinx near the thumb pad. The top of the hand, arm, and syrinx were polished.

Description and Reconstruction

These fragments preserve a half-life-size left hand holding a syrinx. The fingers are extended straight across the width of the instrument, so that the hand is flat. The mouth piece is held between the index finger and the thumb, projecting from the inner side of the hand. On the back, the thumb extends across the width of the pipes and is turned sideways so that its inner side is pressed against the pipes exposing the pad of the thumb. The piece is modeled to show the rounded back of the hand, the ridges of skin around the knuckles, and the pad of the thumb. The smooth modeling of the hand and lower arm suggests that the figure was probably youthful.

The hand does not extend straight from the wrist but is angled to the left and bent inward. Because this leftward tilt and the inward bend of the wrist are not a natural resting position, it is unlikely that the figure held the pipes at his side.

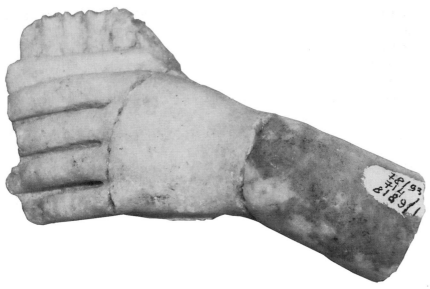

Fig. 61   Cat. 19: *Left hand holding a syrinx.*

Fig. 62   Cat. 19: *Left hand holding a syrinx, palm side.*

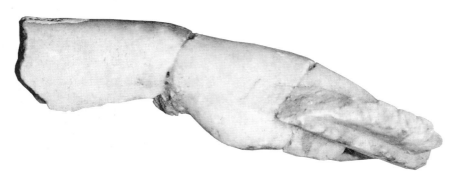

Fig. 63   Cat. 19: *Left hand holding a syrinx, right profile.*

Instead, the position of the hand indicates that the figure held the syrinx up to his face, as though he were about to play it. Because the right side of the syrinx is complete, the figure held the instrument with his left hand only. The hand was probably meant to be seen from the front and sides only.

Identification

Pan and Daphnis (in the sculptural type depicting Pan teaching Daphnis how to play the syrinx) are the two mythological figures most frequently depicted holding syrinxes. There are multiple representations of Pan, both standing and seated, which show the god holding and sometimes playing the syrinx.[44] Not enough of the Paneion fragment remains to associate this hand with any particular standing or seated Pan type, nor do these representations fall into clearly defined types.[45] Instead, because of the position and youthful appearance of the Paneion hand, it is tempting to identify this fragment, at least tentatively, with the sculptural group of Pan teaching Daphnis to play the syrinx, which is a commonly reproduced, well-defined, sculptural type (Marquardt 1995: 182–206). This is one of three Pan-related sculptures found at the sanctuary.

Comparanda, Workshop, and Date

Because this piece is so fragmentary, it is impossible to identify comparanda, determine a date, and associate it with a workshop.

SMALL-SCALE STATUETTES

20 — TORSO OF A DANCING SATYR

Exc. nos. 85/92/705/7804/1 (torso) (figs. 64–67)

Preservation and Material

H. 0.29 m; W. 0.13 m; D. 0.07 m; reconstructed H. 0.52 m.

White marble; medium-sized, closely-packed crystals. Isotopic analyses associate the marble with three quarries in Asia Minor: Afyon, Aphrodisias, or Uşak.

The piece is broken at the neck, left shoulder, and below the buttocks. Missing are the head, right hand, left shoulder and arm, both legs, and genitalia. There is damage to all joins, both breasts, the area below the left breast, the lower abdomen at the left of the navel, the middle of the back to the left of the spine, and the right buttock. The lower abdomen and pubic region were covered with a fine, plaster-like substance, removed during cleaning. The back of the torso is smoothed, not polished, and not fully modeled. The left leg shown in the photograph was erroneously associated with and attached to sculpture.

Technique

Chisel lines delineate details of the nodule atop the right shoulder, the curly pubic hair, the spine, individual strands of hair within the tail, and the separation between the buttocks. A small, shallow drill hole (Diam. 0.3 cm) indicates the navel. The front of the piece is highly modeled and polished, while the back is smoothed.

Description and Reconstruction

These fragments preserve the torso and right arm of a small-scale male figure with a tail. The gesture and posture shift the axes of the shoulders and hips into opposing diagonals to create a dynamic, moving figure. The upper torso turns toward the right. The right arm, held away from the torso, extends down the side of the body and is bent at a ninety-degree angle, so that the forearm extends toward the viewer. Although the left arm no longer remains, the left side of the torso is stretched and elongated, and the left pectoral is higher than the right. Consequently, the right side of the torso curves inward, its muscles shortened and bulging. At the chest, the central axis of the body curves toward the right. There is a depression in the side of the left buttock, indicating its tensed muscles. The right buttock, relaxed and rounded, protrudes farther back than the left.

The torso is highly modeled with bulging muscles, a virtuoso rendering of mature male anatomy. Especially emphasized are the depression between the clavicles, the muscles of the right shoulder and arm, the folds of musculature beneath the armpit, the depressions between and beneath the breasts,

the folded muscles of the right side of the torso, the pelvic girdle, the muscles of the left thigh, the scapula, the muscles along the spine, and the tensed and relaxed buttocks.

The posture and gesture may be partially reconstructed from the musculature and remaining portions of the arms and legs. The dimple and tensed muscles of the left buttock indicate that the figure supported its weight on its left leg. The full, rounded form of the right buttock and its position behind the left one suggest that the free right leg must have extended behind the body. Not enough of the thighs are preserved to determine whether the right leg crossed behind the left or extended straight behind the body. The position of the left pectoral above the right one and the elongated left side of the torso indicate that the left arm was probably extended upward above the figure's head,

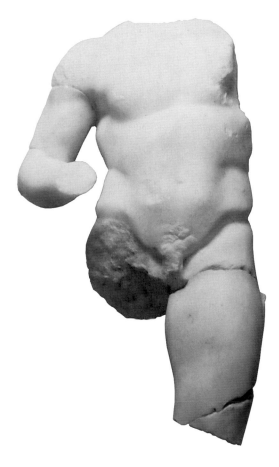

Fig. 64   Cat. 20: Torso of a dancing satyr, front (left leg not original).

Fig. 65   Cat. 20: Torso of a dancing satyr, back, enlarged to show details.

either slightly in front of his body or to his left side. The form of the preserved right trapezius muscle suggests that the head of the figure either faced directly forward or turned toward the left to look at the raised left arm.

The back of the torso was smoothed, not polished, and is not fully modeled. The spine is indicated by a single line that runs from the base of the neck down the back. Below the mid-point of the back, this vertical line forks into two roughly horizontal lines, which extend from the center of the back outward to its sides, indicating the separation of the lower back from the buttocks. Beneath this fork, a tail, shaped like a reversed S, is carved in relief. Below this tail, a tiny triangular impression begins the linear separation of the buttocks.

A leaf-shaped projection (L. 4.5 cm) is carved on the back of the right shoulder, rising 0.5 cm off the back of the shoulder and 0.3 cm off the front. It has a 0.2 cm wide rim and an abraded, pointed tip. Its surface is not flat, but ripples with the flow of the shoulder muscles. A similarly-shaped symmetrical area appears on the left shoulder, but its surface is now broken away.

The position of the tail, an important iconographic feature, suggests that the piece was meant to be viewed not only from the front and sides, but also from the back.

Identification

This figure may be identified as a satyr primarily on its tail, but also on its nudity, mature musculature, posture (with its weight on its left leg and the free right leg extended behind the body), and gesture (with the left arm extended upward

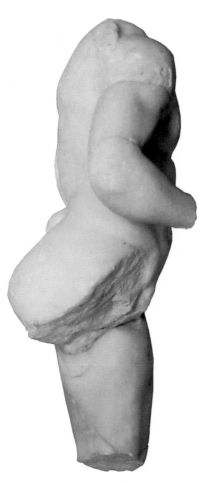

Fig. 66   Cat. 20: Torso of a dancing satyr, right profile (left leg not original).

Fig. 67   Cat. 20: Torso of a dancing satyr, left profile (left leg not original).

above the figure's head, either slightly in front of his body or to his left side). Both the posture and gesture are related to that of the dancing faun from the House of the Faun in Pompeii (Smith 1991: 129, fig. 151; Bieber 1955: 39, figs. 95–96), the bronze satyr from Nikomedia (Philipp 1987: 131–43), and numerous examples of tail-chasing satyrs (Büsing and Büsing 1991: 31–39). All of these sculptural types are related to the Borghese Faun, the prototype of which is attributed to Lysippos or one of his pupils and dated to late fourth or early third century BC (Bieber 1955: 39, fig. 94; Pollitt 1986: 53; Ridgway 1990a: 324). Thus, the Paneion dancing satyr constitutes one of the seven statues found at the sanctuary that may be associated with sculptural types thought to have been created in the Hellenistic period.

The comparison of the Paneion dancing satyr to the satyr from the House of the Faun in Pompeii and the Borghese Faun suggests further details of its posture, costume, and attributes. The figure may have stood elevated on the balls of both feet as do the Borghese Faun and the dancing faun from Pompeii. The leaf-shaped projection (H. 0.5 cm; L. 4.5 cm), carved on the back of the right shoulder, that ripples with the flow of the shoulder muscles and the now broken, but similarly-shaped symmetrical area on the left shoulder, probably represented the ends of a lappet or ribbon, which may have been tied around the satyr's head, perhaps to secure a wreath.

Representations of Pan-related subjects such as this satyr are expected at a sanctuary of Pan, and two other such sculptures have been found at the Paneion: the left hand holding a syrinx possibly from a group of Pan teaching Daphnis to play the pipes (cat. 19) and a tree trunk with a hanging syrinx almost certainly associated with a sculpture of a satyr either alone or in a group (cat. 18).

Comparanda, Workshop, and Date

The Paneion satyr is somewhat similar to that from Caesarea Maritima (Gersht 1987: cat. 32) in terms of posture, gesture, and the modeling of the torso. The most diagnostic technical feature of the Paneion satyr is the manner in which the spine is carved with a single chisel line, ending just above the buttocks in a triangular fork, into which an S-shaped tail is nestled. Such geometric rendering of the spine and tail is rare, but has several parallels in two pieces from Aphrodisias: the Pan of a *spinario* group (inv. no. 67–559; Erim 1967: 69; Mellink 1968: 143, pl. 55, 6) and the satyr of the small group of a satyr and young Dionysos (Erim 1974; Smith 1996: 60–63, fig. 62; Smith 1998: 255–57, fig. 7). Although neither group has been assigned a date, the small satyr and young Dionysos group is definitively associated with the sculptor's workshop discovered to the north of the Odeon, which is thought to have functioned from the first half of the third century AD into the fourth century (Rockwell 1991). Furthermore, based on the stylistic and technical features, the sculptor of the small group of a satyr and young Dionysos from Aphrodisias may have been active in the mid-second century AD (Smith 1996: 63, n. 53; Smith 1998: 258–59). Therefore, the Paneion satyr may be associated with the sculptural workshops at Aphrodisias, although it is difficult to determine a date for it. Isotopic analyses of the marble associate it with Afyon, Aphrodisias, or Uşak, all in Asia Minor.

21 — TORSO AND LEGS OF A "WEARY HERAKLES"

Exc. nos. 82/90/183/1567/1 (torso); 78/93/714/8163/3 (legs) (figs. 68–70)

Preservation and Material

H. 0.13 m; W. 0.10 m; reconstructed H. not determinable.

White marble; small, glittering, closely-packed crystals.

The piece is broken through the abdomen and support, and a joining fragment preserving the legs was found separately. Missing are the head, arms, most of the torso, left knee, both ankles and feet, upper and lower portion of the support, and base. The piece is eroded overall, and there is damage to the side of the right hip and details on the front of the support. Dark brown accretions cover the right side of torso, both legs, and the front of the support.

Technique

The piece is not carefully carved. The cursory workmanship seems attributable to rapid execution and the tiny scale rather than to incomplete carving. A chisel line indicates the separation between the buttocks. A shallow drill channel divides the figure from the support. Broad tool strokes indicate anatomical details, such as the pelvic girdle, the genitalia, and the division between the thighs. The marble between the thighs was never carved away. Ridges of chisel strokes are left on the piece, especially on the areas depicting the musculature of the legs.

Description and Reconstruction

These fragments preserve the lower torso and crossed legs of a tiny nude male figure. The figure leans to his left against a support with his weight on his right leg. The free left leg crosses in front of the right at the middle of the shin. Correspondingly, the left hip is dropped and the right is thrust outward to the side. This contrapposto stance creates a tilted axis in the hips, visible from the front in

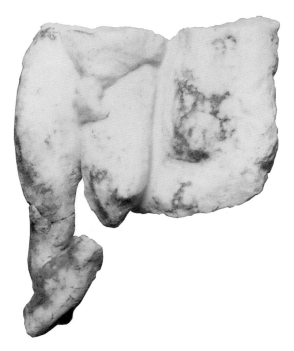

Fig. 68   Cat. 21: Torso and legs of a "Weary Herakles," front.

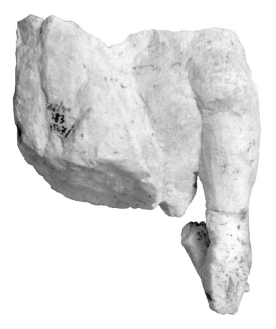

Fig. 69   Cat. 21: Torso and legs of a "Weary Herakles," back.

Fig. 70   Cat. 21: Torso and legs of a "Weary Herakles," right profile.

the pelvic girdle and from behind in the buttocks. A drill line, which separates the left thigh from the adjacent support, also heightens the curving contour of the left side of the body.

Although it is not carefully worked, the preserved portion of the body is modeled to give the figure a mature, muscular appearance. The iliac crest is clearly delineated. The muscles of the thighs and calves are emphasized. In addition, the right buttock is shown as especially rounded and tensed, since it supports the weight of the hulking figure. The genitalia, carved as a large arc-shaped protrusion, are not naturalistically represented; however, their size and shape further emphasize the maturity of the figure.

Both the front and left side of the support are heavily eroded and abraded and, like the remainder of the piece, they do not seem to have been carefully carved. On the right half of the support, there is a raised rectangular area (L. 5.2 cm; W. 3.0 cm). This area is surrounded by a small rim and at its bottom half is carved with raised details, now too abraded and encrusted to discern. To the left and adjacent

to this raised rectangular area, there is a columnar area (L. 2.7 cm), resting atop a wider base (L. 1.0 cm; W. 1.5 cm). Because the majority of the support is missing, it is difficult to know for sure what these areas represented. The left side of the support is too abraded and broken to preserve any of its original carving, although it does contain a single shallow drill channel running down its length.

The back of both the figure and the support are less worked than the front. The separation between the buttocks and thighs is cursorily rendered. A tiny V-shaped area is carved on the lower back, above the buttocks. The poor preservation of the back of the support makes it difficult to discern whether this surface is chipped or merely eroded. The figure was meant to be seen from the front and right sides only.

Identification

The heroic nudity, emphatic musculature, crossed legs, hip-shot pose with lowered left hip, and wide support adjacent to the left side of the body all identify this statuette as a Herakles related to the Copenhagen/Dresden and Farnese types (Palagia 1988; Krull 1985; Moreno 1982). The Copenhagen/Dresden or so-called "Weary Herakles" type, representing the aged hero, tired from his labors, is thought to have been given sculptural form by a Polykleitan follower around 360 BC (Palagia 1988: 762). The Farnese type, perhaps created by Lysippos around 325–320 BC, is thought to have been derived from this representation (Palagia 1988: 762–65) and possesses fuller anatomical features, more elongated proportions, and a stance with the left leg advanced so far in front of the right that the legs are almost crossed. Thus, the Paneion Herakles is one of seven Roman-period versions of well-known Hellenistic types dedicated at the Sanctuary of Pan.

Two features of the Paneion Herakles differ from the majority of Copenhagen/Dresden and Farnese types. The fully-crossed legs are not a regular feature of either type.[46] As well, there are only a few renditions of the Herakles Farnese in which the support is carved adjacent to the left side of the body as on the Paneion example; instead, most of these figures are adjacent to their supports only at their upper torsos (statuette from Compiègne in the Musée Vivenel, Moreno 1982: 514, no. B.6.9, fig. 102; statuette in the Thasos Museum, no. 2446; Boardman et al. 1988: 764, Heracles no. 707).

The comparison of the Paneion Herakles to the Copenhagen/Dresden and Farnese types suggests possible reconstructions for the posture, gesture, and details of the support. The head probably turned to the left and looked downward. The right foot stood flat atop the base; however, the left foot rested only on its ball. The left arm, which in examples of both types hangs down along the outer edge of the support, may be represented by the columnar area on the front of the Paneion support. The right hand must have rested on the hip, since there is no evidence of any attachment point on the right buttock where the typical Herakles Farnese rests his right hand, holding the apples of the Hesperides.[47] The small chip in the outer edge of the right hip may indicate that this was an attachment point for the right hand. The support was probably wedged tightly beneath the left armpit and may have consisted of a lion skin draped over a club, which rested atop a rock. In the Paneion Herakles, the raised rectangular area on the right side of the support may have been a lion skin draped atop a club. The now-abraded

details at its lower end may be understood as the front paws of the lion, which typically hang in front of the gathered pelt even with or above the level of Herakles' left knee. The widening base at the bottom of the Paneion support may depict the top of a rock.

The Farnese type was one of the most popular images of Herakles in the Roman period and as such has a wide distribution (Vermeule 1975: 323–32). Both the Farnese type and the related "Weary Herakles" have been found in a variety of media throughout the Levant from the Hellenistic period onward (Downey 1969: 1–2, 9–11). Three-dimensional marble representations of the hero-god are, however, rare. Another marble Herakles Farnese, this one just over life-size, was recently discovered at Beth Shean/Scythopolis in the excavations of the bath building (Gabi Mazor, personal communication, 1995).

Comparanda, Workshop, and Date

Because of the small size of this figure, its low degree of finish, and the lack of any diagnostic, stylistic, or technical features, it is impossible to locate comparanda or determine a date or workshop association for the Paneion Herakles.

22 — TORSO OF AN EROS

Exc. no. 85/92/705/7832/3 (figs. 71–74)

Preservation and Material

H. 0.11 m; W. 0.09 m; reconstructed H. not determinable.

White marble; medium, closely-packed, sparkling crystals.

The piece is broken at the neck and below the buttocks. Missing are the head, top of the right shoulder, right arm from the elbow down, left arm, lower abdomen, legs, and most of the wings. There is a wide break along the edge of the left wing (W.

3.3 cm). Dark brown accretions cover the broken surfaces on the front and top of the piece.

Technique

Few tool marks appear on the figure's front. Drill channels separate the right forearm from the torso and the inner face of the right wing from the side of the torso. A series of drill holes divide the inner face of the left wing from the left arm. Chisel lines divide the outer face of the left wing from the back and denote the separation between the buttocks. The front of the figure is highly polished

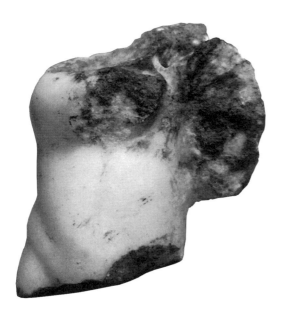

Fig. 71   Cat. 22: Torso of an Eros, front.

Fig. 72   Cat. 22: Torso of an Eros, back.

Fig. 73   Cat. 22: Torso of an Eros, right profile.

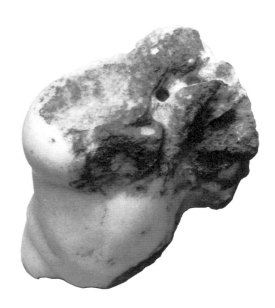

Fig. 74   Cat. 22: Torso of an Eros, top.

and slippery, while the back, buttocks, and wings are unpolished and only roughly shaped.

Description and Reconstruction

This piece preserves a winged torso of a tiny figure. The small, plump figure extends its right arm across its upper body, reaching upward toward the left shoulder. This right arm is held tightly against the chest. From the shoulder, the broken left arm, nestled in front of the wing, extends upward, continuing the line of the right arm. Thus, the upper torso of the figure twists toward the left. Little of the posture remains except for a small portion of the right thigh, which extends outward diagonally from the hip.

The front and right side of the piece are delicately modeled to show a chubby figure. Emphasized areas include the plump stomach, the fatty roll of flesh on the right hip, the bulge of the right thigh, and the rounded right buttock. This modeling is especially visible in right profile view. In accordance with the twist of the torso, the central axis of the body, indicated by a delicate depression on the front of the torso, runs down the center of the figure and, at the lower abdomen, curves toward the right. No navel is indicated.

The back of the figure, including the wings, is roughly shaped and smoothed. The left buttock appears more compact and tensed, while the right buttock is larger, more rounded, and extends outward toward the right. The wings are not positioned symmetrically on either side of the spine. The right wing emerges immediately to the side of the spine and seems to have extended almost directly behind the figure. The left wing springs from the far left edge of the back and curves toward the front of the figure, so that its inner face forms a backdrop for the left arm. The left wing is thicker than the right (Left wing: approx. 2.0 cm across break; right wing: 1.2 cm across break). Because both wings are broken away close to their bases (the right more so than the left), it is impossible to say more about their position and surface articulation.

The preserved portion of the torso suggests some details of the figure's posture. The figure stood with its weight supported on the left leg, as shown by the more compact, tensed left buttock.

The free right leg was either crossed in front of the left or extended outward toward the side. The later seems more likely, since the curve of the body's central axis toward the left would necessitate counter-balance, which might come from pulling the lower abdomen toward the right. Thus, the figure's weight would have been shifted entirely to the left in accordance with his gesture.

The unpolished and roughly-shaped back, buttocks, and wings indicate that the piece was meant to be seen from the front. The delicate modeling of the right side suggests that it was also meant to be viewed from the right or three-quarter-right.

Identification

The wings and chubby stature of this figure identify it as Eros. The larger narrative context of this piece is difficult to determine, because the figure is so fragmentary and because its posture and gesture do not associate it with any one of the established Eros/Amor/Cupid types (Augé and De Bellefonds 1986b). The most diagnostic features of the statuette are the chubby, infant-like proportions of the torso, the gesture of the right arm (held tightly against its chest, extended across its upper body, reaching upward toward the left shoulder), and the placement of the wings, with the right wing emerging immediately to the side of the spine and extending almost directly behind the figure and the left wing springing from the far left edge of the back and curving toward the front of the figure, so that its inner face forms a backdrop for the left arm. Representations of Eros with this distinctive stature, age, and gesture include the armed Eros, the sleeping Eros, playful scenes of Eros holding a variety of animals, and Eros as a companion to Aphrodite (Blanc and Gury 1986: 1046–47). The Paneion Eros is not comparable to the Lysippan bow stringer for two reasons: the famous fourth-century BC work represents a slender adolescent Eros rather than a chubby infant; furthermore, the gesture of the Lysippan Eros differs significantly from the Paneion statuette in that the right arm reaches down and across the torso rather than upward and across the chest. If the Paneion example represents a sleeping Eros, he would have been either standing or resting solely on his left side along the break in the left wing, since the back of the piece is not damaged and thus could not have been attached to a rock or other resting surface. The gesture of the Paneion piece is somewhat comparable to the statue of Eros with a rabbit, found in one of the terrace houses at Ephesos and dated to the second century AD, which offers an example of Eros holding an animal (Eichler 1961: 70; Erdemgil 1989: 31).

This Paneion piece may have been part of a multi-figured sculptural group for several reasons: the leftward posture and gesture show that the figure focused on something at its left; the diminutive scale makes it likely that the piece was a subsidiary element in a group; and the broken surface along the side of the left wing, as well as the disparity between the finish of the right and left sides, may indicate that the figure was attached to another sculptural element along its left side.

Comparanda, Workshop, and Date

Because of the small scale and poor preservation of the piece, it is difficult to locate comparanda.

The slippery, glossy polish on the front and right sides of this statuette may associate this figure with the late fourth and early fifth centuries AD, when sculptures were given this distinctive high polish (Stirling 2005: 108). Its diminutive scale and possible inclusion in a multi figured sculptural group also connect the Paneion Eros with the genre of late antique mythological statuettes (Stirling 2005: 2–3, 104–5) that are thought to have been produced by Asiatic sculptors, perhaps in the sculptural workshops of Aphrodisias, Ephesos, and Constantinople (Stirling 2005: 117–29). If the Paneion Eros was a subsidiary figure in one of these late antique sculptural groups, it may be dated to the late fourth or early fifth centuries AD and associated with one of these Asiatic production centers. This would make the piece one of two statues discovered at the sanctuary that are dated stylistically to the late fourth or early fifth centuries AD (along with the forequarters of a bovine, cat. 25), a period for which there is no epigraphic evidence for the dedication of statuary at the sanctuary.

Fig. 75   *Cat. 23: Base of a statuette of Kybele or Dea Syria, front. Photo IAA, by permission.*

23 — BASE OF A STATUETTE OF KYBELE OR DEA SYRIA

Exc. no. 82/90/183/1585/1 (fig. 75)

Preservation and Material

H. 0.07 m; W. 0.12 m; D. 0.11 m; reconstructed H. not determinable.

White limestone.

The piece is broken just above the feet of the figures and through the base, preserving the left side of the base, left foot of the woman, and lower portion of the front of the animal's body. There is damage to the woman's left foot and the hem of the chiton. The back of the statue is not carved in three dimensions but is smoothed to a flat plane, perpendicular to the top of the base.

Technique

The coarse-grained material preserves many tool marks, but there is no evidence of drillwork. Chisel lines denote the folds in the woman's chiton and the toes of the animal. A small flat chisel was used to smooth the front, left, and back edges of the base. A toothed scraper was used to smooth the left side of the animal and the base around it. The top of the base is not level, but rises up to meet the figures and is carved lower on the left side than at the front.

Description and Reconstruction

This fragment preserves the base of a statuette that included at least two figures — a draped woman and a four-legged animal seated or lying against her left side. The woman's chiton falls to the ground in a distinctive pattern. Its rippling hem extends to the base between the legs, but is pulled up to rest on top of the left foot. On the outer side of the left foot, the drapery cascades downward toward the base in a smoother, less rippling curve. The left foot, turned outward, is shown as a sort of slipper without any indication of toes.

The four-legged animal is nestled against the left side of the woman, so that the left portion of her drapery covers part of the animal's front right foot. Three of the four feet of the animal are depicted; the back right foot and entire right side of the animal are not shown, since they are completely enveloped by the woman's drapery. The pattern of the animal's front paws echoes the ripples in the hem of the woman's chiton. Each front foot has four toes that end in triangular points; each toe has a central ridge. The animal lies with its hind legs folded against its sides, so that the back left foot and leg are carved in relief against the side of the animal's body. Between the two front feet, a small portion of the chest and belly of the animal is preserved, pressed against the top of the base. Judging from the remaining portion of the animal's body, the piece was not subtly modeled.

The figures occupy the entire base. The woman's left foot and drapery protrude over the front of the base. On the left, the animal's front paw is flush with the edge of the base. At the back, the statue is not carved in three dimensions, but is smoothed to a flat plane, perpendicular to the top of the base. Thus, details such as the tail of the animal and the back of the woman were never rendered. Because the front and left side are finished, but the back is not, the piece was meant to be seen from the front and sides only. The flat back may indicate that the piece was meant to be displayed against a wall.

Identification

The distinctive pattern of the hem, the rounded shape of the left foot, and the accompanying four-legged animal identify the figure as either Kybele or Dea Syria with her attendant animal, the lion (Naumann-Steckner 1983; Rein 1993). It is impossible to determine whether this figure represents Kybele or her Syrian counterpart, Dea Syria or Atargatis, since the most-common representations of Dea Syria adopt the iconography of Kybele (Drijvers 1986: 357–58). Although the Levantine context of the sanctuary and the local material of this statuette suggest that this sculpture may represent the Semitic Dea Syria, the overwhelmingly Hellenized character of the sanctuary and the Graeco-Roman nature of its sculptural dedications make it difficult to rule out the possibility that this statuette depicted the Greek goddess Kybele. Whether she was Kybele or Dea Syria, the statuette may be reconstructed as a goddess seated on a throne, wearing a girt chiton and himation, and flanked by at least one, probably two seated lions (Naumann-Steckner 1983: 247–53). Typically, the goddess would have held a *tympanum* in her left hand and a *patera* in her right. The small scale of the statue suggests that it was dedicated at the sanctuary as a votive offering.

Comparanda, Workshop, and Date

The Paneion Kybele or Dea Syria is most comparable to a marble statue of Kybele from Selendi in Lydia in the geometric rendering of the ripples of its drapery, the pattern of the hem line along the base and on top of the left foot, the rendering of the goddess' left foot and the toes of the lion, and the position of the figures on the base (*CCCA* 1: 139–40, no. 471, pl. 103). However, the Paneion statuette differs in its material, the relative scales of the lion and goddess (the lion is larger in proportion to the goddess on the Paneion example), and the proximity of the lion to the goddess (the drapery of the Selendi goddess does not spill onto the right foot of the lion as on the Paneion example). This fragment is the only three-dimensional sculpture made of limestone discovered at the Sanctuary of Pan. This local material, along with the geometric execution of the work, indicates that the piece was carved in the Levant by a craftsman trained in native sculpting traditions. The fragmentary nature of this piece makes it impossible to determine a stylistic date for it.

24 — MALE HEAD (PORTRAIT OF AN EMPEROR?)

Exc. no. 78/93/716/8116/1 (figs. 76–78)

Preservation and Material

H. 0.06 m; W. 0.05 m; D. 0.05 m; reconstructed H. not determinable.

White marble.

The piece is broken at the base of the neck. There is damage to the right eyebrow, ears, wreath, hair behind the wreath, and neck strut. Dark brown accretions cover the right side.

Technique

Chisel lines denote the details of the physiognomy, hairstyle, and headdress. The surface of the face is polished. The back of the head is not fully carved.

Description and Reconstruction

This fragment preserves a tiny head carved in a highly unnaturalistic style. The bulbous chin and the large headdress give the head an oval shape. The facial features and hairstyle are carved asymmetrically to indicate a turn of the head toward the left. The center and left side of the face are broader and flatter than the right. The left ear is carved flat against the side of the head in contrast to the right ear, which sticks out. The cleft in the chin is positioned to the left of center.

The facial features are rendered geometrically with short chisel strokes. The eyebrows are arched protrusions of marble. The inset eyes are almond-shaped with two chisel lines indicating both the upper and the lower lids. The eyeballs bulge. The arch of the eyebrows continues into the side lines of the nose, which has a simple triangular form. The

Fig. 76   Cat. 24: Male Head (Portrait of an
Emperor?), three-quarter.

Fig. 77   Cat. 24: Male Head (Portrait of an
Emperor?), right profile.

Fig. 78   Cat. 24: Male Head (Portrait of an
Emperor?), left profile.

mouth is made of two raised sections of marble with a chisel line between, indicating the division between the lips. Beneath the mouth, a depression highlights the square chin, which protrudes from the plane of the face. All of the features are concentrated at the center of the facial plane, which, in addition to their geometric rendering, adds to the unnaturalistic and disproportionate appearance of the face.

While the face is not intricately modeled, the cheekbones are prominently rendered. The head sits on a thick neck whose right side has undulations to show musculature. A V-shaped area just beneath the chin indicates the Adam's apple.

The hairstyle consists of three rows of patterned bands followed by a smoothed flat band. The front-most band is carved with a chevron pattern, flat against the head, and provides an arched frame for the forehead. Behind this, two raised bands are carved with diagonal incisions; those on the band closer to the forehead run in one direction, those on the next band run opposite. Behind these patterned areas is a smoothed band. A chisel line runs from the back of the smooth band down the center of the head, indicating a central part.

The first band, carved flat with chevron patterns, may be understood as a ring of short hair, combed forward to provide an arched frame for the face. The two raised bands behind this ring of hair may depict a schematic wreath composed of either laurel or oak leaves. In this case, the diagonal incisions would separate individual leaves.

The back of the head is not fully carved in three dimensions and has a large rectangular neck strut at the nape of the neck (H. 4.0 cm; W. 1.6 cm; D. 2.5 cm). Judging from the unfinished state of the back of the head, the figure was meant to be seen from the front and in three-quarter view only.

Identification

This head, though carved in a highly unnaturalistic style, may be identified as a portrait rather than a representation of an ideal figure, because it has highly specific physiognomic features, such as the prominent cheekbones and the square, protruding, cleft chin. Since the laurel or oak wreath is an attribute more common to emperors than

Fig. 79   Cat. 25: Forequarters of a bovine, front.

Fig. 81   Cat. 25: Forequarters of a bovine, right profile.

Fig. 80   Cat. 25: Forequarters of a bovine, back.

Fig. 82   Cat. 25: Forequarters of a bovine, left profile.

private individuals (Stout 1994: 82), the head may represent an imperial personage. However, any further identification of the subject on the basis of physiognomy and style is difficult, because the piece is so cursorily carved and so small in scale.

Comparanda, Workshop, and Date

Because the workmanship of this sculpture is so cursory, it is difficult to locate comparanda or assign it a date on the basis of stylistic features. The schematic, geometric representation of the facial features, their unnaturalistic proportions, and their confinement to the center of the face make it unlikely that this piece was carved by a sculptor trained in the Graeco-Roman tradition. Instead, the piece was probably carved by a craftsman who was not familiar with Graeco-Roman conventions or with carving marble, but instead was trained in local Levantine sculptural traditions. Interestingly, the Paneion male head has several of the technical characteristics common to the life-size ideal heads found at the sanctuary, namely the large neck strut and the distortion of the facial features to indicate a turn of the head. It is the only marble sculpture discovered at the sanctuary likely to have been manufactured locally.

25 — FOREQUARTERS OF A BOVINE

Exc. no. 78/93/716/8240/1 (figs. 79–82)

Preservation and Material

H. 0.10 m; L. 0.12 m; W. 0.05 m; reconstructed H. not determinable.

White marble; small, closely-packed, highly translucent, glittering crystals. Isotopic analyses associate the marble with one of two quarries in Asia Minor, either Denizli or Afyon.

The piece is broken through the body. Missing are the tips of the horns, left ear, lower stomach, hind portion of the body, and legs. There is damage to the right side of the nose and nostril. There is a flat break on the left side of the body with a drill channel running along the bottom of the break to denote the separation between the left side of the animal and a once-adjacent figure. There is an oval depression carved between the eyes (W. 1.4 cm; H. 1.6 cm). A portion of a drill channel (D. 2.0 cm) with rusty residue inside remains on the vertical break through the torso. Heavy, dark brown accretions once covered the entire right side of piece, but before study, they were removed by bathing in acid solution (3–5% EDTA) and scraping the surface with a scalpel and toothbrush. The entire piece was coated with Hagesan ("HG") to "restore" the smooth, shiny surface.

Technique

Few tool marks appear on the surface of the figure. Chisel lines denote the base of the horns, a series of short nicks around the horns, outlines of the arc-shaped ears, the upper and lower eyelids, lunate nostrils, and the mouth. Tiny drill holes create the pupils. The vertical break through the torso is worked with a point and may have been a join surface. The degree of original surface polish is impossible to determine, since the piece was cleaned and coated before study.

Description and Reconstruction

This piece preserves the head and torso of a small-scale bovine. The head is carved in three dimensions with both sides of the face equally detailed. However, the left flank of the animal, from the shoulder back, is broken as though the animal had been attached originally to a relief background or another figure along this side. A drill channel, which runs along the bottom of this break, denotes the separation between the left side of the animal and a relief background or once-adjacent figure.

The animal turns its head slightly to the right. The head is crowned by two short horns encircled by vertical incisions. Below the horns, arc-shaped ears nestle against the head, following the line of the eyebrows. The thick-lidded almond-shaped eyes are widely separated. Tiny circular pupils are drilled into the eyeballs just below the upper lids, so that the animal seems to look upward. The corners of the eyes are inset to indicate tear ducts. Between the eyes, there is a shallow oval depression (W. 1.4 cm; H. 1.6 cm). This oval indentation must have been part of the original design rather than a later addition or a break, because of its regularity of position and outline. The animal has an elongated, rounded snout with lunate nostrils carved on its front. A thin mouth is indicated beneath the snout.

The body is delicately modeled. A flap of skin running down the chest narrows realistically to a pointed ridge. The head is more clearly distinguished from the body on the right side than on the left because of its rightward turn. Other anatomical features that are highlighted include a flat area on the back, the outline of the right shoulder, and the slimming of the stomach toward the underside of the animal. Since the modeling is so smooth and does not emphasize the musculature of the shoulders and neck, the animal has a docile look.

Because the animal was attached either to a relief background or to another figure on its left side, and because it turns its head slightly toward the right, the piece was meant to be viewed primarily in right profile. However, the equal finish of both sides of the head and the inclusion of such details as eyes, nostrils, and the oval depression on its front indicate that the animal may also have been meant to be viewed head on.

The animal seems to have been part of a three-dimensional multi-figured group rather than a relief. The equal carving of both sides of the head and the frontal vantage point would have been unlikely if the animal had been attached to a relief where it would have been viewed in profile only. Also, the piece seems too three-dimensional to have been part of a relief (greatest preserved W. ca. 5.0 cm).

The two remaining iconographic details, the incisions encircling the animal's horns and the oval depression between the creature's eyes, are enigmatic. The nicks may represent a tiny wreath wrapped round the animal's horns. However, their cursory nature makes it more likely that these incisions show hair sprouting from the animal's head. The oval depression between the eyes may have been carved to accommodate a gem or glass paste inlay. In this respect, this piece may be compared to the fragment of an *ependytes* of the Artemis of Ephesos also from the sanctuary (cat. 16), since it is punctuated by similar oval, rectangular, and square depressions (for a discussion of the evidence for the inlay of marble statuary, see cat. 16).

Identification

The drilled pupils, statuette scale, and animal subject matter associate this piece with the genre of multi-figured late antique mythological statuettes (Stirling 2005: 2–3, 98–102, 104–6). While cows and bulls appear in numerous mythological, religious, and pastoral figural groups, based on its posture and attributes, the Paneion bovine most likely belonged either to a representation of Orpheus charming the animals or to one of Herakles during or after his encounter with the cattle of Geryon (Todisco 1990). There are several three-dimensional marble representations of Orpheus charming the animals, one of which comes from the Levantine city of Byblos,[48] though none of these include a bovine. Alternately, the Paneion bovine may have been part of a representation of Herakles and the theft of the cattle of Geryon. Although scenes from this labor are rarely represented in three dimensions, Herakles is commonly shown on Greek vases resting among docile cattle and their calves in rocky settings (Brize 1990: 73–85). Several reliefs, including a Hellenistic votive relief probably from Kyzikos (Boardman et al. 1990: 80, Herakles no. 2535c) and a second-century AD sarcophagus from the Black Sea (Boardman et al. 1990: 80, Herakles no. 2536a=2652), also show Herakles accompanied by bulls.

Another fragment that preserves the rear quarters of a cow or bull was discovered at the Paneion (cat. 26). While the hindquarters are comparable to the piece discussed here in scale, degree of carving, finish, direction of motion, and piecing, the two fragments do not join. Thus, there seem to have been at least two marble representations of bovines at the sanctuary, perhaps from the same figural group.

Comparanda, Workshop, and Date

In terms of style, the Paneion bovine is most comparable to the head of a bovine from a Roman villa in Gaul, which is thought to have come from a late antique multi-figured mythological statuette. The Gallic piece is dated to the late fourth century AD and is believed to have been carved by an Asiatic sculptor (Stirling 1994: 213–14, no. SGM 14, fig. 39). Like the Gallic bovine, the Paneion example has widely-spaced eyes with thick upper lids and drilled pupils positioned such that the animal looks upward (though the Gallic example has lunate pupils rather than circular ones). While the nostrils and mouth of the Paneion statuette are indicated, they are not heavily-drilled like those of the Gallic example. The two examples are less comparable in terms of posture and therefore in the type of composition from which they come, since the Gallic example turns its head sharply to the right while looking up toward the left. Based on the stylistic similarities between the Paneion bovine and the Gallic example, this piece may be dated to the late fourth century AD. The Paneion bovine is, therefore, one of two sculptures discovered at the sanctuary that may be associated with the genre of late antique mythological statuettes and are therefore probably dated to the late fourth or early fifth centuries AD (see also the torso of an Eros, cat. 22).

Because the statuette may be associated with the genre of late mythological statuettes, it may be attributed to the Asiatic workshops at Aphrodisias, Ephesus, and Constantinople, which are thought to have produced these distinctive sculptures (Stirling 2005: 117–29). Isotopic analyses of the marble also associate the piece with two quarries in Asia Minor.

26 — HINDQUARTERS OF A BOVINE

Exc. no. 78/93/714/8191/2 (figs. 83–86)

Preservation and Material

H. 0.13 m; W. 0.07 m; reconstructed H. not determinable.

White marble; tiny, glittering, closely-packed crystals.

The piece is broken or cut vertically through the torso, just before the back legs. Missing are the top of the back on the right side, lower part of the legs and tail, and feet. There is damage to the tail, joint of the right leg, and left side. There are small areas of dark brown encrustations overall. Traces of red paint remain on the right leg.

Technique

Few tool marks remain. A chisel line separates the tail from the rump. The vertical cut through the torso is leveled to effect a join, and the join surface is angled toward the right. The right side of the animal is fully carved and polished; however, the left side was not completely worked and is covered with point marks.

Description and Reconstruction

This piece preserves the rump, tail, and back legs of a small-scale bovine. The back left leg is positioned slightly in front of the right. The long tail springs from the top of the rear end. As it flows down the posterior of the animal between the legs, the tail widens and curves toward the right (W. 1.0 at top, 3.0 cm at bottom).

The right side of the animal is delicately modeled. The muscles and bones of the joint in the right leg are clearly indicated. The ridge along the center of the back and the point from which the tail springs are also emphasized. In contrast, the left

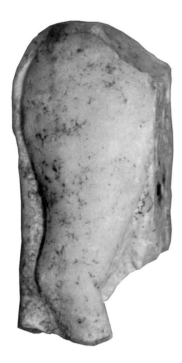

Fig. 83   Cat. 26: Hindquarters of a bovine, right profile.

Fig. 84   Cat. 26: Hindquarters of a bovine, left profile.

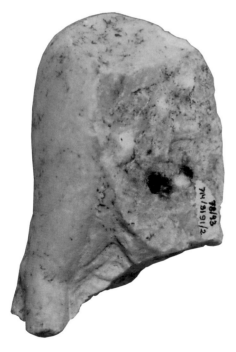

Fig. 85   Cat. 26: Hindquarters of a bovine, three-quarter.

Fig. 86   Cat. 26: Hindquarters of a bovine, back.

side of the animal was never fully carved, but was shaped to show the silhouette of the hind quarters. Because of the unfinished state of the left side and the semi-finished rear and tail, the animal was meant to be seen in right profile view only.

The leveled cut through the animal's torso and the tenon preserved in it suggest that this fragment was meant to be joined to another to complete the representation of a bovine. Although the left side of the figure was never fully carved, because it was at least roughed out, the fragment is more likely to have been part of a three-dimensional statuette rather than a relief. The swish of the tail toward the right side, the position of the left back leg in front of the right, and the angling of the leveled join surface suggest that the animal turned its head and forequarters toward the right.

Identification

Too little of this piece remains to allow discussion of its broader narrative context or comparanda.

However, another fragment of a bovine, which is comparable to this one in scale, stance, degree of finish, and marble type, was discovered at the Paneion (cat. 25). This fragment and the piece discussed here are similar in size, the rightward turn of their bodies, the full carving of their right sides, the unfinished state of their left sides, and the use of piecing. However, the join surfaces of these two pieces do not match. Thus, despite their similarities, the two fragments do not come from the same figure. There were, therefore, at least two statuette-sized sculptural representations of bovines dedicated at the Sanctuary of Pan at Caesarea Philippi, presumably as part of multi-figured votive groups.

Comparanda, Workshop, and Date

Because this piece is so fragmentary, it is impossible to locate comparanda or determine a date or workshop association on the basis of stylistic and technical details.

27 — FRAGMENT OF A MALE HEAD

Exc. no. 78/93/712/7981/1 (fig. 87)

Preservation and Material

H. 0.08 m; W. 0.05 m; reconstructed H. not determinable.

White marble.

The piece preserves the left side of a head, including a portion of the crown, left ear, and back of the head. Dark brown accretions cover the top of the head, and there are small areas of brown encrustation overall.

Technique

Light chisel lines delineate the curls of hair and details of the cartilage surrounding the ear canal. A drill hole marks the center of the ear. The hair is smoothed and may have been polished.

Fig. 87   Cat. 27: Fragment of a male head, left profile.

Description and Reconstruction

This fragment preserves the left side of a head of a small-scale male figure, including the hair and the left ear. Because none of the face or neck is preserved, it is impossible to say anything about the position of the head. The hairstyle consists of many tight curls, shown as small blobs, lying close to the head. The curls are not rendered in detail, and no individual strands of hair are shown. This short hair covers the entire preserved portion of the head, extending down to the middle of the ear both in front and behind.

The ear is rendered simply but with some detail, including the ear canal and the cartilage surrounding it. The small preserved portion of the back of the head is carved with as much detail as the front, indicating that the piece was meant to be seen from all sides. Based on the details of the ear and the finish of the hairstyle, much attention was lavished on this piece.

Identification

Because so little of this piece is preserved, it is impossible to determine what subject it represents; however, Herakles and Hermes (Siebert 1990) are the ideal figures who are most-commonly represented with comparable hairstyles. Certainly, either of these gods would be at home in the Sanctuary of Pan, since there is evidence for sculptural representations of both at the site: Herakles, in a statuette version of the "Weary Herakles" (cat. 21), and Hermes, in an inscription that records the dedication of a statue of this god (Isaac in press: no. 1a).

Comparanda, Workshop, and Date

Because so little of this piece remains, it is impossible to locate comparanda, determine a date, or associate it with a workshop based on stylistic or technical characteristics.

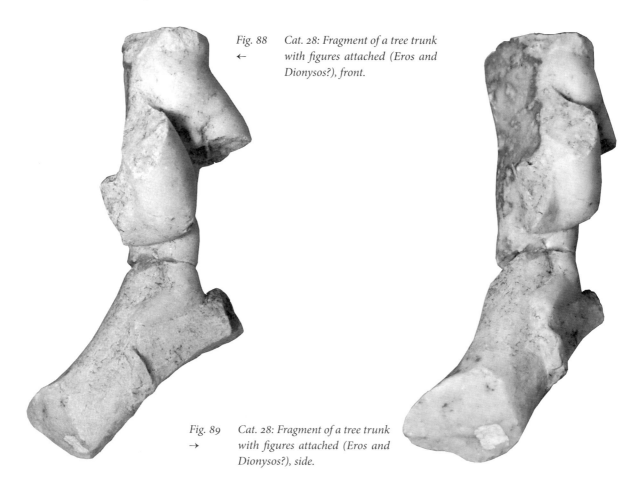

Fig. 88   Cat. 28: Fragment of a tree trunk
←   with figures attached (Eros and
           Dionysos?), front.

Fig. 89   Cat. 28: Fragment of a tree trunk
→   with figures attached (Eros and
           Dionysos?), side.

28 — FRAGMENT OF A TREE TRUNK WITH FIGURES ATTACHED (EROS AND DIONYSOS?)

Exc. nos. 85/92/192/7088/1 (upper portion); 85/92/705/7827/1 (lower portion) (figs. 88–90)

Preservation and Material

H. 0.28 m; L. 0.10 m; W. 0.11 m; reconstructed H. not determinable.

White marble; large, chunky, translucent crystals.

The piece consists of two joining fragments and is broken at the top through the upper torso of the small figure and top of the branch and at the bottom through the tree trunk. The smaller figure is missing its head, shoulders, both arms and hands, left leg, and foot. Only the left elbow and a small part of the arm of the larger figure remain. The lower branch is broken after the fork, and there is damage to the base of the lower branch. Dark brown accretions cover the back and right side.

Technique

Chisel lines delineate the back of the smaller figure's body from the tree branch. Drill channels separate the lower torso of the smaller figure from the upper arm of the larger figure and the thighs of the smaller figure. There are two drill holes on the vertical tree branch: one behind the shoulders of the smaller figure on the left, the other near the lower abdomen of the smaller figure on the right. Chisel work is left along the branches of the trunk. Marks of a toothed scraper are left on the underside of the smaller figure's calf. The front of both figures is polished.

Description and Reconstruction

This fragment belonged to a sculpture that depicted at least two human figures. The preserved portion of the tree trunk forks into two branches above the bottom break. A nude male figure is carved in high relief leaning his right side against the more vertical of these two branches and resting his right foot at the crux of the fork on the more horizontal branch. A fragment of the left elbow and lower arm of a second, larger figure crosses in front and on top of the right knee, thigh, and abdomen of the smaller nude male figure. The lower preserved portion of the tree trunk, including the fork, is carved in three dimensions. However, the right side of the upper, vertical branch, along which the nude male is positioned, was never fully shaped to delineate the right side of the nude figure and the back of the arm of the larger figure from the tree branch.

The small nude male figure twists his upper torso toward the right in the direction of the larger figure. He leans forward over his planted right foot, which bears his weight. Although the shoulders and arms are missing, the area just below the top

Fig. 90   Cat. 28: Fragment of a tree trunk with figures attached (Eros and Dionysos?), back.

break is modeled to show that the figure reached his left arm across his upper chest and out toward the right. It is impossible to determine whether the right arm was depicted and, if so, what gesture it made, because this part of the figure is missing.

From the chest, the front of the torso swells to form a chubby belly, balanced by an arching back. Modeling indicates a fatty roll below the belly, the iliac crest, and the genitalia. At the back, only the rounded left buttock is carved, since the right one melded into the tree branch. The right leg is vaguely modeled to show a chubby thigh, the bend behind the knee, calf muscles, and an ankle. Although the front of the right foot is slightly damaged, it is clear that the toes were never individually delineated. Instead the right foot melds into the tree trunk in a diagonal slope. On the back, only the uppermost portion of the left thigh is preserved beneath the left buttock.

The stance of the smaller figure may be partially reconstructed. The toothed scraper marks visible on the back of the calf indicate that the left thigh was probably pressed tightly against the right one, which would have limited the sculptor's access to the calf. The small portion of the left thigh remaining below the left buttock and the drill channel below the genitalia that separated the thighs indicate that the left leg was positioned behind the right one. This left leg probably rested on an extension of the now-missing horizontal branch on which the right leg rests. Like the right leg, the left one may have borne the weight of the figure. Alternately, it could have rested only the ball of the foot on the branch.

The arm of the second, larger figure crosses in front of the smaller figure at an angle. It is bent at the elbow and positioned so that its upper arm is perpendicular to the axis of the body of the smaller figure. The lower arm extended upward along the line of the smaller figure's torso. The break through the upper arm on the right side of the tree branch indicates that the arm extended forward toward the branch and that the larger figure stood behind the branch.

Because the right side of the vertical tree branch is not completely worked, the piece was probably meant to be seen from the front and right sides only. Not much of the larger figure may be reconstructed, though it seems that its lower arm probably extended upward above the smaller figure's head.

Identification

It is difficult to determine what subjects are represented, because this piece is so fragmentary. As noted above, this statue was a sculptural group that included at least two figures — the smaller nude male figure climbing on the tree trunk and a larger figure who stood slightly behind the tree trunk and reached forward toward it. The smaller figure may be tentatively identified as Eros by his chubby stature, his nudity, and his small scale in relation to the larger figure. The sculptural subject most commonly accompanied by a support shaped like a tree trunk with Erotes climbing in its branches is Dionysos (Augé and De Bellefonds 1986a). If this fragment may be associated with a statue of Dionysos, it would be one of three sculptural representations of the god found at the sanctuary, along with the head of Dionysos (cat. 7) and the fragment of a head wearing a wreath (cat. 8). As well, the smaller figure in this fragment is comparable to the torso of an Eros found at the sanctuary (cat. 22) in its stature and technique.

Comparanda, Workshop, and Date

A Dionysos in the Villa Albani includes a subsidiary Eros whose posture, gesture, and location on the tree trunk are comparable to those of the Eros on the Paneion fragment (*DAIR* Fiche No. 27, F2). Dionysos stands with his weight on his right leg, his left leg crossed over his right, and his left elbow resting on top of a tree trunk, which is wrapped in vines laden with bunches of grapes. At the base of the trunk, a Pan competes with an Eros for a bunch of grapes. Tiny Erotes climb throughout the vines. At the top of the trunk, an Eros stands with his right side against the trunk and reaches across his chest with his right arm to grab a cluster of grapes. His stance is similar to the Eros on the Paneion fragment: his right foot is planted on top of a cluster of grapes, and his left foot extends behind him to rest on another branch. Although Dionysos' left arm is bent similarly to the elbow of the larger figure preserved on the Paneion fragment, it does not cross in front of the torso of the Eros as on our piece.

It is unusual that the elbow of the larger figure on the Paneion fragment comes in such close proximity to the smaller, subsidiary figure. In most free-standing sculptures, the supports rise no higher than the mid-torsos of the main figures and the main figures rest their elbows on top of these supports. Thus, it is rare, on free-standing statuary, to find a bent elbow of the main figure positioned level with or below a subsidiary figure as on the Paneion example. In is not uncommon, however, to find such overlapping figures in two genres of sculpture: table stands and late antique mythological statuettes. Spreading trees with subsidiary figures climbing in their branches are a well-known characteristic of late antique mythological statuettes (Stirling 2005: 104–5).

For example, a late antique statuette of the birth of Adonis from the villa of Montmaurin has, as reconstructed by Stirling, a tiny infant running in its branches (Stirling 2005: 37–39, 40–45, figs. 17, 20). In addition, a table stand on display in the Athens National Museum shows Dionysos framed by a spreading tree (Athens National Museum no. 5706). In the branches of the tree, to the right of the god, a small subsidiary figure of Eros stands level with Dionysos' shoulder and above the god's right hand.

If the Paneion fragment of a tree trunk was associated with a late antique mythological statuette, then the piece would be datable to the late fourth or early fifth centuries AD and would probably have originated in the sculptural workshops of Asia Minor, which are thought to have produced these sculptural groups (Stirling 2005: 117–29).

29 — FRAGMENT OF BASE WITH HUMAN AND ANIMAL FEET (DIONYSOS OR SATYR?)

Exc. no. 78/93/716/8066/1 (two joining fragments) (figs. 91–94)

Preservation and Material

H. 0.09 m; L. 0.23 m; W. 0.18 m; reconstructed H. not determinable.

White marble; medium-sized, glittering crystals. Isotopic analyses associate the marble with several quarries in Asia Minor: Ephesos, Afyon, Aphrodisias, or Miletos.

The piece preserves the right portion of the base, bottom of two human feet, and lower portion of a seated animal including its front left foot. There is damage to the front edge of the base. Dark brown accretions cover the top of the piece and the back edge of the base. The piece is broken and abraded overall. There is a dark red spot on the upper edge of the left human foot.

Technique

The piece is worked largely with a chisel to denote the joints of the toes, the toe-nails, the separations

between toes, the separation of the feet from the base, and the front half of the human foot from the body of the animal. The top of the base is mostly smoothed; however, some tool marks remain.

Description and Reconstruction

This fragment preserves part of the base of a statuette that depicted at least two figures — one human and one animal. All that remains of the statuette is the "footprint" of a left human foot (L. 6.5 cm), the corresponding right human foot (L. 6.5 cm), the lower portion of the body of a seated animal, its front left paw, and, between this paw and the left human foot, an unidentifiable oval-shaped protrusion.

The barefoot human stands on the base, his out-turned feet positioned 4.0 cm apart, his left foot farther forward than his right. The feet are not naturalistically rendered, nor are they subtly modeled. There is no indication of their arches, and the toes are proportionately long (2.0 cm).

An animal sits to the left of the human figure. The front half of its right side is adjacent to the hu-

Fig. 91   Cat. 29: Fragment of a base with human and animal feet (Dionysos or satyr?), front.

Fig. 92   Cat. 29: Fragment of a base with human and animal feet (Dionysos or satyr?), back.

Fig. 93   Cat. 29: Fragment of a base with human and animal feet (Dionysos or satyr?), top.

man. The remaining lower portion of the animal's body is shaped like a rectangle (W. 7.6 cm; L. 9.6 cm) with feet protruding from the front and a nodule indicating the tail at the back. Indentations in the hind of the animal (1.0 cm up from the base) may indicate the animal's haunches; however, no back legs or feet are indicated, although the animal's left side is preserved to a height of 3.0 cm. The preserved portion of the left leg of the creature is broad. The left foot has a paw with four segmented, elongated toes. Each toe has a central ridge. Between the left foot of the animal and the left foot of the human, where the right foot of the animal should be, there is an oval-shaped broken surface (L. 5.0 cm; W. 4.3 cm). This protrusion is too large and not appropriately-shaped to be the remains of the now-missing right foot of the animal; thus, the animal may have rested its right foot on top of a prop.

The finished sides of the base show that it was unevenly-shaped with curved edges. On the front edge of the base, below the left foot of the animal, there is an unidentifiable protrusion (L. 3.0 cm). The piece was probably meant to be viewed from the front and sides only.

Identification

The presence of an animal suggests that this piece represents an ideal figure rather than a portrait, because portraits do not often include animals, while several ideal figures have animals as attributes.

The stance, bare foot, and absence of drapery falling on top of the foot suggest that the figure may be conjecturally identified as Dionysos or a satyr. Since most goddesses (except Aphrodite and Artemis) are clothed in long gowns, the absence of drapery on the foot of this figure makes it likely that this statuette represented a male deity or mythological character. The identity of the animal may be suggested by its broad lower leg, its segmented, elongated toes, and the possibility that it rested its right foot

on top of a prop. The shape of the animal's paw indicates that it was probably a lion, panther, or griffin. Both Dionysos and satyrs are commonly depicted with panthers seated to one side resting their front paws on various props (for example a *kantharos*, a ball, or a rabbit; Pochmarski 1990). Comparable statue types include the Dionysos from Cyrene (Gasparri 1986: 435, Dionysos no. 119a) and the satyr in the Villa Albani in Rome (Bieber 1955: 139, fig. 568).

If this statuette represents a satyr, it would be one of four sculptures found at the sanctuary that have Pan-related subjects (see also cats. 18, 19, and 20). If it represents Dionysos, it would constitute at least a third if not a fourth or fifth representation of this deity from the sanctuary (see also cats. 7, 8, 12, and 28).

Comparanda, Workshop, and Date

Because this piece is so fragmentary, it is difficult to locate comparanda or determine a date or workshop association based on stylistic or technical features. Isotopic analyses of the marble, however, associate it with several quarries in Asia Minor.

Fig. 94 Cat. 29: Fragment of a base with human and animal feet (Dionysos or satyr?), top.

ward and was frequently shown with a cloak fastened atop his left shoulder and encircling his upper chest (Sichtermann 1988). Adonis might be considered a likely identification for the Paneion figure, since he is a Near Eastern god thought to have his origins in Phoenicia and was honored with temples and festivals throughout the Levant, including those at Dura-Europos and Byblos (Servais-Soyez 1981: 222). However, it is unlikely that the Paneion youthful nude god represents Adonis, since he was rarely depicted in three-dimensional statuary during the Roman period but was more commonly shown on sarcophagi and in wall paintings. The Paneion figure probably does not represent a young satyr, since the three standard types, the flute-playing, resting, and wine-pouring satyrs, have postures and gestures that are distinctly different from the Paneion youthful nude god. Furthermore, these satyrs are not usually shown entirely nude, but often wear an animal skin. Finally, the gesture of Paneion figure's right arm is not comparable to that of the Apollo Lykeios or the Dionysos Lykeios, since these types reach straight upward rather than laterally like the Paneion figure.

26   The elongated element is identified as a stylized *loutrophoros* rather than a column for several reasons. The *loutrophoros* covered by drapery is a common attribute accompanying Aphrodite. Although there are several Aphrodite types supported by architectural elements, their supports tend to be squared pillars rather than columns, and these Aphrodites are generally half-draped or fully clothed as opposed to nude. For Aphrodites with square pillars, see the so-called Venus Marina (Delivorrias et al. 1984: Aphrodite no. 554), the "propped" Aphrodite (Delivorrias et al. 1984: Aphrodite no. 572), and variants of the Aphrodite of Agen (Delivorrias et al. 1984: Aphrodite no. 717).

27   The other sculptures from the sanctuary that are based on Hellenistic types are the torso of a nymph (cat. 11), the Artemis Rospigliosi (cat. 15), the Artemis of Ephesos (cat. 16), the torso of a dancing satyr (cat. 20), the "Weary Herakles" (cat. 21), and the base of a statuette of Kybele or Dea Syria (cat. 23).

28   The chiton was not carved with any indication of how the sleeves were fastened. Pins may have been shown in paint.

29   These boots were worn to protect the leg during horseback-riding and are commonly shown on Amazons and the goddess Artemis. For a well-known example, see the Artemis on the Pergamene altar (Morrow 1985: 123–24, 132). For definitions, origins, development during the Greek period, and

adaptation by the Romans, see Morrow 1985: 60–61, 64–66, 82, 87–89, 123–24, 132, 148–50, 178.

30   Morrow 1985: 65.

31   The particular *embas* shown on this figure is one of the plainer types common in the fifth and fourth centuries BC. In addition to the continuation of this type, much more elaborate versions are documented from the Hellenistic period onward. The relatively simple depiction of the *embas* on the Paneion Artemis may be due to the fact that the lower third of the sculpture was not worked in great detail.

32   For examples of the position of the head, see the Cyrene Artemis (Beschi 1959: fig. 83), the Palazzo Rospigliosi Artemis (Beschi 1959: fig. 89), and the Samos Artemis (Grotemeyer and Schmidt 1928: 276, pl. 6).

33   Beschi argues that the running Artemis type was originally created for the Lesser Attalid dedication on the Athenian Acropolis and should therefore be associated with a Gigantomachy (Beschi 1959: 284–97).

34   For a well-preserved example of these gestures, see the Artemis (identified, however, as a Versailles type) found at Saint-George-de-Montagne outside of Bordeaux (Stirling 2005: 30–37, figs. 4–6; Stirling 1996: 108–11, fig. 3; Stirling 1994: 194–97, figs. 17–20; Simon and Bauchhenss 1984b: Artemis/Diana 376; Gazda 1981: 150–55, figs. 35–37, 39–40).

35   For example, see the Cyrene Artemis (Beschi 1959: 255–60, figs. 83–85).

36   See the Cyrene Artemis (Beschi 1959: 255–60, figs. 83–85) and the Samos Artemis (Grotemeyer and Schmidt 1928: 276, pl. 6).

37   Hornum argues that a griffin shown with the spoked wheel should be associated solely with Nemesis (1993: 24–32).

38   Cima and La Rocca 1986: 105–28.

39   While oval-shaped gems are the most common, a variety of differently-shaped gems were found, including rectangular ones (Cima and La Rocca 1986: 120–21).

40   Cima and La Rocca 1986: 121–22.

41   In contrast, the *ependytes* of the Aphrodite of Aphrodisias are only divided into three or four horizontal zones, and those of Jupiter Heliopolitanus are decorated with registers of varying sizes and shapes, which are not laid out regularly over the garment (Fleischer 1973: 170, 348, respectively); the skirts of the Aphrodite of Aphrodisias and Jupiter Heliopolitanus have fields on all sides (Fleischer 1973: 91, 346), and griffins are not featured at all on the *ependytes* of the Aphrodite of Aphrodisias,

whose subjects tend to be restricted to Selene, Helios, Hera, Zeus, the three Graces, Aphrodite, Erotes, and various sea-related creatures such as Tritons and dolphins (Fleischer 1973: 170–75); in only one instance is a griffin recorded by Fleischer on an *ependytes* of a Jupiter Heliopolitanus (Fleischer 1973: 346–57, 350).

42 Fleischer explains the appearance of non-Nemesis-specific griffins and other animals on the *ependytes* of the Artemis of Ephesos as a mixture of Orientalizing creatures and those which were known in Greece from the seventh century BC onward (1973: 98–99).

43 For a famous example, see the syrinx and *lagobolon* hanging on the support accompanying the group of the young satyr holding the infant Dionysos in the Naples National Museum (Pozzi 1989: 156–57, no. 19).

44 Several different types of standing Pan are shown holding syrinxes. These include the Pan from Lappas in the Iraklion Museum, classified by Marquardt as Pan in his guise as leader of the goats (Marquardt 1995: 97–98, pl. 14, 1); the Pan from Cyrene who lifts a syrinx to his mouth with his right hand, classified by Marquardt as a Pan shown alone (Marquardt 1995: 35, pl. 5,1; Paribene 1959: 122, no. 349, pl. 159); and the Pan on the front of the Ostia Attideion, which is classified by Marquardt as a Pan figure used as an architectural support (Marquardt 1995: 105, pl. 15,3). One of the more well-known examples of the seated Pan playing a syrinx is in the Sofia Museum (Marquardt 1995: 91, pl. 13, 3). For a catalogue and discussion of the sculptural type of the seated, syrinx-playing Pan, see Marquardt 1995: 84–96.

45 Because it is uncloaked, the Paneion left hand holding a syrinx (cat. 19) may not be associated with the well-known type of a standing, cloaked Pan holding a syrinx, an example of which is in the Athens National Museum (from Sparta, no. 252).

46 For a Herakles Farnese with the left leg crossed behind the right, see the votive relief from Athens (National Archaeological Museum no. 1456; Boardman et al. 1988: 763, Herakles no. 684; Krull 1985: 293–94, no. 203). Moreno notes this cross-legged stance on the Herakles from the Telephos frieze of the Pergamene Altar, on one of the eponymous heroes on the east frieze of the Parthenon, in Scopas' Pathos, and on several of the main figures on a fourth-century BC Athenian grave stele (Moreno 1982: 466–67, figs. 88–89). He believes that the Telephos frieze Herakles may be seen as a precursor to one of the Herakles Farnese sub-types, the Herakles Farnese-Pitti type (Moreno 1982: 435–62, 465).

47 Palagia classifies examples with this gesture as "The Farnese Herakles: Variant A" (1988: 764).

48 Examples of marble sculptures representing Orpheus charming the animals include a first-century BC piece found in the Tiber at Rome (Garezou 1994: 96, Orpheus no. 162); a table stand (?) from the baths at Lepcis Magna (Garezou 1994: 94, Orpheus no. 143b); a table stand from the Nymphaeum at Byblos in the Beirut National Museum (Garezou 1994: 94, Orpheus no. 143a; Picard 1947: 266–68, fig. 2; Lauffray 1940: 29–30, pl. 5); an acroterion from Aegina in the Byzantine Museum of Athens (Picard 1947: 272–73); and an acroterion from Istanbul in the Istanbul Archaeological Museum (Mendel 1914, 2: 420–23, no. 651).

Appendix 1

Findspots for Sculptural Fragments Discovered in Dumps Associated with the Tripartite Building

General Findspot	Locus #	Piece	Cat. No.
Ashlar dump inside entrance of Tripartite Building			
	702	Artemis Rospigliosi, torso	15
	705	Artemis Rospigliosi, base	15
	705	Head of Athena or Roma	3
	705	Head of Apollo or a Muse	6
	705	Head of Zeus or Asklepios	4
	705	Head of a goddess wearing a *stephane*	5
	705	Fragment of a face of a goddess	9
	705	Torso of a nymph	11
	705	Torso of a youthful nude god	12
	705	Left leg and support of a Capitoline/Medici Aphrodite	13
	705	Torso of a dancing satyr	20
	705	Torso of an Eros	22
	705	Fragment of a base with tree trunk and right foot	17
	712	Crest of an Attic helmet	10
	712	Artemis Rospigliosi, fragments of mantle	15
	712	Fragment of a male head	27
	714	Arm fragment of the Artemis Rospigliosi	15
	714	Fragment of a head wearing a wreath	8
	714	Hindquarters of a bovine	26
	714	Non-joining fragment of base with left foot	17
	192	Head of Athena wearing an Attic helmet	2

General Findspot	Locus #	Piece	Cat. No.
Tripartite Building, ashlar dump outside entrance			
	192	Fragment of the torso of a youthful, nude god	12
	192	Left hand holding a syrinx	19
	192	Fragment of a tree trunk with figures attached (Dionysos ?).	28
	183	Herakles, body	21
	183	Base of a statuette of Kybele or Dea Syria	23
	195	Left leg and support of the Capitoline/Medici Aphrodite, fragments	13
Tripartite Building, ashlar dump in north end of central hall			
	716	Fragmentary head of Dionysos	7
	716	Male head	24
	716	Tree trunk with hanging syrinx	18
	716	Fragment of the *ependytes* of an Artemis of Ephesos	16
	716	Forequarters of a bovine	25
	716	Fragment of base with human and animal feet (Dionysos or satyr ?)	29
	171	Fight shoulder, upper arm, and breast	14

Appendix 2

Findspots for Sculptural Fragments Discovered Throughout the Site

General Findspot	Locus #	Piece	Cat. No.
Tripartite Building, western hall, uppermost layer of excavation	150	Hair fragment	–
Tripartite Building, early Islamic installations against the sides of the deposit inside	156 & 157	Head of Roma or Athena	1
Tripartite Building, early Islamic installations against the sides of the deposit inside	156 & 157	Torso of the nymph, fragment of the drapery	11
Tripartite Building, early Islamic installations against the sides of the deposit inside	156 & 157	Fragments and chips (5)	–
Apsidal Court, Mamluk layers above court	678, 692, 692A, 693	Small fragments (4 marble, 1 limestone)	–
Apsidal Court, above the flight of stairs to the north of the central niche	699	Body fragment	–
Apsidal Court, service area behind niche	689A	Colossal thumb or toe	–
Apsidal Court, late Roman deposit in room behind the apse	750	Unidentifiable fragment	–
Augusteum, southwestern area, above destruction layers of building	439	Fragment of a finger or tree branch	–
Augusteum, just outside the cella atop natural rock	445	Fragment of a finger or toe	–
Court of Pan and the Nymphs, Topmost layer of excavation	300	Unidentifiable marble fragment	–
Temple of Zeus, pronaos, Mamluk layers	228	Fragment of the rim of a marble bowl	–
Temple of Zeus, southeastern corner, Mamluk and early Islamic layers	205	Drapery fragment	–

General Findspot	Locus #	Piece	Cat. No.
Temple of Zeus, northern wall, early Islamic layers	213 & 216	Small unidentifiable fragments (3)	–
Temple of Zeus, early Islamic tomb placed into the center of the northern wall	224	Unidentifiable fragment	–
Temple of Zeus, atop northern area of the eastern wall	218	Chips (3)	–
Temple of Zeus, Mamluk ash layer in central area of the naos	261	Fragment of finger	–
Court of Nemesis, Mamluk layers atop floor in southern area	202	Limb fragment	–

Appendix 3

Small, Non-Restorable Sculptural Fragments Discovered at the Sanctuary of Pan

MARBLE FRAGMENTS

Hands (2 Life-Size Right and Left Hands; 5 Statuette Hands)	7
Fingers	12
Feet	4
Arm and Leg Fragments	13
Body Fragments	7
Hair Fragments	4
Drapery Fragments	22
Tree Trunk Fragments	7
Pine Needle and Cone Bunches	6
Bowls (5 Distinguishable Individual Bowls; 1 Platter)	24
Unknowns	49
Chips	56
TOTAL	211

LIMESTONE FRAGMENTS

Unknown	6

Fig. 95   Portrait bust of Antinous, AD 130–138, marble, said to have been found at Caesarea Philippi/Panias. European Private Collection. Original photograph courtesy of Sotheby's, Inc. © 2010.

Appendix 4

Bust of Antinous from Caesarea Philippi / Panias

In the mid-1800s, M. Pérétié, then the chancellor of the French consulate in Beirut, amassed a collection of antiquities from all parts of Syria, which included bronzes, terracottas, jewelry, precious stones, metals, and other items. Among the objects in his collection was an over-life-size bust of Antinous bearing an inscription on its pedestal, which he reportedly discovered at Caesarea Philippi. Although the inscription was published in 1879 by M. Beaudouin and E. Pottier in a *Bulletin de Correspondence Hellénique* article on the inscriptions from Pérétié's collection, the bust itself does not seem to have been published until 1906, after it had passed into the Collection De Clercq and was catalogued by A. de Ridder in his *Collection De Clercq IV: Les Marbres, Les Vases Peints et Les Ivoires*. In 1983, the piece appeared on the art market via a dealer in Würzburg, Germany. In 1991, the bust was re-published by H. Meyer in his monograph on Antinous types (Meyer 1991: 99–100, pls. 88, 4–5 and 89); subsequently, the piece has been published by C. Vout (2005; 2007; Vout and Curtis 2006). The bust recently entered the art market again and was sold by Sotheby's as part of its auction of the collection of the late Clarence Day; it sold on December 7, 2010, to a private collector for US\$23,826,500.

The following brief catalogue entry is largely a summary of Meyer's analysis of the piece with some additions of my own. Since I have not seen the piece myself, I do not include any description or reconstruction here.

BUST OF ANTINOUS (fig. 95)

FINDSPOT: "Panias" (Beaudouin and Pottier 1879: 259; see below under "Identification").

SCALE: Over life-size.

HEIGHT: 1.08 m; face: 0.30 m; from chin to breast stand: 0.67 m; foot to break: 0.11 m.

WIDTH: 0.78 m (De Ridder 1906: 39).

MATERIAL: white, large-crystalled, glittering marble, yellowish patina.

Technique

The hair of the locks is subdivided into thick locks partly by drill channels with some wide, empty spaces left between locks. The eyebrows are sketched in. The pupils are undrilled and there is no indication of tear ducts. The lower lip is polished. The edge of the bust from shoulder to shoulder curves outward.

Condition

The foot and greater part of the inscription plaque were once broken away from the bust, but have been restored and are held in place with thick binder. There is some damage to the two join areas. Missing are the nose, upper lip, large locks on both the right and left ears, and two locks on the right temple. There are occasional nicks throughout the hair.

Inscription

"To the hero Antinous/M. Loukkios Phlakkos" (Isaac in press: 20, no. 25)

Identification

Meyer classifies this bust as one of a group of Antinous portraits closely indebted to the principal type. He notes that it is the only portrait of Antinous outside of coin portraits that is identified by an inscription. It is one of only two portraits of the heroized youth found in the Near East; the other Antinous portrait, which was discovered in the early 1900s at Caesarea Maritima but is now lost, preserved only a battered head.

It should be noted here that a debate concerning the original findspot of the piece has developed in the scholarship, such that Vout in her multiple publications of the piece refers to it as "assumed to have been discovered in Syria" (Vout 2005: 85) or "discovered in Syria" (Vout and Curtis 2006: 29; 2010: 77, fig. 23), but is not more specific. Although the earliest publication of the piece states that it was found at "Panias," some scholars argue that this piece could have been discovered at the "Baniyas" in Syria, north of Tartus, which was known as Balanea and Claudia Leucas (after the emperor Claudius) in Roman times. The confusion arises in part due to the modern Arabic names of the two sites in question: ancient Caesarea Philippi/Panias is named Banias in an Arabized version of Panias, while Balanea/Claudia Leucas is named Baniyas after the nearby river, Nahr Baniyas. Especially because the northern Syrian Baniyas or Balanea was not associated with the Greek god Pan and so was not referred to in ancient or modern times as Panias, it seems that Pottier and Beaudouin meant to refer to Caesarea Philippi when they cited the findspot as "Panias." Therefore, until further research can be done on the Perétié collection to determine whether we can establish a better provenience for the bust of Antinous, I follow the earliest reported findspot of "Panias" and associate the piece with Caesarea Philippi/Panias.

Although no specific findspot within Caesarea Philippi/Panias is known for this bust, Meyer argues that because of the inscription, the piece must have been intended for a public building or some local communal place rather than a private context (Meyer 1991: 99). Two further points may be made in support of this argument. First, the over-life-size scale makes the piece more likely to have been a public dedication. Second, Pérétié is more likely to have discovered this sculpture around the rock scarp of the sanctuary terrace than anywhere else in the city or its territory, since this was the only feature of ancient Caesarea Philippi exposed and identifiable at this time.

Comparanda, Workshop and Dating

Although Meyer does not assign this bust to any particular workshop, he compares it to a bust of Pertinax from Antioch-on-the-Orontes (Inan and Alföldi-Rosenbaum 1979: 112–13, no. 62, pls. 55, 67, 1; Brinkerhoff 1970: 7–13, figs. 3–4). Both have a similar technical peculiarity: their edges are curved from shoulder to shoulder as was more common on bronze busts.

This bust is dated sometime between the years AD 130 and 138, which coincide, respectively, with the death and symbolic resurrection of Antinous and the end of the reign of Hadrian, since this period is known to have been the era during which the majority of Antinous portraits were carved (Lambert 1984: 209).

Select Bibliography

Vout 2005: 85, pl. II, 1–2; Vout 2007: 77, fig. 23; Vout and Curtis 2006: 20, fig. 5; Meyer 1991: 99–100, pls. 88, 4–5 and 89, no. I 77; von Heintze 1971: 397; Clairmont 1966: 41, no. 9; De Ridder 1906: 39–40, pls. 15–17, no. 35; Beaudouin and Pottier 1897: 259.

Bibliography

Al-Bashaireh, K.
2003 Geological and Geochemical Study of Building Materials at Ancient Gadara (Um Qais), NW Jordan. M.A. thesis, Yarmouk University, Irbid.
2011 Provenance of Marbles from the Octagonal Building at Gadara "Umm-Qais," Northern Jordan. *Journal of Cultural Heritage* 12: 317–22.

Albertson, F. C.
1988 A Portrait of Marcus Aurelius from Syro-Palestine. *Damaszener Mitteilungen* 3: 1–9.
2004 The Creation and Dissemination of Roman Imperial Portrait Types: The Case for Marcus Aurelius Type IV. *Jahrbuch des Deutschen Archäologischen Instituts* 119: 259–306.

Aliquot, J.
2008a *Inscriptions grecques et latines de la Syrie 11: Mont Hermon (Liban et Syrie)*. Bibliothèque archéologique et historique 183. Beyrouth: Institut français du Proche-Orient.
2008b Sanctuaries and Villages on Mt Hermon during the Roman Period. Pp. 73–96 in *The Variety of Local Religious Life in the Near East in the Hellenistic and Roman Periods*, Religions in the Graeco-Roman World 164, ed. T. Kaizer. Leiden: Brill.

Alroth, B.
1989 *Greek Gods and Figurines: Aspects of the Anthropomorphic Dedications*. Uppsala Studies in Ancient Mediterranean and Near Eastern Civilizations 18. Uppsala: Acta Universitatis Upsaliensis.

Asgari, N.
1978 The Roman and Early Byzantine Marble Quarries of Proconnesus. Pp. 467–80 in *Proceedings of the Xth International Congress of Classical Archaeology* 1, ed. E. Akurgal. Ankara: Türk Tarih Kurumu.

Ashmole, B.
1929 *A Catalogue of the Ancient Marbles at Ince Blundell Hall*. Oxford: Clarendon.

Attanasio, D.; Armiento, G.; Brilli, M.; Emanuele, M. C.; Platania, R.; and Turi, B.
2002 Multimethod Provenance Determination: Isotopic, ESR and Petrographic Discrimination of Fine-Grained White Marbles. Pp. 141–48 in *Interdisciplinary Studies on Ancient Stone – ASMOSIA VI, Proceedings of the Sixth International Conference of the Association for the Study of Marble and Other Stones in Antiquity, Venice, June 15–18, 2000*, ed. L. Lazzarini. Padova: Bottega d'Erasmo.

Attanasio, D.; Brilli, M.; and Ogle, N.
2006 *The Isotopic Signature of Classical Marbles*. Rome: L'Erma di Bretschneider.

Augé, C., and De Bellefonds, P. L.
1986a Dionysos (In Peripheria Orientali). *LIMC 3*: 514–31.
1986b Eros. *LIMC 3*: 850–952.

Aurenhammer, M.
1990 *Die Skulpturen von Ephesos, Bildwerke aus Stein: Idealplastik 1*. Forschungen in Ephesos 10.1. Vienna: Österreichische Akademie der Wissenschaften.

Avida, U.
1978 *Aphrodite: A Greek Goddess*. The Israel Museum, Jerusalem Catalogue 184. Jerusalem: Israel Museum.

Avi-Yonah, M.
1962 Scythopolis. *Israel Exploration Journal* 12: 123–34.
1966 *The Holy Land From the Persian to the Arab Conquests (536 BC to AD 640): A Historical Geography*. Grand Rapids, MI: Baker Book House.

Balestrazzi, E. Di Filippo
1997　Roma. *LIMC 8*: 1048–68.

Bartman, E.
1992　*Ancient Sculptural Copies in Miniature*. Leiden: Brill.
1996　The Praxitelean Afterlife in Roman Ideal Sculpture (Abstract). *American Journal of Archaeology* 100: 389.

Bass, G. F.
1966　*Archaeology Under Water*. New York: Thames and Hudson.

Beaudouin, M., and Pottier, E.
1879　Collection de M. Péretié: Inscriptions. *Bulletin de Correspondance Hellénique* 3: 257–71.

Becker, L., and Kondoleon, C. (eds.)
2005　*The Arts of Antioch: Art Historical and Scientific Approaches to Roman Mosaics and a Catalogue of the Worcester Art Museum Antioch Collection*. Worcester, MA: Worcester Art Museum.

Belayche, N.
2001　*Iudaea-Palaestina: The Pagan Cults in Roman Palestine (Second to Fourth Century)*. Tübingen: Mohr Siebeck.

Berlin, A. M.
1999　The Archaeology of Ritual: The Sanctuary of Pan at Banias/Caesarea Philippi. *Bulletin of the American Schools of Oriental Research* 315: 27–45.
2003　Banias Is Still the Best Candidate. *Biblical Archaeology Review* 29.5: 22–24.

Bernett, M.
2007a　*Der Kaiserkult in Judäa unter den Herodiern und Römern: Untersuchungen zur politischen und religiösen Geschichte Judäas von 30 v. bis 66 n. Chr*. Tübingen: Mohr Siebeck.
2007b　Roman Imperial Cult in the Galilee: Structures, Functions, and Dynamics. Pp. 337–56 in *Religion, Ethnicity and Identity in Ancient Galilee: A Region in Transition*, eds. J. Zangenberg, H. W. Attridge, D. B. Martin. Tübingen: Mohr Siebeck.

Beschi, L.
1959　Nuove Repliche dell'Artemide Tipo Rospigliosi. Pp. 256–97 in *Sculture Greche e Romane di Cirene*, ed. C. Anti. Padova: Cedam.

Bieber, M.
1915　*Die Antiken Skulpturen und Bronzen des Königlichen Museum Fridericianum in Cassel*. Marburg: Elwert.
1955　*The Sculpture of the Hellenistic Age*. New York: Columbia University.

Blanc, N., and Gury, F.
1986　Amor, Cupido. *LIMC 3*: 952–1049.

Boardman, J.; Brize, P.; Felten, W.; Kokkorou-Alewaras, G.; Laurens, A.-F.; Palagia, O.; Smallwood, V.; Todisco, L.; and Woodford, S.
1990　Herakles. *LIMC 5*: 1–192.

Boardman, J.; Palagia, O.; and Woodford, S.
1988　Herakles. *LIMC 4*: 728–838.

Bol, P. C.; Hoffmann, A.; and Weber, T.
1990　Gadara in der Dekapolis: Deutsche Ausgrabungen bei Umm Qais in Nordjordanien 1986 bis 1988. *Archäologischer Anzeiger*: 193–266.

Borgeaud, P.
1988　*The Cult of Pan in Ancient Greece*. Chicago: University of Chicago.

Bowder, D.
1978　*The Age of Constantine and Julian*. New York: Barnes and Noble.

Bowersock, G. W.
1978　*Julian the Apostate*. Cambridge, MA: Harvard University.
1983　The Arabian Ares. Pp. 43–47 in *Tria Cordia: Scritti in onore di Arnaldo Momigliano*, ed. E. Gabba. Como: Edizioni New Press.
1990　*Hellenism in Late Antiquity*. Ann Arbor, MI: University of Michigan.

Braemer, F.
1990　Les relations commerciales et culturelles de Carthage avec l'orient romain à partir de documents sculptés. Pp. 175–98 in *Carthage et son territoire dans l'antiquité. Histoire et archéologie de l'Afrique du Nord. Tome I. Actes du IVe colloque international sur l'histoire et l'archéologie de l'Afrique du Nord: réuni dans le cadre du 113e Congrès national des sociétés savantes, Strasbourg, 5–9 avril 1988*. Paris: Editions du CTHS.

Bravi, A.
2011 Le immagini negli spazi pubblici di Perge in epoca adrianea. Pp. 302–18 in *Roman Sculpture in Asia Minor. Proceedings of the International Conference to celebrate the 50th Anniversary of the Italian Excavations at Hierapolis in Phrygia, held on May 24–26, 2007, in Cavallino (Lecce)*, Journal of Roman Archaeology Suppl. 80, ed. F. D'Andria and I. Romeo. Portsmouth, RI: Journal of Roman Archaeology.

Brinkerhoff, D. M.
1970 *A Collection of Sculpture in Classical and Early Christian Antioch*. New York: New York University.
1978 *Hellenistic Statues of Aphrodite: Studies in the History of their Stylistic Development*. New York: Garland.

Brinkmann, V., and Wünsche, R.
2007 *Gods in Color: Painted Sculpture of Classical Antiquity: Exhibition at the Arthur M. Sackler Museum, Harvard University Art Museums, in cooperation with Staatliche Antikensammlungen and Glyptothek Munich, Stiftung Archäologie Munich, September 22, 2007-January 20, 2008*. Munich: Stiftung Archäologie/Glyptothek.

Brize, P.
1990 Herakles: L. Herakles and Geryon (Labor X). *LIMC 5*: 73–85.

Bru, H.
2008 Némésis et le culte impérial dans les provinces syriennes. *Syria* 85: 293–314.

Budde, L., and Nicholls, R.
1964 *A Catalogue of the Greek and Roman Sculpture in the Fitzwilliam Museum, Cambridge*. Cambridge: Fitzwilliam Museum.

Burrell, B.
2006 False Fronts: Separating the Aedicular Facade from the Imperial Cult in Roman Asia Minor. *American Journal of Archaeology* 110: 437–69.

Burton, J. H.
2010 Religion, Society, and Sacred Space at Banias: A Religious History of Banias/Caesarea Philippi, 21 BC–AD 1635. Ph.D. dissertation, Texas Tech University.

Büsing, A., and Büsing, H.
1991 Ein neuer Paniskos vom Typus des 'Schwänzchenhaschenden Satyr.' Pp. 31–39 in *Stips Votiva: Papers Presented to C. M. Stibbe*, ed. M. Gnade. Amsterdam: Allard Pierson Museum, University of Amsterdam.

Cabrol, F., and Leclercq, H.
1925 Hémorroïsse. Cols. 2200–2209 in *Dictionnaire d'Archéologie Chrétienne et de Liturgie* 6, 2. Paris: Letouzey et Ané.

Cima, M., and La Rocca, E. (eds.)
1986 *Le Tranquille Dimore degli Dei: La Residenza Imperiale degli Horti Lamiani*. Venice: Marsilio.

Çimak, F. (ed.)
2000 *Antioch Mosaics*. Istanbul: Turizm Yayınları.

Clairmont, C. W.
1966 *Die Bildnisse des Antinous: Ein Beitrag zur Porträtplastik unter Kaiser Hadrian*. Rome: Schweizerisches Institut.

Claridge, A.
1988 Roman Statuary and the Supply of Statuary Marble. Pp. 139–52 in *Ancient Marble Quarrying and Trade*, British Archaeological Reports, International Series 453, ed. J. C. Fant. Oxford: B.A.R.
1990 Ancient Techniques of Making Joins in Marble Statuary. Pp. 135–62 in *Marble: Art Historical and Scientific Perspectives on Ancient Sculpture*. Malibu: J. Paul Getty Museum.

Clerc, G., and Leclant, J.
1994 Sarapis. *LIMC* 7: 666–92.

Coleman, M., and Walker, S.
1979 Stable Isotope Identification of Greek and Turkish Marbles. *Archaeometry* 21: 107–12.

Colledge, M. A. R.
1976 *The Art of Palmyra*. London: Thames and Hudson.

Craig, H., and Craig, V.
1972 Greek Marbles: Determination of Provenance by Isotopic Analysis. *Science* 176: 401–3.

Crowfoot, J. W.; Crowfoot, G. M.; and Kenyon, K. M.
1957 *The Objects from Samaria*. Samaria-Sebaste 3. London: Palestine Exploration Fund.

Dar, S.
1991   A Relief of Aphrodite from Paneas, Israel. *Journal of the British Archaeological Association* 144: 116–18.
1993   *Settlements and Cult Sites on Mount Hermon, Israel: Ituraean Culture in the Hellenistic and Roman Periods.* Oxford: Tempus Reparatum.

Davaris, D.
n.d.   *Kos Museum Exhibits List.* N.p.

De Grazia, C. E.
1973   Excavations of the American School of Classical Studies at Corinth: The Roman Portrait Sculpture. Ph.D. dissertation, Columbia University.

Delivorrias, A.; Berger-Doer, G.;
and Kossatz-Deissmann, A.
1984   Aphrodite. *LIMC* 2: 2–151.

Dentzer, J. M.
1991   Le sanctuaire de Sî. Hellénisation et cultures indigènes dans la Syrie intérieure. L'exemple du sanctuaire de Sî. Pp. 269–77 in *Ho Hellenismos Sten Anatole: Praktike a Diethnous Archaiologikon Synedrion, Delphi 6–9 (Nov. 1986).* Athens: Europaiko politistiko Kentro Delphon.

De Ridder, A.
1906   *Collection de Clercq Catalogue 4: Les Marbres, Les Vases Peints et Les Ivoires.* Paris: Leroux.

Despinis, G.; Stefanidou Tiveriou, Th.; and Voutiras, E.
1997   *Catalogue of Sculpture in the Archaeological Museum of Thessaloniki* I. Athens: National Bank Cultural Foundation.

Deubner, O.
1934   *Hellenistische Apollogestalten.* Athens: Hestia.

Dodge, H.
1988   Palmyra and the Roman Marble Trade: Evidence from the Baths of Diocletian. *Levant* 20: 215–30.
1991   Ancient Marble Studies: Recent Research. *Journal of Roman Archaeology* 4: 28–50.

Dodge, H., and Ward-Perkins, B. (eds.)
1992   *Marble in Antiquity: Collected Papers of J. B. Ward-Perkins.* Archaeological Monographs of the British School at Rome 6. London: British School at Rome.

Downey, S. B.
1969   *The Excavations at Dura-Europos 3, Part 1, Fasc. 1. The Heracles Sculpture.* New Haven: Yale University.
2008   The Role of Sculpture in Worship at the Temples of Dura Europos. Pp. 413–35 in *The Sculptural Environment of the Roman Near East: Reflections on Culture, Ideology, and Power.* Interdisciplinary Studies in Ancient Culture and Religion 9, eds. Y. Z. Eliav, E. A. Friedland, and S. Herbert. Leuven: Peeters.

Dresken-Weiland, J.
1991   *Reliefierte Tischplatten aus theodosianischer Zeit.* Studi di antichità cristiana 44. Vatican City: Pontificio Istituto di archeologia cristiana.

Drijvers, H. J. W.
1978   *De Matre Inter Leones Sedente*: Iconography and Character of the Arab Goddess Allât. Pp. 331–51 in *Hommages à Maarten J. Vermaseren, Études préliminaires aux religions orientales dans l'Empire romain,* 3 vols., eds. M. B. de Boer and T. A. Edridge. New York: Brill.
1986   Dea Syria. *LIMC* 3: 355–58.
1995   Inscriptions from Allât's Sanctuary. *ARAM* 7: 109–19.

Dumser, E.A.
2006   The *Aeternae Memoriae* Coinage of Maxentius: An Issue of Symbolic Intent. Pp. 106–18 in *Imaging Ancient Rome: Documentation—Visualization—Imagination,* Journal of Roman Archaeology Suppl. 61, eds. L. Haselberger and J. Humphrey. Portsmouth, RI: Journal of Roman Archaeology.

Dussaud, R.
1936   Cultes cananéens aux sources du Jourdain. D'après les textes de Ras Shamra'. *Syria* 17: 283–95.

Eğilmez, E. T.
1980   Darstellungen der Artemis als Jägerin aus Kleinasien. Ph.D. dissertation, Johannes Gutenberg-Universität, Mainz.

Eichler, F.
1961   Die österreichischen Ausgrabungen in Ephesos im Jahre 1960. *Anzeiger der Österreichischen Akademie der Wissenschaften, Wien, Philologisch-historische Klasse* 9: 65–75.

El Fakharani, F.
1975   Das Theater von Amman in Jordanien. *Archäo-logischer Anzeiger* 90: 377–403.

Elsner, J.
1998   *Imperial Roman and Christian Triumph: The Art of the Roman Empire AD 100-450.* New York: Oxford University.
2000   Between Mimesis and Divine Power: Visuality in the Greco-Roman World. Pp. 45–69 in *Visuality Before and Beyond the Renaissance: Seeing as Others Saw,* ed. R. S. Nelson. New York: Cambridge University.

Erdemgil, S.
1989   *Ephesus Museum Catalogue.* Istanbul: Hitit Color.

Erim, K. T.
1967   Aphrodisias: Results of the 1967 Campaign. *Türk Arkeoloji Dergisi* 16,1: 67–79.
1974   The Satyr and Young Dionysus Group from Aphrodisias. Pp. 767–75 in *Mansel'e Armağan (Mélanges Mansel).* Ankara: Türk Tarih Kurumu.

Erim, K. T., and Roueché, C. M.
1982   Sculptors from Aphrodisias: Some New Inscriptions. *Papers of the British School at Rome* 50: 102–15.

Erlich, A.
2009   The Image of Kybele in the Land of Israel in the Hellenistic Period. Pp. 22–34 and 281* in *Eretz-Israel 29, Ephraim Stern Book* (in Hebrew with English abstract).

Estienne, S.
2010   *Simulacra deorum* versus *ornamenta aedium*: The Status of Divine Images in the Temples of Rome. Pp. 257–71 in *Divine Images and Human Imaginations in Ancient Greece and Rome,* ed. J. Mylonopoulos. Leiden: Brill.

Faedo, L.
1994   Mousa, Mousai. *LIMC 7*: 991–1013.

Felletti Maj, B. M.
1951   'Afrodite Pudica:' Saggio d'Arte Ellenistica. *Archeologia classica* 3: 33–65.

Filges, A.
1999   Marmorstatuetten aus Kleinasien. Zur Ikonographie, Funktion und Produktion antoninischer, serverischer und späterer Idealplastik. *Istanbuler Mitteilungen* 49: 377–430.

Fine, S.
2005   *Art and Judaism in the Greco-Roman World: Toward a New Jewish Archaeology.* New York: Cambridge University.

Fischer, M. L.
1988   Marble Imports and Local Stone in the Architectural Decoration of Roman Palestine: Marble Trade, Techniques and Artistical Taste. Pp. 161–70 in *Classical Marble: Geochemistry, Technology, Trade,* eds. N. Herz and M. Waelkens. Boston: Kluwer.
1991   Figured Capitals in Roman Palestine, Marble Imports and Local Stones: Some Aspects of 'Imperial' and 'Provincial' Art. *Archäologischer Anzeiger*: 119–44.
1994   Historical and Philological Observations on *Marmorarii* in Byzantine Palestine in the Light of two Greek Inscriptions. *Mediterranean Language Review* 8: 20–38.
1998   *Marble Studies: Roman Palestine and the Marble Trade.* Xenia 40. Konstanz: Universitätsverlag Konstanz.
2002   Marble Studies in Israel since Lucca 1988: A Balance as the Millennium Turns. Pp. 317–24 in *ASMOSIA 6. Interdisciplinary Studies on Ancient Stone. Proceedings of the Sixth International Conference of the Association for the Study of Marble and Other Stones in Antiquity, Venice, June 15–18, 2000,* ed. L. Lazzarini. Padova: Bottega d'Erasmo.
2009a   Marble from Pentelicon, Paros, Thasos and Proconnesus in Ancient Israel: An Attempt at a Chronological Distinction. Pp. 399–412 in *ASMOSIA 7. Proc. 7th Conf. 2003 (Thasos).* Bulletin de Correspondance Hellénique, Suppl. 51, ed. Y. Maniatis. Paris: Thorin et fils.
2009b   Sculpture in Roman Palestine: Import and Local Production, An Overview. Pp. 401–15 in *Les ateliers de sculpture régionaux: techniques, styles et iconographie. Actes du Xe Colloque international sur l'art provincial romain, Arles et Aix-en-Provence, 21–23 mai 2007,* ed. V. Gaggadis-Robin, A. Hermary, M. Reddé, and C. Sintes. Aix-en-Provence: Centre Camille-Jullian.

Fischer, M. L., and Grossmark, T.
1996   Marble Import and *Marmorarii* in Eretz Israel during the Roman and Byzantine Periods. Pp. 319–52 in *Classical Studies in Honor of David*

Sohlberg, ed. R. Katzoff. Ramat Gan: Bar-Ilan University.

Fischer, M. L.; Magaritz, M.; and Pearl, Z.
1992   Isotopic and Artistic Analysis of Corinthian Marble Capitals from Caesarea: A Case Study. Pp. 214–21 in *Caesarea Papers: Staton's Tower, Herod's Harbour, and Roman and Byzantine Caesarea*, Journal of Roman Archaeology Suppl. 5, ed. R. L. Vann. Ann Arbor, MI: Journal of Roman Archaeology.

Fischer, M. L., and Pearl, Z.
1998   Excursus III: Provenance of Marble Imported to Roman Palestine: A Geochemical, Petrographic and Artistic Analysis. Pp. 247–62 in *Marble Studies: Roman Palestine and the Marble Trade*, Xenia 40, ed. M. L. Fischer. Konstanz: Universitätsverlag Konstanz.

Fischer, M. L., and Stein, A.
1994   Josephus on the Use of Marble in Building Projects of Herod the Great. *Journal of Jewish Studies* 45: 79–85.

Fisher, C. S.
1938   Buildings of the Christian Period: I – The Baths of Placcus. Pp. 265–69 in *Gerasa: City of the Decapolis*, ed. C H. Kraeling. New Haven: Yale University.

Fleischer, R.
1971   Artemisstatuette aus dem Hanghaus II in Ephesos. *Jahreshefte des Österreichischen Archäologischen Instituts in Wien* 49, Beih. 2: 172–88.
1972–75   Skulpturenfunde. Pp. 420–67 in *Grabungen in Ephesos von 1960 – 1969 bzw. 1970.* Jahreshefte des Österreichischen Archäologischen Instituts in Wien, Beiblatt 50: 225–558.
1973   *Artemis von Ephesos und Verwandte Kultstatuen aus Anatolien und Syrien.* Leiden: Brill.
1984   Artemis Ephesia. *LIMC 2*: 755–63.

Foerster, G.
1997   Review of *"Peopled" Scrolls in Roman Architectural Decoration in Israel*, by A. Ovadiah and Y. Turnheim. *Journal of Roman Archaeology* 10: 557–60.

Foss, C.
1977   Archaeology and the "Twenty Cities" of Byzantine Asia. *American Journal of Archaeology* 81: 469–86.

Fraser, P. M.
1972   *Ptolemaic Alexandria* 1–3. Oxford: Clarendon.

Friedland, E. A.
1997   Roman Marble Sculptures from the Levant: The Group from the Sanctuary of Pan at Caesarea Philippi (Panias). Ph.D. dissertation, University of Michigan.
1999   Graeco-Roman Sculpture in the Levant: The Marbles from the Sanctuary of Pan at Caesarea Philippi (Banias). Pp. 7–22 in *The Roman and Byzantine Near East: Some Recent Archaeological Research*, Vol. 2. Journal of Roman Archaeology Suppl. 31, ed. J. H. Humphrey. Portsmouth, RI: Journal of Roman Archaeology.
2003   The Roman Marble Sculptures from the North Hall of the East Baths at Gerasa. *American Journal of Archaeology* 107: 413–48.
2008   Visualizing Deities in the Roman Near East: Aspects of Athena and Athena-Allat. Pp. 315–50 in *The Sculptural Environment of the Roman Near East*, eds. Y. Z. Eliav, E. A. Friedland, and S. Herbert. Leuven: Peeters.
in press   Marble Sculpture in the Roman Near East: Remarks on Import, Production, and Impact. Pp. 55–73 in *Ateliers and Artisans in Roman Art and Archaeology*, eds. T. M. Kristensen and B. Poulson, Journal of Roman Archaeology Suppl. Portsmouth, RI: Journal of Roman Archaeology.

Friedland, E. A., and Tykot, R. H.
2010   The Quarry Origins of Nine Roman Marble Sculptures from Amman/Philadelphia and Gadara. *Annual of the Department of Antiquities of Jordan* 54: 177–87.
2012   Quarry Origins, Commission, and Import of the Marble Sculptures from the Roman Theater in Philadelphia/Amman, Jordan. Pp. 52–60 in *Interdisciplinary Studies in Ancient Stone: Proceedings of the IX Association for the Study of Marble and Other Stones in Antiquity (ASMOSIA) Conference (Tarragona, 2009).* Tarragona: Institut Catala d'Arqueologia Classica (ICAC).

Frova, A.
1966   *Scavi di Caesarea Maritima.* Rome: L'Erma di Bretschneider.

Fuchs, M.
1987   *Untersuchungen zur Ausstattung römischer Theater in Italien und den Westprovinzen des Imperium Romanum.* Mainz: von Zabern.

1992 *Römische Idealplastik*. Glyptothek München Katalog der Skulpturen 6. Munich: Beck.

Fullerton, M. D.
1990 *The Archaistic Style in Roman Statuary*. Mnemosyne Suppl. 110. Leiden: Brill.

Garezou, M.-X.
1994 Orpheus. *LIMC 7*: 81–105.

Gasparri, C.
1986 Dionysus. *LIMC 3*: 414–514.

Gawlikowski, M.
1977 Le Temple d'Allat à Palmyre. *Revue Archéologique*: 253–74.
1983 Le sanctuaire d'Allat à Palmyre: Aperçu préliminaire. *Annales Archéologiques Arabes Syriennes* 33: 188–89.
1989 Les temples dans la Syrie à l'époque hellénistique et romaine. Pp. 323–46 in *Archéologie et histoire de la Syrie*, 2. *La Syrie de l'époque achéménide à l'avènement de l'Islam*, eds. J.-M. Dentzer and W. Orthmann. Saarbrücken: Saarbrücker Druckerei und Verlag.
1996 The Athena of Palmyra. *Archeologia Warszawa* 47: 21–32.
1998 Les sanctuaires du Proche-Orient romain dans la recherche récente. *Topoi* 8: 31–52.
2008 The Statues of the Sanctuary of Allat in Palmyra. Pp. 397–411 in *The Sculptural Environment of the Roman Near East*, eds. Y. Z. Eliav, E. A. Friedland, and S. Herbert. Leuven: Peeters.

Gazda, E. K.
1981 A Marble Group of Ganymede and the Eagle from the Age of Augustine. Pp. 125–78 in *Excavations at Carthage 1977: Conducted by the University of Michigan* 6, ed. J. H. Humphrey. Ann Arbor, MI: Kelsey Museum, University of Michigan.
1986 Review of *Syrische Grabreliefs Hellenistischer und Römischer Zeit: Fundgruppen und Probleme*, by K. Parlasca, and *Funerary Portraiture of Roman Palestine: An Analysis of the Production in Its Culture-Historical Context*, by I. Skupinska-Løvset. *American Journal of Archaeology* 90: 138–40.

Geiger, J.
2008 *The First Hall of Fame: A Study of the Statues in the Forum Augustum*. Leiden: Brill.

Gendelman, P., and Gersht, R.
2010 Crafts and Craftsmen in Roman and Byzantine Caesarea. *Michmanim* 22: 27–48 (Hebrew with English abstract).

Gercke, P.
1968 Satyrn des Praxiteles. Ph.D. dissertation, Hamburg.

Gergel, R. A.
1991 The Tel Shalem Hadrian Reconsidered. *American Journal of Archaeology* 95: 231–51.

Germann, K.; Holzmann, G.; and Winkler, F. J.
1980 Determination of Marble Provenance: Limits of Isotopic Analysis. *Archaeometry* 22: 99–106.

Gersht, R.
1984 The Tyche of Caesarea Maritima. *Palestine Exploration Quarterly* 116: 110–14.
1987 The Sculpture of Caesarea Maritima. Ph.D. dissertation, Tel Aviv University (Hebrew with English abstract).
1991 Dionysiac Sarcophagi from Caesarea Maritima. *Israel Exploration Journal* 41: 145–56.
1995a The Importation of Sculpture to Caesarea. Pp. 34–38 in *Caesarea: A Mercantile City by the Sea*, Ruben and Edith Hecht Museum, University of Haifa, Catalogue 12, ed. O. Rimon. Haifa: Haifa University.
1995b Seven New Sculptural Pieces from Caesarea. Pp. 108–20 in *The Roman and Byzantine Near East: Some Recent Archaeological Research*, Journal of Roman Archaeology Suppl. 14, ed. J. H. Humphrey. Ann Arbor, MI: Journal of Roman Archaeology.
1996a Imported Marble Sarcophagi from Caesarea. *Asaph* 2: 13–26.
1996b Representations of Deities and the Cults of Caesarea. Pp. 305–24 in *Caesarea Maritima: A Retrospective After Two Millennia*, ed. K. G. Holum and A. Raban. Leiden: Brill.
1996c Roman Copies Discovered in the Land of Israel. Pp. 433–50 in *Classical Studies in Honor of David Sohlberg*, ed. R. Katzoff. Ramat-Gan: Bar-Ilan University.
1996d Three Greek and Roman Portrait Statues from Caesarea Maritima. *'Atiqot* 28: 99–113.
2008 Caesarean Sculpture in Context. Pp. 509–38 in *The Sculptural Environment of the Roman Near East*, eds. Y. Z. Eliav, E. A. Friedland, and S. Herbert. Leuven: Peeters.

Gersht, R., and Pearl, Z.
1992 Decoration and Marble Sources of Sarcophagi from Caesarea. Pp. 224–44 in *Caesarea Papers: Staton's Tower, Herod's Harbour, and Roman and Byzantine Caesarea*, Journal of Roman Archaeology, Suppl. 5, ed. R. L. Vann. Ann Arbor, MI: Journal of Roman Archaeology.

Glaukler, P.
1895 *Musée de Cherchel*. Catalogue des Musées et Collections Archéologiques de l'Algérie et de la Tunisie 4. Paris: Leroux.

Gordon, R.
1979 The Real and the Imaginary: Production and Religion in the Graeco-Roman World. *Art History* 2: 5–34.

Gorgoni, C.; Lazzarini, L.; Pallante, P.; and Turi, B.
2002 An Updated and Detailed Mineropetrographlc and C-0 Stable Isotopic Reference Database for the Main Mediterranean Marbles Used in Antiquity. Pp. 115–31 in *ASMOSIA 5. Interdisciplinary Studies on Ancient Stone. Proceedings of the Fifth International Conference of the Association for the Study of Marble and Other Stones in Antiquity*, Museum of Fine Arts, Boston, June 1998, eds; J. J. Herrmann, N. Herz and R. Newman. London: Archetype.

Gounari, E. G.
2003 Ἡ εικονογραιθία της Ρώμης στην αρχαία τέχνη. Thessaloniki: University Studio.

Graindor, P.
1915 Les Cosmètes du Musée d'Athènes. *Bulletin de Correspondance Hellénique* 39: 241–401.

Grainger, J.
1990 *The Cities of Seleukid Syria*. Oxford: Oxford University.

Grotemeyer, P., and Schmidt, E.
1928 Die Entstehungszeit der Artemis Rospigliosi. *Jahrbuch des Deutschen Archäologischen Instituts* 43: 269–80.

Hachlili, R.
1988 *Ancient Jewish Art and Archaeology in the Land of Israel*. Leiden: Brill.

Hajjar, Y.
1977 *La triade d'Héliopolis-Baalbek: son culte et sa diffusion à travers les textes littéraires et les documents iconographiques et épigraphiques* 1–2. Leiden: Brill.
1985 *La triade d'Héliopolis Baalbek: iconographie, théologie, culte et sanctuaires*. Montreal: University of Montreal.
1988 Heliopolitani Dei. *LIMC* 4: 573–92.
1990a Divinités oraculaires et rites divinatoires en Syrie et en Phénicie à l'époque gréco-romaine. *Aufstieg und Niedergang der römischen Welt* II 18.4: 2236–320.
1990b Dieux et cultes non héliopolitains de la Béqa', de l'Hermon et de l'Abilène à l'époque romaine. *Aufstieg und Niedergang der römischen Welt* II 18.4: 2509–604.

Halm-Tisserant, M., and Siebert, G.
1997 Nymphai. *LIMC* 8: 891–902.

Hampe, R., and Krauskopf, I.
1981 Alexandros. *LIMC* 1: 494–529.

Hänlein-Schäfer, H.
1985 *Veneratio Augusti: Eine Studie zu den Tempeln des ersten römischen Kaisers*. Rome: L'Erma di Bretschneider.

Hannestad, N.
1998 The Daidalos Group in Amman, or Transporting Marble Sculpture in Late Antiquity. Pp. 513–20 in *Studies in the History and Archaeology of Jordan 7*. Amman: Department of Antiquities.
1999 How Did Rising Christianity Cope with Pagan Sculpture? Pp. 173–204 in *East and West: Modes of Communication, Proceedings of the First Plenary Conference at Merida*, eds. E. K. Chrysos and I. N. Wood. Leiden: Brill.

Hartal, M.
2008 Banias. *NEAEHL* 5: 1592–93.
2009 *Paneas. Volume 4. The Aqueduct and the Northern Suburbs*. Israel Antiquities Authority Reports 40. Jerusalem: Israel Antiquities Authority.

Havelock, C. M.
1995 *The Aphrodite of Knidos and Her Successors: A Historical Review of the Female Nude in Greek Art*. Ann Arbor, MI: University of Michigan.

Heiderich, G.
1966   Asklepios. Ph.D. dissertation, Freiburg.

Heimann, A., and Porat N.
1995   The Excavations of the Sanctuary of Pan (Banias): Geological Reports. *Geological Survey of Israel Report* GSI/5/95: 9–25.

Hekler, A.
1912   *Greek and Roman Portraits*. New York: Putnam.

Helbig, W.
1963–1972 *Führer durch die öffentlichen Sammlungen klassischer Altertümer in Rom* 1–4. 4th ed. Tübingen: Wasmuth.

Herrmann, J. J.
1990   Thasos and the Ancient Marble Trade: Evidence from American Museums. Pp. 73–100 in *Marble: Art Historical and Scientific Perspectives on Ancient Sculpture*. Malibu: J. Paul Getty Museum.

Herz, N.
1987   Carbon and Oxygen Isotopic Ratios: A Data Base for Classical Greek and Roman Marble. *Archaeometry* 29: 35–43.
1990   Stable Isotope Analysis of Greek and Roman Marble: Provenance, Association, and Authenticity. Pp. 101–10 in *Marble: Art Historical and Scientific Perspectives on Ancient Sculpture*. Malibu: J. Paul Getty Museum.

Herz, N., and Waelkens, M. (eds.)
1988   *Classical Marble: Geochemistry, Technology, Trade*. Boston: Kluwer.

Herz, N., and Wenner, D. B.
1978   Assembly of Greek Marble Inscriptions by Isotopic Methods. *Science* 199: 1070–72.
1981   Tracing the Origins of Marble. *Archaeology* 34.5: 14–21.

Hill, G. F.
1914   *Catalogue of the Greek Coins of Palestine*. London: British Museum.

Hillers, D. R., and Cussini, E.
1996   *Palmyrene Aramaic Texts*. Baltimore, MD: Johns Hopkins University.

Hollinshead, M. B.
2002   Extending the Reach of Marble: Struts in Greek and Roman Sculpture. Pp. 117–52 in *The Ancient Art of Emulation. Studies in Artistic Originality and Tradition from the Present to Classical Antiquity*. Memoirs of the American Academy in Rome, Suppl. 1, ed. E. K. Gazda. Ann Arbor, MI: University of Michigan.

Holtzmann, B.
1984   Asklepios. *LIMC 2*: 863–97.

Holum, K. G.
2006   Review of *Art in the Public and Private Spheres in Roman Caesarea Maritima*, by Y. Turnheim and A. Ovadiah. *Journal of Roman Archaeology* 19: 659–60.

Holum, K. G., and Hohlfelder, R. L. (eds.)
1988   *King Herod's Dream: Caesarea on the Sea*. New York: Norton.

Hopfe, L. M.
1990   Caesarea Palaestinae as a Religious Center. *Aufstieg und Niedergang der römischen Welt* II 18.4: 2380–411.

Hörig, M.
1984   Dea Syria-Atargatis. *Aufstieg und Niedergang der römischen Welt* II 17.3: 1536–81.

Hornum, M. B.
1993   *Nemesis, the Roman State, and the Games*. Leiden: Brill.

Humphrey, J. H. (ed.)
1995   *The Roman and Byzantine Near East: Some Recent Archaeological Research*. Journal of Roman Archaeology, Suppl. 14. Ann Arbor, MI: Journal of Roman Archaeology.

Iliffe, J. H.
1932   A Portrait of Vitellius (?) in Rock Crystal. *Quarterly of the Department of Antiquities in Palestine* 1: 153–54.
1933a   A Copy of the Crouching Aphrodite. *Quarterly of the Department of Antiquities in Palestine* 2: 110–12.
1933b   Third-Century Portrait Busts. *Quarterly of the Department of Antiquities in Palestine* 2: 11–14.
1934   A Bust of Pan. *Quarterly of the Department of Antiquities in Palestine* 3: 165–66.

1951   A Heroic Statue from Philadelphia-Amman. Pp.
         705–12 in *Studies Presented to David Moore Rob-*
         inson 1, ed. G. E. Mylonas. St. Louis: Washington
         University.

Inan, J.
1975   *Roman Sculpture in Side*. Ankara: Türk Tarih
         Kurumu.

Inan, J., and Alföldi-Rosenbaum, E.
1979   *Römische und frühbyzantinische Portätplastik*
         aus der Türkei: Neue Funde. Mainz: von Zabern.

Inan, J., and Rosenbaum, E.
1966   *Roman and Early Byzantine Portrait Sculpture*
         in Asia Minor. London: Oxford University for
         the British Academy.

Isaac B.
in press   Inscriptions from Banias. In *Paneion I:*
             Excavations at the Sanctuary of Pan at Caesarea
             Philippi-Banyas, Final Report, Israel Antiquities
             Authority Report Series, ed. Z. U. Maʾoz. Jerusa-
             lem: Israel Antiquities Authority.

Israeli, Y.
1992   Marble Sculptures from Roman Israel. *Minerva*:
         14–19.

Jalabert, L.
1906   Inscriptions grecques et latines: Monuments
         relatifs au Culte d'Esculape. *Mélanges de la*
         Faculté orientale de Beyrouth 1: 157–61.

Jidejian, N.
1971   *Sidon Through the Ages*. Beirut: Dar el-Mashreq.

Kadman, L.
1961   *The Coins of Akko Ptolemais*. Tel Aviv: Schocken.

Kahil, L.
1984   Artemis. *LIMC* 2: 618–753.

Kaizer, T.
2002   *The Religious Life of Palmyra: A Study of the*
         Social Patterns of Worship in the Roman Period.
         Oriens et Occidens 4. Stuttgart: Steiner.

Kane, S. E., and Carrier, S. C.
1988   Relationships Between Style and Size of Statu-
         ary and the Availability of Marble at Cyrene. Pp.

197–206 in *Classical Marble: Geochemistry, Tech-*
         nology, Trade, eds. N. Herz, and M. Waelkens.
         Boston: Kluwer.
1992   Relationships Between Style and Size of
         Statuary and the Availability of Marble in the
         Eastern Roman Empire. Pp. 121–25 in *Ancient*
         Stones: Quarrying, Trade and Provenance, eds.
         M. Waelkens, N. Herz, and L. Moens. Leuven:
         Leuven University.

Kapossy, B.
1969   *Brunnenfiguren der hellenistischen und römi-*
         schen Zeit. Zürich: Juris.

Kondoloeon, C. (ed.)
2000   *Antioch: The Lost Ancient City*. Princeton, NJ:
         Princeton University.

Kossatz-Deissmann, A.
1988   Hera. *LIMC* 4: 659–719.
1994   Paridis Iudicium. *LIMC* 7: 176–88.

Krencker, D., and Zschietzschmann, W.
1938   *Römische Tempel in Syrien*. Berlin: de Gruyter.

Kropp, A.
2009   King – Caesar – God: Roman Imperial Cult
         among Near Eastern Client Kings in the Julio-
         Claudian Period. Pp. 99–150 in *Lokale Identität*
         im römischen Nahen Osten: Kontexte und Pers-
         pektiven, Erträge der Tagung "Lokale Identität im
         Römischen Nahen Osten", Münster 19.-21. April
         2007, eds. M. Blömer, M. Facella, and E. Winter.
         Wiesbaden: Steiner.

Krull, D.
1985   *Der Herakles vom Typ Farnese: Kopienkritische*
         Untersuchung einer Schöpfung des Lysipp. New
         York: Lang.

Lambert, R.
1984   *Beloved and God: The Story of Hadrian and*
         Antinous. London: Weidenfeld and Nicolson.

Lambrinudakis, W.; Bruneau, P.; Palagia, O.;
Daumas, M.; Kokkorou-Alewras, G.:
and Mathiopoulou-Tornaritou, E.
1984   Apollon. *LIMC* 2: 183–327.

Lancha, J., and Faedo L.
1994   Mousa, Mousai/Musae. *LIMC* 7: 1013–59.

La Rocca, E.
1990   Iuno. *LIMC* 5: 814–56.

Larson, J. L.
2001   *Greek Nymphs: Myth, Cult, Lore*. New York: Oxford University Press.

Lauffray, J.
1940   Une fouille au pied de l'acropole de Byblos. *Bulletin du Musée de Beyrouth* 4: 7–36.

Lazzarini L.; Ponti, G.; Martinez, M. P.; Rockwell, P.; and Turi, B.
2002   Historical, Technical, Petrographic and Isotopic Features of Aphrodisian Marble. Pp. 163–68 in *ASMOSIA 5. Interdisciplinary Studies on Ancient Stone. Proceedings of the Fifth International Conference of the Association for the Study of Marble and Other Stones in Antiquity*, Museum of Fine Arts, Boston, June 1998, eds. J. J. Herrmann, N. Herz and R. Newma. London: Archetype.

Leibovitch, J.
1958   Le griffon d'Erez et le sens mythologique de Némésis. *Israel Exploration Journal* 8: 141–48.

Levi, D.
1947   *Antioch Mosaic Pavements* 1–2. Princeton, NJ: Princeton University.

Lichtenberger, A.
2003   *Kulte und Kultur der Dekapolis. Untersuchungen zu numismatischen, archäologischen und epigraphischen Zeugnissen*. Abhandlungen des Deutschen Palästina-Vereins 29. Wiesbaden: Harrassowitz.

Linant de Bellefonds, B.
1992   Nemesis (in peripheria orientali). *LIMC* 6: 770–73.

Lippold, G.
1918   Musengruppen. *Mitteilungen des Deutschen Archäologischen Instituts, Römische Abteilung* 33: 64–102.

Longfellow, B.
2011   *Roman Imperialism and Civic Patronage: Form, Meaning, and Ideology in Monumental Fountain Complexes*. New York: Cambridge University.

Mägele, S.
2011   The Sculptural Evidence of Sagalassos in its Urban Context. Pp. 319–35 in *Roman Sculpture in Asia Minor, Proceedings of the International Conference to Celebrate the 50th Anniversary of the Italian Excavations at Hierapolis in Phrygia, Held on May 24–26, 2008, in Cavallino (Lecce)*. Journal of Roman Archaeology Suppl. 80, eds. F. D'Andria and I. Romeo. Portsmouth, RI: Journal of Roman Archaeology.

Magness, J.
1990   Some Observations on the Roman Temple at Kedesh. *Israel Exploration Journal* 40: 173–81.

Manderscheid, H.
1981   *Die Skulpturenausstattung der kaiserzeitlichen Thermenanlagen*. Berlin: Mann.

Manfra, L.; Masi, U.; and Turi, B.
1975   Carbon and Oxygen Isotope Ratios of Marbles from Some Ancient Quarries of Western Anatolia and Their Archaeological Significance. *Archaeometry* 17: 215–21.

Mansuelli, G. A.
1958   *Galleria degli Uffizi: Le sculture* 1–2. Rome: Istituto poligrafico dello Stato, Libreria dello Stato.

Maʿoz, Z.
1989–90   Banias, Temple of Pan – 1989. *Explorations and Surveys in Israel* 9: 85–86.
1993a   Banias. *NEAEHL* I: 136–43.
1993b   Banias, Temple of Pan – 1991/1992. *Explorations and Surveys in Israel* 13: 2–7.
1994–99   Coin and Temple: The Case of Caesarea Philippi-Paneas. *Israel Numismatic Journal* 13: 90–102.
2007   *Baniyas in the Greco-Roman Period: A History Based on the Excavations*. Archaostyle Scientific Research Series 3. Qazrin: Archaostyle.
2008   Banias. *NEAEHL* 5: 1587–90.
in press   *Paneion I: Excavation at the Sanctuary of Pan at Caesarea Philippi-Banyas, Final Report*. Israel Antiquities Authority Report Series. Jerusalem: Israel Antiquities Authority.

Marcadé, J.
1957   Sculptures Argiennes. *Bulletin de Correspondance Hellénique* 81: 405–74.

Marcadé, J., and Raftopoulou, É.
1963   Sculptures Argiennes (2). *Bulletin de Correspondance Hellénique* 87: 33–187.

Marquardt, N.
1995   *Pan in der hellenistischen und kaiserzeitlichen Plastik*. Bonn: Habelt.

Marvin, M.
1993   Copying in Roman Sculpture: The Replica Series. Pp. 161–88 in *Roman Art in Context: An Anthology*, ed. Eve D'Ambra. Englewood Cliffs, NJ: Prentice Hall.

Mattingly, D. J.
2011   *Imperialism, Power, and Identity: Experiencing the Roman Empire*. Princeton, NJ: Princeton University.

Matz, F.
1968   *Die dionysischen Sarkophage* 1. Berlin: Gebr. Mann.

Mellink, M. J.
1968   Archaeology in Asia Minor. *American Journal of Archaeology* 72: 125–47.

Mellor, R.
1975   *THEA ROME: The Worship of the Goddess Roma in the Greek World*. Hypomnemata 42. Göttingen: Vandenhoeck & Ruprecht.

Mendel, G.
1912–14   *Catalogue des Sculptures Grecques, Romaines et Byzantines* 1–3. İstanbul: İstanbul Arkeoloji Müzeleri.

Merker, G. S.
1987   A Statuette of Minerva in the Rockefeller Museum, Jerusalem. *Eretz-Israel: Archaeological, Historical and Geographical Studies* 19: 15–20.

Meshorer, Y.
1982   *Ancient Jewish Coinage*. Vol. 2: *Herod the Great through Bar Cochba*. New York: Dix Hills.
1984–85   The Coins of Caesarea Paneas. *Israel Numismatic Journal* 8: 37–58.

Metropolitan Museum of Art
1986   *Treasures of the Holy Land: Ancient Art from the Israel Museum*. New York: Metropolitan Museum of Art.

Meyer, H.
1991   *Antinoos: Die archäologischen Denkmäler unter Einbeziehung des numismatischen und epigraphischen Materials sowie der literarischen Nachrichten. Ein Beitrag zur Kunst- und Kulturgeschichte der hadrianisch-frühantoninischen Zeit*. Munich: Fink.

Millar, F.
1993   *The Roman Near East, 31 BC–AD 337*. Cambridge, MA: Harvard University.

Miltner, F.
1959   Vorläufiger Bericht über die Ausgrabungen in Ephesos. *Jahreshefte des Österreichischen archäologischen Instituts in Wien* 44: 315–80.

Moens, L.; Roos, P.; De Rudder, J.; De Paepe, P.; Van Hende, J.; and Waelkens, M.
1990   Scientific Provenance Determination of Ancient White Marble Sculptures Using Petrographic, Chemical, and Isotopic Data. Pp. 111–24 in *Marble: Art Historical and Scientific Perspectives on Ancient Sculpture*. Malibu: J. Paul Getty Museum.

Moreno, P.
1982   Il Farnese Ritrovato ed Altri Tipi di Eracle in Riposo. *Mélanges de l'École française de Rome, Antiquité* 94: 379–526.

Morrow, K. D.
1985   *Greek Footwear and the Dating of Sculpture*. Madison, WI: University of Wisconsin.

Mussche, H. F.
1961   Recherches sur la sculpture gréco-romaine au Liban et en Syrie Occidentale d'Alexandre le Grand à Constantin. Pp. 437–42 in *Atti del Settimo Congresso Internazionale di Archeologia Classica*. Rome: L'Erma di Bretschneider.

Mylonopoulos, J.
2010   *Divine Images and Human Imaginations in Ancient Greece and Rome*. Leiden: Brill.

Najbjerg, T.
2001   Sculpture from Antioch. Pp. 172–271 in *Roman Sculpture in the Art Museum, Princeton University*, ed. J. M. Padgett. Princeton, NJ: The Art Museum, Princeton University.

Naumann-Steckner, F.
1983 *Die Ikonographie der Kybele in der phrygischen und der griechischen Kunst.* Tübingen: Wasmuth.

Netzer, E.
1981 Herod's Building Projects: State Necessity or Personal Need? Pp. 48–61 in *The Jerusalem Cathedra: Studies in the History, Archaeology, Geography and Ethnography of the Land of Israel* 1, ed. L. I. Levine. Jerusalem: Yad Izhak Ben-Zvi Institute.
2003 A Third Candidate: Another Building at Banias. *Biblical Archaeology Review* 29.5: 25.

Neudecker, R.
1988 *Die Skulpturenausstattung römischer Villen in Italien.* Mainz: von Zabern.

Norris, F. W.
1990 Antioch on-the-Orontes as a Religious Center, 1: Paganism before Constantine. *Aufstieg und Niedergang der römischen Welt* II 18.4: 2322–79.

Ovadiah, A., and Mucznik, S.
2009 *Worshiping the Gods: Art and Cult in Roman Eretz Israel.* Leiden: Alexandros.

Ovadiah, A.; Roll, I.; and Fischer, M.
1993 The Roman Temple at Kedesh in Upper Galilee: A Response. *Israel Exploration Journal* 43: 60–63.

Ovadiah, A., and Turnheim, Y.
1994 *"Peopled" Scrolls in Roman Architectural Decoration in Israel: The Roman Theatre at Beth Shean, Scythopolis.* Rivista di archeologia Suppl. 12. Rome: L'Erma di Bretschneider.

Overman, J. A.; Olive, J.; and Nelson, M.
2003 Discovering Herod's Shrine to Augustus: Mystery Temple Found at Omrit. *Biblical Archaeology Review* 29.2: 40–67.
2007 A Newly Discovered Herodian Temple at Khirbet Omrit in Northern Israel. Pp. 177–95 in *The World of Herods: Volume 1 of the International Conference, The World of the Herods and the Nabataeans, Held at the British Museum, 17–19 April 2001*, ed. N. Kokkinos. Stuttgart: Steiner.

Palagia, O.
1988 I. Herakles Alone – C: Classical and Hellenistic Greek, and Roman. *LIMC* 4: 738–90.

Panzanelli, R. (ed.)
2008 *The Color of Life: Polychromy in Sculpture from Antiquity to the Present.* Los Angeles: J. Paul Getty Museum.

Paribeni, E.
1959 *Catalogo delle sculture di Cirene. Statue e rilievi di carattere religioso.* Rome: L'Erma di Bretschneider.

Parker, A. J.
1992 *Ancient Shipwrecks of the Mediterranean and the Roman Provinces.* British Archaeological Reports, International Series 580. Oxford: B.A.R.

Parlasca, K.
1989 La sculpture grecque et la sculpture d'époque romaine impériale en Syrie. Pp. 537–56 in *Archeologie et histoire de la Syrie* II: *La Syrie de l'époque achéménide à l'avènement de l'Islam*, eds. J.-M. Dentzer and W. Orthmann. Saarbrücken: Saarbrücker Druckerei und Verlag.

Pearl, Z.
1989 Archaeological Marble in Israel: Chemical and Mineralogical Analysis. M.Sc. thesis, Weizmann Institute of Science. Rehovot, Israel.

Pearl, Z., and Magaritz, M.
1991a The Marble Source of the Tel Naharon-Scythopolis Heads. *'Atiqot* 20: 46–48.
1991b Stable Isotopes and the Roman Marble Trade: Evidence from Scythopolis and Caesarea, Israel. Pp. 295–303 in *Stable Isotope Geochemistry: A Tribute to Samuel Epstein, The Geochemical Society*, Special Publication 3, eds. H. P. Taylor, Jr., J. R. O'Neil, and I. R. Kaplan. San Antonio, TX: Geochemical Society.

Pensabene, P.
1997 Marmi d'importazione, pietre locali e committenza nella decorazione architettonica di eta severiana in alcuni centri delle province *Syria et Palestina e Arabia. Archeologia Classica* 49: 275–422.
2011 Su alcuni aspetti produttivi delle "scuole" di scultura di Docimio, Afrodisia e Nicomedia. Pp. 37–61 in *Roman Sculpture in Asia Minor. Proceedings of the International Conference to Celebrate the 50th Anniversary of the Italian Excavations at Hierapolis in Phrygia, Held on May 24–26, 2008, in Cavallino (Lecce)*, Journal of Roman Archaeology Suppl. 80, eds. F. D'Andria

and I. Romeo. Portsmouth, RI: Journal of Roman Archaeology.

Pentia, M.; Herz, N.; and Turi, B.
2002 Provenance Determination of Classical Marbles: A Statistical Test Based on 87Sr/86Sr, 18O/16O, and 13C/12C Isotopic Ratios. Pp. 219–26 in *ASMOSIA 6. Interdisciplinary Studies on Ancient Stone. Proceedings of the Sixth International Conference of the Association for the Study of Marble and Other Stones in Antiquity, Venice, June 15–18, 2000*, ed. L. Lazzarini. Padova: Bottega d'Erasmo.

Pernier, L.
1931 L'Artemision di Cirene. *Africa Italiana* IV: 228.

Perry, E. E.
1995 Artistic Imitation and the Roman Patron, with a Study of Imitation in the Ideal Sculptures of Herodes Atticus. Ph.D. dissertation, University of Michigan.

Philipp, H.
1987 Eine Hellenistische Satyrstatuette aus Izmit (Nikomedia). *Archäologischer Anzeiger*: 131–43.

Picard, C.
1947 Sur l'Orphée de la fontaine monumentale de Byblos. *Orientalia Christiana Periodica* 13: 266–81.

Pinkwart, D.
1965 *Das Relief des Archelaos von Priene und die "Musen des Philiskos."* Kallmünz: Lassleben.

Pochmarski, E.
1990 *Dionysische Gruppen: Eine typologische Untersuchung zur Geschichte des Stützmotivs.* Sonderschriften des Österreichischen Archäologischen Instituts 19. Vienna: Österreichisches Archäologisches Instituts.

Pollitt, J. J.
1986 *Art in the Hellenistic Age.* New York: Cambridge University.

Pozzi, E. (ed.)
1989 *Le Collezioni del Museo nazionale di Napoli 1, 2: La scultura greco-romana, Le sculture antiche della collezione Farnese, Le collezioni monetali, Le oreficerie, La collezione glittica.* Roma: De Luca.

Prayon, F.
1982 Projektierte Bauten auf römischen Münzen. Pp. 319–30 in *Praestant Interna. Festschrift für Ulrich Hausmann*, eds. B. von Freitag gen. Löringhoff, D. Mannsperger, and F. Prayon. Tübingen: Wasmuth.

Preger, T.
1901 *Scriptores Originum Constantinopolitanarum* 1. Leipzig: Teubner.

Price, M. J., and Trell, B. L.
1977 *Coins and Their Cities: Architecture on the Ancient Coins of Greece, Rome, and Palestine.* Detroit: Wayne State University.

Prittwitz und Gaffron, H. H. v.
1988 *Der Wandel der Aphrodite: Archäologische Studien zu weiblichen halbbekleideten Statuetten des späten Hellenismus.* Bonn: Habelt.

Queyrel, A.
1992 Mousa, Mousai. *LIMC* 6: 657–81.

Reich, R.
1996 A Hellenistic Statue of Daedalus and Icarus Discovered in Philadelphia/Amman. *Qadmoniot* 29: 39–43 (Hebrew).

Reid, S. K.
2005 *The Small Temple: A Roman Imperial Cult Building in Petra, Jordan.* Piscataway, NJ: Gorgias.

Rein, M. J.
1993 The Cult and Iconography of Lydian Kybele. Ph.D. dissertation, Harvard University.

Richardson, P.
1996 *Herod: King of the Jews and Friend of the Romans.* Columbia, SC: University of South Carolina.

Ridgway, B. S.
1981 Sculpture from Corinth. *Hesperia* 50: 422–48.
1984 *Roman Copies of Greek Sculpture: The Problem of the Originals.* Ann Arbor, MI: University of Michigan.
1990a *Hellenistic Sculpture I: The Styles of ca. 331–200 BC.* Madison, WI: University of Wisconsin.
1990b Metal Attachments in Greek Marble Sculpture. Pp. 185–206 in *Marble: Art Historical and Scientific Perspectives on Ancient Sculpture.* Malibu: J. Paul Getty Museum.

Robert, L., and Robert, J.
1950   *Hellenica, Recueil d'épigraphie, de numismatique et d'antiquités grecques 9: Inscriptions et reliefs d'Asie Mineure.* Paris: Adrien-Maisonneuve.

Rockwell, P.
1991   Unfinished Statuary Associated with a Sculptor's Studio. Pp. 127–42 in *Aphrodisias Papers 2: The Theater, a Sculptor's Workshop, Philosophers, and Coin-Types*, Journal of Roman Archaeology, Suppl. 2, eds. R. R. R. Smith and K. T. Erim. Ann Arbor, MI: Journal of Roman Archaeology.
1993   *The Art of Stoneworking: A Reference Guide.* New York: Cambridge University.

Roll, I.
1983   The Roman Road System in Judaea. Pp. 136–61 in *The Jerusalem Cathedra: Studies in the History, Archaeology, Geography and Ethnography of the Land of Israel 3*, ed. L. I. Levine. Jerusalem : Yad Izhak Ben-Zvi Institute.
2002   Crossing the Rift Valley: The Connecting Arteries Between the Road Networks of Judaea/Palaestina and Arabia. Pp. 215–30 in *Limes XVIII: Proceedings of the XVIIIth International Congress of Roman Frontier Studies, Held in Amman, Jordan (September 2000)*, ed. Philip Freeman. British Archaeological Reports, International Series 1084. Oxford: Archaeopress.

Rosenbaum, E.
1960   *A Catalogue of Cyrenaican Portrait Sculpture.* London: Oxford University.

Rosenthal-Heginbottom, R.
2010   The Cult of Nemesis: The Griffin in Marble and Clay. Pp. 213–21 in *Excavations at Dor: Figurines, Cult Objects and Amulets, 1980–2000 Seasons*, ed. E. Stern. Jerusalem: Israel Exploration Society.

Russell, B.
2008   The Dynamics of Stone Transport between the Roman Mediterranean and Its Hinterland. *Facta. A Journal of Roman Material Culture Studies*: 107–26.
2011   *Lapis transmarinus*: Stone-Carrying Ships and the Maritime Distribution of Stone in the Roman Empire. Pp. 139–55 in *Maritime Archaeology and Ancient Trade in the Mediterranean*, Oxford Centre for Maritime Archaeology, Monog. 6, eds. D. Robinson and A. Wilson. Oxford: Institute of Archaeology.

Sartre, M.
1991   *L'Orient romain: Provinces et sociétés provinciales en Méditerranée orientale d'Auguste aux Sévères (31 avant J.-C.–235 après J.-C.).* Paris: Seuil.

Sadurska, A., and Bounni, A. (eds.)
1994   *Les sculptures funeraires de Palmyre.* Rome: L'Erma di Bretschneider.

Schmidt-Colinet, A.
1985   Skulpturen aus dem Nymphäum von Apamea/Syrien. *Archäologischer Anzeiger*: 119–33.

Schneider, C.
1999   *Die Musengruppe von Milet.* Milesische Forschungen 1. Mainz: von Zabern.

Schürer, E.
1973–87   *The History of the Jewish People in the Age of Jesus Christ (175 BC–AD 135)* 1–3. Edinburgh: Clark.

Sebesta, J. L., and Bonfante, L. (eds.)
1994   *The World of Roman Costume.* Madison, WI: University of Wisconsin.

Servais-Soyez, B.
1981   Adonis. *LIMC* 1: 222–29.

Seyrig, H.
1932   Antiquités syriennes. Monuments syriens du culte de Némesis, 6. La Némésis de Doura. *Syria* 13: 53–61.

Sichtermann, H.
1988   Ganymedes. *LIMC* 4: 154–69.

Siebert, G.
1990   Hermes. *LIMC* 5: 285–387.

Simon, E.
1994   Poseidon. *LIMC* 7: 446–79.

Simon, E., and Bauchhenss, G.
1984a   Apollo. *LIMC* 2: 363–464.
1984b   Artemis/Diana. *LIMC* 2: 792–855.

Skupinska-Løvset, I.
1983   *Funerary Portraiture of Roman Palestine: An Analysis of the Production in Its Culture-Historical Context.* Gothenburg: Åström.

1999   *Portraiture in Roman Syria: A Study in Social and Regional Differentiation within the Art of Portraiture.* Łódź: Wydawn. Uniwersytetu Łódzkiego

Smith, M.
1974   On the Wine God in Palestine (Gen. 18, Jn. 2, and Achilles Tatius). Pp. 815–29 in *Salo Wittmayer Baron Jubilee Volume on the Occasion of his Eightieth Birthday* 2, eds. S. Lieberman and A. Hyman. Jerusalem: American Academy for Jewish Research.

Smith, R. R. R.
1991   *Hellenistic Sculpture: A Handbook.* London: Thames and Hudson.
1996   Archaeological Research at Aphrodisias, 1989–1992. Pp. 10–72 in *Aphrodisias Papers 3: The Setting and Quarries, Mythological and Other Sculptural Decoration, Architectural Development, Portico of Tiberius, and Tetrapylon,* Journal of Roman Archaeology Suppl. 20, eds. C. Roueché and R. R. R. Smith. Ann Arbor, MI: Journal of Roman Archaeology.
1998   Hellenistic Sculpture under the Roman Empire: Fishermen and Satyrs at Aphrodisias. Pp. 253–60 in *Regional Schools in Hellenistic Sculpture: Proceedings of an International Conference Held at the American School of Classical Studies at Athens, March 15–17, 1996,* eds. O. Palagia and W. D. E. Couleson. Oxford: Oxbow Books.
2007   Statue Life in the Hadrianic Baths at Aphrodisias, AD 100–600: Local Context and Historical Meaning. Pp. 203–35 in *Statuen in der Spätantike,* Spätantike, frühes Christentum, Byzanz Reihe B. Studien und Perspectiven 23, eds. F. A. Bauer and C. Witschel. Wiesbaden: Reichert.
2011   Marble Workshops at Aphrodisias. Pp. 62–76 in *Roman Sculpture in Asia Minor. Proceedings of the International Conference to Celebrate the 50th Anniversary of the Italian Excavations at Hierapolis in Phrygia, Held on May 24–26, 2008, in Cavallino (Lecce),* Journal of Roman Archaeology Suppl. 80, eds. F. D'Andria and I. Romeo. Portsmouth, RI: Journal of Roman Archaeology.

Smith, R. R. R., and Erim, K. T. (eds.)
1991   *Aphrodisias Papers 2: The Theater, a Sculptor's Workshop, Philosophers, and Coin-Types.* Journal of Roman Archaeology, Suppl. 2. Ann Arbor, MI: Journal of Roman Archaeology.

Sobel, H.
1990   *Hygieia: Die Göttin der Gesundheit.* Darmstadt: Wissenschaftliche Buchgesellschaft.

Sobocinski, M. G.
in press   Visualizing Architecture Then and Now: *Mimesis* and the Capitoline Temple of Jupiter Optimus Maximus, in *A Companion to Roman Architecture,* eds. R. Ulrich and C. Quenemoen. Malden, MA: Wiley-Blackwell.

Sourdel, D.
1952   *Les cultes du Hauran à l'époque romaine.* Institut français d'archéologie de Beyrouth: Bibliothèque archéologique et historique 53. Paris: Imprimerie nationale.

Squarciapino, M. F.
1943   *La scuola di Afrodisia.* Rome: Govern. di Roma.
1991   La scuola di Aphrodisias (dopo 40 anni). Pp. 123–26 in *Aphrodisias Papers 2: The Theater, a Sculptor's Workshop, Philosophers, and Coin-Types.* Journal of Roman Archaeology, Suppl. 2. Ann Arbor, MI: Journal of Roman Archaeology.

Starcky, J.
1981   Allath. *LIMC* 1.1: 564–70.

Stemmer, K.
1976   Ein Asklepios-Kopf in Amman. *Annual of the Department of Antiquities of Jordan* 21: 33–39.

Stewart. A. F.
1993   *Faces of Power: Alexander's Image and Hellenistic Politics.* Berkeley, CA: University of California.

Stillwell, R. (ed.)
1938   *Antioch on-the-Orontes 2: The Excavations 1933-1936.* Princeton, NJ: Princeton University.
1941   *Antioch-on-the-Orontes 3: The Excavations 1937–1939.* Princeton, NJ: Princeton University.

Stirling, L. M.
1994   Mythological Statuary in Late Antiquity: A Case Study of Villa Decoration in Southwest Gaul. Ph.D. dissertation, University of Michigan.
1996   Gods, Heroes, and Ancestors: Sculptural Decoration in Late-Antique Aquitania. *Aquitania* 14: 209–30.
2005   *The Learned Collector: Mythological Statuettes and Classical Taste in Late Antique Gaul.* Ann Arbor, MI: University of Michigan.

Stout, A. M.
1994   Jewelry as a Symbol of Status in the Roman Em-
        pire. Pp. 77–100 in *The World of Roman Costume*,
        eds. J. L. Sebesta and L. Bonfante. Madison, WI:
        University of Wisconsin.

Stuart, M.
1939   How Were Imperial Portraits Distributed
        Throughout the Roman Empire? *American
        Journal of Archaeology* 43: 601–17.

Stucky, R. A.
1993   *Die Skulpturen aus dem Eschmun-Heiligtum bei
        Sidon*. Antike Kunst, Beiheft 17. Basel: Vereini-
        gung der Freunde antiker Kunst.

Sturgeon, M. C.
1975   A New Group of Sculptures from Ancient
        Corinth. *Hesperia* 44: 280–301.
1987   *Sculpture* I: *1952–1967*. Isthmia: Excavations by
        the University of Chicago under the Auspices
        of the American School of Classical Studies at
        Athens 4. Princeton, NJ: American School of
        Classical Studies at Athens.
1989   Roman Sculptures from Corinth and Isthmia:
        A Case for a Local "Workshop." Pp. 114–21 in
        The Greek Renaissance in the Roman Empire,
        Bulletin of the Institute of Classical Studies of
        the University of London 55, eds. S. Walker and
        A. Cameron. London: University of London,
        Institute of Classical Studies.
1995   The Corinth Amazon: Formation of a Roman
        Classical Sculpture. *American Journal of Archae-
        ology* 99: 483–505.
2003   Sculpture at Corinth, 1896–1996. Pp. 351–68 in
        Corinth, the Centenary, 1896–1996, Corinth 20,
        eds. C. K. Williams and N. Bookidis. Princeton,
        NJ: American School of Classical Studies at
        Athens.

Todisco, L.
1990   Herakles: H. Herakles and the Cretan Bull (La-
        bor 7). *LIMC* 5: 59–67.

Trillmich, W.
1973   Bemerkungen zur Erforschung der römischen
        Idealplastik. *Jahrbuch des Deutschen Archäolo-
        gischen Instituts* 88: 247–82.
1979   Eine Jünglingsstatue in Cartagena und Überle-
        gungen zur Kopienkritik. *Madrider Mitteilungen*
        20: 339–60.

Trombley, F. R.
1993–94   *Hellenic Religion and Christianization, c.
           370–529*. Leiden: Brill.

Tzaferis, V.
1992a   Cults and Deities Worshipped at Caesarea
         Philippi-Banias. Pp. 190–201 in *Priests, Proph-
         ets, and Scribes: Essays on the Formation and
         Heritage of Second Temple Judaism in Honour of
         Joseph Blenkinsopp*, eds. E. Ulrich, J. W. Wright,
         R. P. Carroll, and P. R. Davies. Sheffield: Con-
         tinuum International.
1992b   The "God Who is in Dan" and the Cult of Pan
         at Banias in the Hellenistic and Roman Periods.
         Pp. 128*–35* in *Eretz-Israel* 23 (*Avraham Biran
         volume*). Jerusalem: Israel Exploration Society.
2008   Banias. *NEAEHL* 5: 1590–92.

Tzaferis, V., and Israeli, S.
2008a   *Paneas*. Volume 1: *The Roman to Early Islamic
         Periods. Excavations in Areas A, B, E, F, G and H*.
         Israel Antiquities Reports 37. Jerusalem: Israel
         Antiquities Authority.
2008b   *Paneas*. Volume 2: *Small Finds and Other Studies*.
         Israel Antiquities Reports 38. Jerusalem: Israel
         Antiquities Authority.

Tsafrir, Y. and Foerster, G.
1997   Urbanism at Scythopolis-Bet Shean in the
        Fourth to Seventh Centuries. *Dumbarton Oaks
        Papers* 51: 85–146.

Urman, D.
1985   *The Golan: A Profile of a Region During the
        Roman and Byzantine Periods*. British Archaeo-
        logical Reports, International Series 269. Oxford:
        B.A.R.

Van Voorhis, J.
1998   Apprentices' Pieces and the Training of Sculptors
        at Aphrodisias. *Journal of Roman Archaeology*
        11: 175–92.
2008   The Training of Marble Sculptors at Aphrodisias.
        Pp. 121–35 in *Roman Portraits from Aphrodisias*,
        eds. R. R. R. Smith and J. L. Lenaghan. Istanbul:
        Yapı Kredi Yayınları.

Vermeule, C. C.
1974   *The Goddess Roma in the Art of the Roman Em-
        pire*. Cambridge, MA: n.p.
1975   The Weary Herakles of Lysippos. *American
        Journal of Archaeology* 79: 323–32.

1981   *Jewish Relationships with the Art of Ancient Greece and Rome:* Judaea capta sed non devicta. Cambridge, MA: Department of Classical Art, Museum of Fine Arts.

Vermeule, C., and Anderson, K.
1981   Greek and Roman Sculpture in the Holy Land. *The Burlington Magazine* 123: 7–19.

Vierneisel-Schlörb, B.
1979   *Klassische Skulpturen des 5. und 4. Jahrhunderts v. Chr.* Glyptothek München: Katalog der Skulpturen 2. Munich: Beck.

Vitto, F.
1991   Two Marble Heads of Goddesses from Tel Naharon-Scythopolis. *'Atiqot* 20: 33–45.

Vollkommer, R.
1988   *Herakles in the Art of Classical Greece.* Oxford University Committee for Archaeology Monograph 25. Oxford: Oxford University Committee for Archaeology.

Von Heintze, H.
1971   Review of *Die Bildnisse des Antinous: Ein Beitrag zur Porträtplastik unter Kaiser Hadrian,* by C. W. Clairmont. *Gnomon* 43: 397.

Vout, C.
2005   Antinous, Archaeology and History. *Journal of Roman Studies* 95: 80–96.
2007   *Power and Eroticism in Imperial Rome.* New York: Cambridge University.

Vout, C. and Curtis, P.
2006   *Antinous: The Face of the Antique.* Leeds: Henry Moore Institute.

Walker, S.
1984   Marble Origins By Isotopic Analysis. *World Archaeology* 16: 204–21.

Ward-Perkins, J. B.
1951   Tripolitania and the Marble Trade. *Journal of Roman Studies* 41: 89–104.
1956   The Hippolytus Sarcophagus from Trinquetaille. *Journal of Roman Studies* 46: 11–16.
1958   Four Roman Garland Sarcophagi in America. *Archaeology* 11: 98–104.
1969   The Imported Sarcophagi of Roman Tyre. *Bulletin du Musée de Beyrouth* 22: 109–45.

1980   The Marble Trade and Its Organization: Evidence From Nicomedia. *Memoirs of the American Academy in Rome* 36: 325–38.

Waywell, G. B.
1971   Athena Mattei. *The Annual of the British School at Athens* 66: 373–82.
1978   *The Free-Standing Sculptures of the Mausoleum at Halicarnassus in the British Museum: A Catalogue.* London: British Museum.

Weber, T.
1990   A Survey of Roman Sculpture in the Decapolis: Preliminary Report. *Annual of the Department of Antiquities of Jordan* 34: 351–53.
1993   *Pella Decapolitana: Studien zur Geschichte, Architektur und bildenden Kunst einer Hellenisierten Stadt des nördlichen Ostjordanlandes.* Abhandlungen des Deutschen Palästinavereins 18. Wiesbaden: Harrassowitz.
1996   Die Statuengruppe Jesu und der Haimorrhoùsa in Caesarea-Philippi. *Damaszener Mitteilungen* 9: 209–16.
1999   Thermalquellen und Heilgötter des Ostjordanlandes in römischer und byzantinischer Zeit. *Damaszener Mitteilungen* 11: 433–51.
2002   *Gadara–Umm Qes I: Gadara Decapolitana. Untersuchungen zur Topographie, Geschichte, Architektur und der Bildenden Kunst einer "Polis Hellenis" im Ostjordanland.* Abhandlungen des Deutschen Palästinavereins 30.1. Wiesbaden: Harrassowitz.
2006   *Sculptures from Roman Syria in the Syrian National Museum at Damascus. I: From Cities and Villages in Central and Southern Syria.* Worms: Wernersche Buchhandlung.
2007   Echoes [*sic*] from Mount Parnassos. Representations of Muses in the Decapolis. Pp. 221–32 in *Studies in the History and Archaeology of Jordan* 9. Amman: Department of Antiquities.

Webster, J.
2001   Creolizing the Roman Provinces. *American Journal of Archaeology* 105: 209–25.

Weiss, C.
1988   Fluvii. *LIMC* 4: 139–48.

Wenning, R.
1983   Hellenistische Skulpturen in Israel. *Boreas* 6: 105–18.

1986 Die Stadtgöttin von Caesarea Maritima. *Boreas* 9: 113–29.

1991 Periods of "Hellenism" in Palestine. Pp. 148–58 in *Ho Hellenismos Sten Anatole: Praktike a Diethnous Archaiologikon Synedrion, Delphoi, 6–9 Nov. 1986.* Athens: Eurōpaiko politistiko Kentro Delphōn.

Wiegand, T.
1900 Antike Sculpturen in Samos. *Mitteilungen des Deutschen Archäologischen Instituts, Athenische Abteilung* 25: 145–214.

Wielgosz, D.
2000 Sculture in marmo proconnesio a Palmira. *Rivista di Archeologia* 24: 96–105.

2001 Sarcofagi attici a Palmira. *Rivista di Archeologia* 25: 167–76.

2008 Marble sculptures from the Archaeological Museum of Bosra. *Marmora* 4: 57–64.

Wielgosz, D.; Lazzarini, L.; Turi, B.; and Antonelli, F.
2002 The Origin of Marble Sculptures from Palmyra. Pp. 389–401 in *ASMOSIA 6. Interdisciplinary Studies on Ancient Stone. Proceedings of the Sixth International Conference of the "Association for the Study of Marble and Other Stones in Antiquity,"* Venice, June 15–18, 2000, ed. L. Lazzarini. Padova: Bottega d'Erasmo.

Will, E.
1950 La date du mithréum de Sidon. *Syria* 27: 261–69.

1965 La Syrie romaine entre l'Occident gréco-romain et l'Orient parthe. Pp. 511–26 in *Le rayonnement des civilisations grecques et romaines sur les cultures périphériques – Huitième Congrès International d'Archéologie Classique (Paris 1963).* Paris: De Boccard.

Wilson, J. F.
2004 *Caesarea Philippi: Banias, The Lost City of Pan.* London: I. B. Tauris.

Zagdoun, M.-A.
1989 *La sculpture archaïsante dans l'art hellénistique et dans l'art romain du Haut-Empire* 1–2. Paris: De Boccard.